How to Document Victims and Locate Survivors of the Holocaust

Avotaynu Monograph Series

How to Document Victims and Locate Survivors of the Holocaust

by Gary Mokotoff

with Foreward by Benjamin Meed

Avotaynu, Inc.
Teaneck, NJ 07666

Requests for permission to make copies of any part of this publication should be addressed to:

Avotaynu, Inc.
P.O. Box 900
Teaneck, NJ 07666

Printed in the United States of America
99 98 97 96 95   5 4 3 2 1

Library of Congress Cataloging in Publication Data

Mokotoff, Gary.
  How to document victims and locate survivors of the holocaust / by Gary Mokotoff.
    p   cm. — (Avotaynu monograph series)
  Includes bibliographical references and index.
  ISBN 0-9626373-8-6 (softcover)
  1. Holocaust, Jewish (1939–1945)—Research—handbooks, manuals, etc. 2. Holocaust survivors—Research—Handbooks, manuals, etc. 3. Holocaust, Jewish (1939–1945)—Archival resources. 4. Holocaust, Jewish (1939–1945)—Library resources. I. Title. II. Series.
D804.3.M65 1995   940.53'18'072—dc20   95-16574
                                                                 CIP

If you were Jewish and living in Poland in 1939, it is unlikely that you would have been alive in 1945. This book is dedicated to the more than 250 members of the Mokotow family murdered in the Holocaust. I know of fewer than 30 survivors.

CONTENTS

ILLUSTRATIONS

Most illustrations in this book are part of the extensive documentation researched and collected by the author on members of the Mokotow family who were either victims or survivors of the Holocaust. In a number of cases, the illustrations show records for the same individuals created at different stages of Holocaust history—for example, both a record of deportation and documentation of death are presented for one individual. These illustrations demonstrate that records do exist that make it possible to document the victims and the survivors of the Holocaust.

FOREWORD

As someone who has devoted almost five decades searching for information about what happened to Mordechai Miedzyrecki, my lost brother, and to numerous other members of my family who perished in the Holocaust, I well understand the significance of tracing family members and documenting accounts of what happened to them.

For those of us who were tragically caught in the Holocaust, our family trees—trees with deep roots and fruitful histories in Europe—have unnaturally short branches, branches severed prematurely, cut well before they had an opportunity to develop. And yet, for many survivors of the Holocaust, and especially for their descendants, investigation of and connecting to the past have taken on ever-growing significance.

Over the years, there have been many attempts to rewrite the history of the Holocaust: to diminish its magnitude, to universalize it, or to deny that it ever took place. It is these attempts that make the significance of documenting the victims and survivors of the Holocaust so very clear.

What better testimony is there to the Holocaust than the names of the individuals who were the victims. What would be the response of the Holocaust deniers regarding the 450,000 Jews deported from the Warsaw ghetto to their deaths at Treblinka if they were presented with a list of the individuals who were murdered? What better tribute to the survival and rebirth of the Jewish people than the names of the survivors who established themselves throughout the world and rebuilt their lives from the ashes of postwar Europe.

It is for this reason that we all have the obligation to document the participants in the Holocaust—the victims through Pages of Testimony at Yad Vashem in Jerusalem and the survivors through the Registry of Jewish Holocaust Survivors at the U.S. Holocaust Memorial Museum in Washington, DC. Only then can future historians have undeniable proof that the Holocaust was an event that happened to people. Only then will the world realize that the Holocaust was more than place names like Auschwitz and Majdanek. More than events such as Kristalnacht, Warsaw Ghetto Uprising, and Death Marches. The Holocaust was people, each individual with a story to tell, sometimes of survival, more likely of death.

Benjamin Meed
President
American Gathering of Jewish Holocaust Survivors

PREFACE

A few years ago, I had the responsibility of maintaining the National Registry of Jewish Holocaust Survivors until it became part of the permanent exhibit at the U.S. Holocaust Memorial Museum in Washington, DC. One day I received a telephone call from an excited staff member of the American Gathering of Jewish Holocaust Survivors. The organization had received a call from a woman who had just discovered, after more than forty years, that her father had survived the Holocaust. "Did the National Registry have any information about him?" The answer was no; he had not registered with them. Out of curiosity, I continued the search for her father's name by referring to my collection of Holocaust research sources. There was his name, in the "List of Survivors—Volume II" published by the Jewish Agency in 1945. I realized that this woman could have found her father years ago. Instead, she was denied his love and companionship for forty years because she did not know that resources were available to determine the fate of Holocaust victims and to help locate Holocaust survivors. Since that incident, my knowledge of resources about individuals caught up in the Holocaust has grown considerably. I have been fortunate to be able to help a number of survivors or their descendants locate information concerning their families.

It was widely believed that the Germans and their collaborators had destroyed all the materials associated with the Holocaust in an effort to hide their crimes. In fact, a wealth of information has survived, and more is uncovered every year. Some records became available shortly after World War II. These have been followed by a steady trickle of additional information throughout the years. But the recent collapse of communism in Central and Eastern Europe has made available a huge number of records. These records had been seized by the Soviet Union and were inaccessible until the collapse of communism. Other formerly communist countries, long reluctant to open their archives, perhaps out of fear that complicity of their countrymen with the Nazi effort would be shown, are now relenting and making their material available.

For this reason, I have decided to write this book—to share my knowledge of what information is available to do Holocaust research. I hope it will allow survivors, their descendants and their collateral relatives to document individuals who were caught up in the maelstrom that is considered by many to be the greatest tragedy in the history of Western civilization.

New documentation of the Holocaust is being discovered on a regular basis. Consequently, there is every indication that this is merely the first edition of this book. Present plans are to update this book periodically as additional resources become available. When conducting your research, always check with the resource sites to determine if they have acquired new information. Holocaust resource sites also share records as they acquire them. If you find that records described in this book are not available locally, ask the facility if it is possible to get a copy of the information either on loan or as a permanent addition to their collection. I encourage readers to write to me in care of Avotaynu, P.O. Box 900, Teaneck, NJ 07666, with information to be added to future editions of this book.

Preparation of this book required the assistance of many people at the facilities mentioned. Their cooperation was generous and made without reservation. Thanks to the following:

Alexander Abraham, Robert Rozett and Yaakov Lozowik at Yad Vashem; at the U.S. Holocaust Research Institute: Valdin Altskan, Sarah Ogilvy and William Connelly; Zachary Baker and Fruma Mohrer of YIVO Institute for Jewish Research; Frank Mecklenberg and Julia Bock of Leo Baeck Institute; Peggy Pearlstein of the U.S. Library of Congress; Paul H. Hamburg, at the Simon Wiesenthal Center in Los Angeles; William Shulman of the Association of Jewish Holocaust Organizations; Barbara Hersche of HIAS; Janice Rosen of the Canadian Jewish Congress.

Special friends made special contributions. Yale Reisner provided the information about the Jewish Historical Institute of Poland. He is working at the Institute by virtue of a special grant from the Ronald S. Lauder Foundation. Sophie Caplan, president of the Australian Jewish Genealogical Society provided the information about resources for locating survivors in Australia.

The numerous friends I have made in the Jewish genealogical community who contributed information and/or advice include Carol Clapsaddle, Jeffrey Cymbler, Peter Lande, Barbara Lightbody, Eileen Polakoff, Sallyann Amdur Sack and Miriam Weiner. Irene Saunders Goldstein, who has edited most of the books published by Avotaynu, Inc., contributed the skills required to convert my ramblings into coherent English.

But most of all, gratitude goes to my wife Ruth, who insisted that I block out time from my busy schedule, one day of every work week, until this project was completed.

Gary Mokotoff
May 1995

How To Do

Holocaust

Research

Konzentrationslager Auschwitz Art der Haft: Sch Jude   Gef. Nr. 184866

Name und Vorname: _Rudzyn Moszek_ Israel

geb.: 3.12.05   zu: _Bendsburg o/s_

Wohnort: _Bendsburg, Wallstr. 21_

Beruf: _Wasserinstallateur_   Rel.: _mos._

Staatsangehörigkeit: _ehem. Polen_   Stand: _verheir._

Name der Eltern: _Joachim, Chaja, geb. Chnanowka_ Rasse: _jüd_

Wohnort: _b. in Bendsburg gest._

Name der Ehefrau: _Saja geb. Koormanter_   Rasse: _jüd._

Wohnort: _Lager Glinhirbrücke, bei Breslau M._

Kinder: _1_   Alleiniger Ernährer der Familie oder der Eltern: _ja_

Vorbildung: _5 Kl. Vollsschule_

Militärdienstzeit: _Uelet. Baon Nowy Dwor_   von — bis _1926-8_

Kriegsdienstzeit: _____   von — bis _____

Grösse: _165_   Gestalt: _stark_   Gesicht: _längl._   Augen: _braun_

Nase: _gerad._   Mund: _mgr._   Ohren: _normal_   Zähne: _1 fehlt 1 gold._

Haare: _gr. mel._   Sprache: _poln. Deutsch_

Ansteckende Krankheit oder Gebrechen: _keine_

Besondere Kennzeichen: _Schnittnarbe auf d. l. Seite d. Halses_

Rentenempfänger: _nein_

Verhaftet am: _10.4.43_   wo: _Bendsburg_

1. Mal eingeliefert: _23.4.44_ RSHA   2. Mal eingeliefert: _____

Einweisende Dienststelle: _____

Grund: _____

Parteizugehörigkeit: _keine_   von — bis _____

Welche Funktionen: _keine_

Mitglied v. Unterorganisationen: _keine_

Kriminelle Vorstrafen: _ang. keine_

Politische Vorstrafen: _ang. keine_

Ich bin darauf hingewiesen worden, dass meine Bestrafung wegen intellektueller Urkundenfälschung erfolgt, wenn sich die obigen Angaben als falsch erweisen sollten.

v. g. u.   Der Lagerkommandant

Rudzyn Moszek

KL/43/43 500.000 3.12.1905.

Auschwitz Prisoner Registration Record. *Documentation of prisoner interned at Auschwitz concentration camp. Thousands of these records have been discovered and are on microfilm at the U.S. Holocaust Memorial Institute in Washington, D.C.*

THE BASICS

The Holocaust has been described as the most documented event in history. Tens of thousands of books depict the circumstances of this great tragedy. Many books provide general histories of the events that transpired during this period; others include the detail of personal accounts of survivors. A wealth of original documents has also survived World War II. They exist in archives throughout the world, and copies of these documents are now being shared among these archives. Recently, with the collapse of the Iron Curtain and communism in Eastern Europe, additional war-era German documents captured by the Soviet government became available to the public.

Most of these books and documents are of little or no interest to persons researching individuals; few of the works identify specific persons. But the small minority of books and documents that do include lists of individuals nevertheless represent a large collection of information about the millions of people affected by the Holocaust.

Documentation during the Holocaust

Germans have had a centuries-old reputation for being meticulous documenters. The period of the Holocaust is no exception. The recording of events falls into three categories: (1) events for which information about individuals was documented, (2) events that were documented without recording specific names of individuals, and (3) events for which there was no documentation.

Events where information about individuals was documented. Documentation exists for persons who were deported to camps. It should be recognized, however, that there were two types of camps: extermination camps and concentration/labor camps. Persons deported to extermination camps, with rare exceptions, were killed immediately. There was no attempt to document these individuals upon their arrival. Examples of extermination camps are Treblinka and Belzec. There are no records of persons who were deported from the Warsaw ghetto to Treblinka or from Lwow to Belzec. Similarly, persons deported to a concentration/labor camp who were killed immediately upon their arrival were not recorded at the camp.

Records were kept, however, of persons who were inmates of concentration camps or labor camps. As one son of a Holocaust survivor caustically

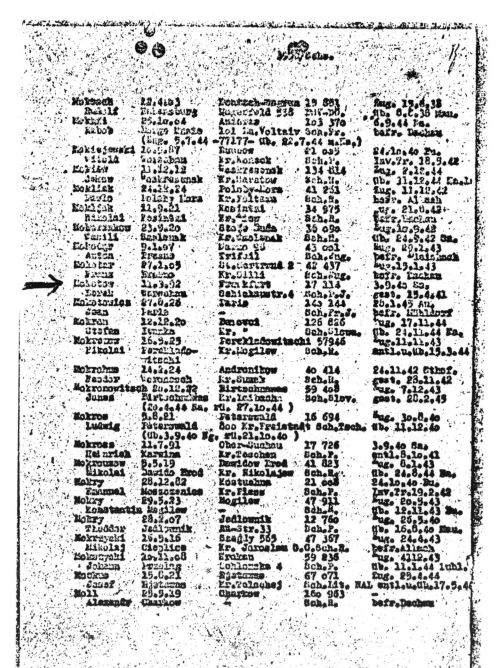

List of Persons Interned at Dachau. Alphabetical list prepared by the U.S. Army.

put it, "They were inventory, and all good businessmen keep track of their inventory." Some of these records survive to this day. They include the individual's name, place of birth, birth date and identification number. Quite often they also include the names of parents and spouse as well as other information, such as occupation and street address before deportation. When death from disease, starvation and/or abuse did not occur on a massive basis in these camps, even these deaths were recorded.

Many documents were destroyed in the late days of the war by the Germans to hide their atrocities. Some of the surviving documents were captured by United States and British liberation forces, however, and have been available to the public for many years—in the United States through the National Archives. Examples include registers from Buchenwald, Mauthausen and Dachau concentration camps. Other surviving documents that were captured by the Soviets have been made available only recently.

Events that were documented without recording specific names of individuals. This category includes the records of the Einsatzgruppen which provide the death dates of more than one million Jews. After Germany invaded the Soviet Union in 1942 (today's Belarus, Lithuania and Ukraine), these mobile killing squads of the German SS had the responsibility of killing every Jew, gypsy and political dissident in the towns captured by the regular German army. Consequently, their reports provide the death dates for almost all the Jews of the town. There are no German records of these events that list individuals.

Events for which there was no documentation. No documentation was made for the following groups:

• Jews sent to extermination camps (as opposed to concentration camps).

• Jews who did not survive the selection at concentration camps because they were considered unsuitable for slave labor—generally, children under 14, adults over age 50 and mothers with children under age 14. These individuals were immediately gassed.

• Jews who hid and were discovered. Invariably they were shot immediately and no records were made of their deaths.

Deportation lists. Independent of which of the above categories apply, there is the possibility of available documentation about individuals through deportation lists. When Jews were sent from one facility to another, the Germans prepared detailed lists of individuals who were transferred. The best known lists are those of Jews deported from France, primarily to Auschwitz. They are published by the Klarsfeld Foundation under the title *Memorial to the Jews Deported from France.* More than 70,000 individuals are listed with names, places of birth and birth dates. Because the book is organized by the dates the trains left France, it is possible to determine the arrival dates at Auschwitz and, consequently, the death dates of individuals who were gassed immediately. Similar memorial books exist for Belgium and Netherlands.

Documentation after the Holocaust

After World War II, with hundreds of thousands of Jews scattered throughout Europe and millions having been murdered, attempts were made to identify the living and the dead so that survivors could locate relatives and friends and know the fate of those who perished. Lists of displaced persons were developed as early as 1943, but the burden of collecting information about both survivors and victims fell upon the International Tracing Service of the International Committee of the Red Cross. This organization still is active and receives thousands of inquiries each year. It is estimated that they hold more than 40 million index cards that record information about specific individuals.

After World War II, the remnant of European Jewry published yizkor books—memorial books—to documeent and remember the towns and townspeople destroyed in the Holocaust. To date, more than one thousand such works have been published. They include articles written by survivors and often provide a great deal of information about specific individuals from the town.

Yad Vashem, the principal repository in the world of Holocaust documentation, in 1955 started a global effort to document each individual murdered in the Holocaust. They asked people with knowledge of these victims to provide Pages of Testimony vouching that the named person was a Holocaust victim. To date, some three million Pages of Testimony are on file at the Hall of Names at Yad Vashem in Jerusalem. Consequently, half of the six million victims have been documented individually through this manuscript collection. The Hall of Names is their cemetery and the Pages of Testimony are their tombstones.

Lists of victims by country, region or camp have been compiled since the war. Best known is the *Gedenkbuch*, a list of 128,000 German Jews murdered in the Holocaust. It was compiled by the German government from surviving records of the war. A comparable book exists for all Dutch Jews. Some compiled lists are for regions (for example, Hajdu County, Hungary), cities (for example, Frankfurt am Main) and camps (for example, Theresienstadt).

Locating Survivors Today

Historically, Jews have banded together for mutual benefit and protection. International and national Jewish social service organizations, such as the Jewish Agency and the Hebrew Immigrant Aid Society (HIAS), helped Holocaust survivors relocate in countries that accepted refugees after World War II. Most of these organizations kept records of the individuals they helped, and some records are accessible to the public. When Jews emigrated from Europe around the turn of the century, they formed landsmanshaftn societies in their new lands that centered around their towns of origin. When Holocaust survivors left Europe, they joined existing societies or created their own new societies. Many of these groups still exist today. Even if they do not, their records have survived and may provide clues to help locate survivors.

Writing to Holocaust Resource Sites

Most facilities do not have the human resources to accommodate requests to do research. You may get them to do the research for you if your request is so specific that it will take them little time to accommodate you. For example, a request to the Yad Vashem archives that you are "looking for information about a Tobias Mokotowski, born about 1900, who lived in Otwock, Poland, before the Holocaust" probably will illicit a polite response that the archives' holdings for the town of Otwock are so extensive, and their human resources are so limited, that it is impossible for them to do the research. However, the following request was processed: "According to the *Guide to Unpublished Materials of the Holocaust Period*, your record group M-1/DN-28/2 contains a list of Jews who lived in Otwock, Poland. Could you please check if there are any persons named Mokotowski on the list." Note that this second request is very specific, identifying where they must go within the archives to locate the information requested.

What if you do not know the exact name of the person? Some facilities will do generic searches, but only on unusual names. Examples are "all persons named Mokotow" or "all persons named Szare from Kalisz." If you are searching for Cohen, you must be more specific. If you are searching for Jacob Cohen, the name is so common that you may have to provide more specific information than just the name.

It is acceptable to write to foreign facilities in your native language. The response may be in their native language. We are now an international community. It is always possible to find someone in your area who can translate the response to your inquiry no matter in which language it is written.

CHECKLIST FOR DOING HOLOCAUST RESEARCH

☐ Read this book to determine the resources available to conduct Holocaust research that apply to your particular situation. Check the index for towns and concentration camps relevant to your specific research. Appendixes A, B and C are not included in the index because they are lists of towns. Check these sections, also.

☐ If you are not familiar with the circumstances surrounding the fate of the Jews of the town where the survivors and/or victims lived before the Holocaust, read a book on the history of the Holocaust that describes these events. Two such books are *Ghetto Anthology* and *Encyclopedia of the Holocaust* (see "Selected Bibliography").

☐ Determine if there is a yizkor book for the town in which the people of interest lived. A list of towns for which yizkor books have been published is in Appendix A. Consult the book to see if there is mention of the individuals or family names you are researching.

☐ If the person(s) is a Holocaust victim and the fate is not known, write to the Hall of Names at Yad Vashem to see if Pages of Testimony have been submitted for that individual.

☐ Check the records of the International Tracing Service for information about survivors and victims, either by writing to them using the Foreign Inquiry Location Service of the American Red Cross or by consulting the microfilm copy at Yad Vashem in person.

☐ Are the persons on victim lists? Where applicable, consult lists that exist for Belgium, France, Germany, Holland, Hungary and other areas.

☐ If searching for a survivor, write a letter to the organizations in various countries that maintain lists of survivors or that assisted survivors in relocating after World War II. They are described in the chapter titled "Locating Survivors."

☐ Contact a local Holocaust Resource Center for information about the latest resources found for Holocaust research. A list of Holocaust Research Centers appears in Appendix E. If the local facility does not have a book or record known to be available elsewhere, ask them to secure a copy of the information for their permanent collection or as a loan copy. New acquisitions are constantly being made and resource sites regularly share their information.

☐ Consider asking for help from a Jewish genealogical society. Their members are researching their families' histories. Because the Holocaust has had such a profound affect on contemporary Jewish families, members have developed expertise in Holocaust research. A list of societies appears in Appendix F.

☐ If you have the option of either going to or writing to a major resource center, go there in person. Many research sites are very conscientious about processing mail inquiries, but the recipient of your request can devote only a limited amount of time to your inquiry. If you go to the facility, you can spend the hours necessary to peruse secondary sources of information. Browse the catalog of the holdings of the facility. See if there is information about any of the towns of interest. Some references may include details about specific individuals that are not obvious in the catalog description of the work. Cataloging is an imperfect process that, to a certain extent, relies on the judgment of the cataloger. An example is Record Group RG-15.019M at the U.S. Holocaust Research Institute. Its description is "Court inquiries about executions and graves in districts, provinces, camps and ghettos"—19 microfilm reels. Its purpose is to document Nazi atrocities in Poland. The names of victims are given in many cases.

☐ When writing to a research facility about a specific individual or family, give as much information as possible—but be concise. Limit your letter to facts about the individual, including exact name, date of birth (even if year only or approximate year), place of birth, names of immediate family members and last known residence address. Any information that can uniquely identify the individual from the thousands, if not millions, of pieces of information at the research site is important. Inadequate information will prompt a rejection of your request, which will only delay your research. Picture yourself at the facility trying to do the research. Could you find the information requested given the information you supplied?

מוקוטוב משה

מצבה למשפחתי שהיתה ואיננה

למרות שכותב רשימה זו הוא בן ואח למשפחה אשר נגזר עליה — חצי
לחיים — וחצי למוות; אמנור באוביקטיביות מלאה ציונים לאלה ממשפחתי
שנרצחו.

אלה שהכירו את אבי ז"ל יצחק מוקוטוב ידעו ויסכימו אתי שהיה זה אדם
יקר במלוא מובן המלה. מפרנסי העיר היה, מעוטי היכולת, "שהתברכה" בהם
עירנו, תמיד מצאו אצלו דלת פתוחה ואוזן קשבת למכלול בעיותיהם. בתור ילד
קטן לא ידעתי מטרת בקורם התכופה אצלנו. מצוות הכנסת כלה קיים אבי ז"ל
גם בנאמנות וגם בשמחה, לא תריסר אחד של זוגות צעירים התחתנו בעירנו,
ובאשר לסידורים החמריים שלהם, דאג אבי ז"ל. כאן עלי להוסיף שאמי תבדל

מוקוטוב יצחק
ובתו ברונקה ז"ל.

לחיים ארוכים היתה מעודדת אותו במפעל אנושי זה בכל מאודה, רגילה היתה
להכין רשימת הנצרכים, זכור לי עדיין משפט של אבי ז"ל כשהיה פונה לאמי:

Yizkor Book Article. *Yizkor books include remembrances by survivors of
those who died in the Holocaust. This article, taken from the yizkor book of
Przedecz, Poland, was written by Moshe Mokotow of Israel. It is titled "A
Monument to My Family Which Was and Is No More." Most yizkor books are
written in Hebrew and Yiddish.*

YIZKOR BOOKS

Background

After World War II, many survivors of the Holocaust published books that memorialized the destroyed Jewish communities of Europe. Called yizkor books (*yizkor* means "memorial" or "remembrance" in Hebrew), they commemorate the victims as well as the Jewish communities. Actually, yizkor books had been published for many years before World War II, but the term has now come to mean specifically Holocaust memorial books. To date, more than one thousand towns have been commemorated in this manner. More than half are associated with the towns of Poland as it existed before World War II, but the percentage represented by today's national boundaries are: Poland, 30%; Germany, 22%; Ukraine, 18%; Belarus, 13%; Hungary, 4%; Lithuania, 3%; Netherlands 3%; Romania, 2%; Slovakia, 2%; Austria, Croatia, Czech Republic, France, Greece, Italy, Latvia, Moldova and Serbia, each 1% or less. A list of towns for which Holocaust yizkor books have been published is found in Appendix A.

Description

Although each yizkor book was written independently, they share a basic common structure. The first section describes the history of the Jewish community of the town from its inception—sometimes hundreds of years ago—to the events of the Holocaust. This history invariably describes the destruction of all Jewish religious property (synagogues, cemeteries, etc.) and the immediate murder or deportation to labor or extermination camps of the Jewish population. A map shows the Jewish section of the town, identifying where the synagogue(s), religious school(s) and other Jewish landmarks once stood. For the historian, this overview provides valuable material about the Jewish communal life of the town. For researchers who want to identify relatives who once lived in the town, pictures of religious, social and welfare organizations may offer clues. The articles and captions associated with the pictures often identify the members.

The next section consists of personal remembrances of survivors about their individual families. They contain a wealth of information about family members, including names, relationships, ages and sometimes birth dates.

יקובובסקי כתריאל

אשתו :   חיה.

בן :   אברהם.

בנות :   פריידה, מיכל.

כתריאל יקובובסקי מיט זיין משפחה, פין פאך אבאשטעלטער שניידער
געווען אפרומער ייד. געדאוואענט אין בית המדרש, און פלעגט לערנען צווישען
מנחה־מעריב ביי ר' לייב לנציצקי אפרק עין יעקב. ער האט געהאט פיינע
אינטעליגענטע קינדער. זיין זין דוד איז געווען פין די גרינדער פין דער פאלקס
ביבליאטעק. ער איז נפטר געווארען אין אמעריקה אין 1972. זייער זוהן משה
אהרון וועלכער איז געווען פין די דיא גרינדער פין דיא שלום עליכם ביבליאטעק
וואוינט אין קאנאדא.

שמעונוביץ הרמן
אשתו, 4 ילדים

הרמן שמעונוביץ, א איידים פין אלטען שפערקע, האט געוואוינט אין
אפאציאטען דירה אין הויז פין קריסט לאפאטקעוויטש. געפארען אויף די מערק
מיט גאלאנטעריע, נאכהער איז ער געווארען אמלמד, און אויף די מערק איז
געפארען זיין פרוי. זיי האבען געהאט פיר קינדער, אשטילע משפחה, נישט
געמישט זיך אין שטעטישע ענינים, דאדורך אויך איז אינז נישט באקאנט זייערע
נעמען.

Yizkor Book "Tombstones." Within yizkor books, families with no
survivors, or whose survivors could not be located, were memorialized by
friends and neighbors in brief passages that include the names of the family
members and a brief description of the family. Where names could not be
remembered, they are left blank, as in the case of the second entry shown
above, which identifies "Herman Shimonovitz, wife and four children." This
page is from the yizkor book of Przedecz, Poland.

Where survivors knew the fate of family members, this may also be included.

The next section of a yizkor book is devoted to describing families with no survivors. These accounts were contributed by neighbors or friends who had known the family. The article is brief—one- or two-paragraph descriptions headed by the names of the father and mother, as well as the names of the children. In cases where the name of a parent could not be remembered, it is left blank. If the children's names were not remembered, the notation might be "three children" or "two sons and a daughter."

The next section may be a necrology—a list of all the victims from the town. The final section includes the names and addresses of survivors of the town, usually organized by country of relocation.

Almost all yizkor books are written in Hebrew and Yiddish. This represents a major challenge to those unversed in these languages, because both the language and the alphabet are unfamiliar. Fortunately, this is not as difficult an obstacle as one might think. The reader is not attempting to read the book for meaning, but rather is looking for something very specific: people's names. Go to the table of contents of a yizkor book. There you find a sequence of words written in Hebrew and Yiddish, aligned at the left margin, and another sequence of words, aligned at the right margin. At the left margin are listed the authors and at the right margin are the titles of the articles. This may seem backwards, but Hebrew and Yiddish are written right to left. Leaf through the book and look at the captions of pictures. A picture of a single person may have two or three words below the picture— the person's name. The caption of a group of ten persons may have many sets of two or three words separated by commas—the names of the persons in the picture. The back of the book consists of pages in table form. It is observed that the table is in sections where the first letter of the first word of each section is identical. This is the necrology listed in alphabetical order by last name.

How to Use a Yizkor Book

How do you find information about specific individuals when you cannot read or do not understand Hebrew or Yiddish? Again, the reader has an advantage that the search is for people's names only. For example, the name Mokotowski, whether it is in Hebrew, Cyrillic, Greek or the Roman alphabet, is written phonetically as *mukutuvski*. To search for a particular name, ask someone knowledgeable in the languages to write in Hebrew and Yiddish its spelling in printed form. Look through the list of authors in the table of contents for the pattern of letters. Read the titles of articles. Scan the captions of pictures of individuals. Check the necrology for names of members of the family. If the name is found, make a copy of the page or the entire associated article and arrange to have it translated. Where do you find someone knowledgeable in Hebrew or Yiddish? Your closest synagogue

ו

זואדקע אברהם, חנה, יודל, הערש, רבקה, אהרן, יוסף, דינה.
זאטמאן אברהם, יהושע, יוסף, ישראל, מענדל, רבקה, מרים פערל,
אסתר רחל לאה, שיינדל, צפורה, מענדל, יוסף אברהם, אליעזר.
וואסערמאן יעקב ומשפחתו, יחיאל ומשפחתו.
וואסערניר מענדל ומשפחתו.
וואסערצוג יעקב, צירל, ברך, ומשפחתו אהרן יונה ומשפחתו.
וואראשאווסקי שלמה יעקב.
וואראשאבסקי אריה ומשפחתו.
וואראשאווער גרשון, שלמה, יעקב, שלמה, יעקב ומשפחותיהם.
וולמאן אליעזר ומשפחתו.
וואלף אהרן ומשפחתו, מאיר.
וואלפאויבין יוסף, צביה.
זוויינבלום הערש דוד, מיכל, אטקע, משה, שרה, רפאל, משה,
שרה, אבא, אסתר, רבקה, פראדל, פיינגע, ישראל, לייבא
הערש, ומשפחותיהם.
וויוסבכארד לוי ומשפחתו.
וויושניע וואלף ומשפחתו.
זויניצקי ישעיהו ומשפחתו, הענער ומשפחתו.

ז

זאכאראבין לייבא, רבקה, פיניע, משה.
זילבער מלכה.
זילבערמעל יעקב, שלמה, רווה ומשפ'.
זילבערשטיין אריה, משה, פישל, פיניע, אלימלך, שרה רויזע,
מאניע, יוסף, מאניס.
זינגער משה ואשתו, פריידע, מרדכי.
זיסקינד פייויל, שמואל לייב, פיניע, יוסף, אסתר מלכה.

ח

חילמאן שלמה זלמן, רבקה, שרה, דורה.
העלדענבערג שמשון דוד ומשפחתו.

ט

טיקאצינסקי שמאי, יחיאל, שמואל, יהושע — ומשפחותיהם.
טעננבוים ישעיהו קלונימוס, איטה, חנוך, מרדכי, בונים, דבורה.
שפרה, נחמה, טענענבוים ישראל, אשתו באלטשע, הילדים:
אהרן, פיינגע, אלחנן.
טעראנגעל אימה, רחל, שלמה.
טראמער יעקב, פרץ.
טראסטערמאן משה, חיה, דוד, לייכל, יצחק, לאה.

י

יום-טוב מענדל, לייטשע, משה, מתתיהו, חיים, יעקב, חנה.
יערוואב שמחה, הערשל, יעקב, אליהו, שלמה, הערשל, רבקה,
פישטשע, וועלויל, חוה, באלטשע, זלמן יוסף ומשפחתו.

ל

לאנגער יוסף, שלום, ומשפחותיהם.
לאנדוי טוביה, פיניע, חיה, פריידע, ישראל הערש, רבקה, רחל.

לעווין יצחק, אסתר גולדע, שיינדל, נחמן, שרגא יחנה.
לאנדרא יחיאל ומשפחתו.
לוסטיג לייזול ואשתו, משה, חנה (שלאנג), אהרן, שרה.
לאקסמאן שמואל, רחל לאה, אלכסנדר, אברהם שלום, אלכסנדר,
איסא, ישראל מענדל, רבקה רייזעל.
ליסינסקי אליעזר, גיטל, אברהם, פיינע, ב"בה.
לעמפער יאסקע.

מ

מאדאנעם בצלאל, מענדל ומשפחותיהם.
מאנדעלאייל לייבא, ומשפחתו.
מאראגאלים אבוש ואשתו.
מאקאטאב יחיאל-טוביה, רחל, דן, משה ומשפחתו, לייבא, אשר.
מיינסטער ישראל הערש, וועלויל.
מיינסטער הערש-דוד.
מינץ משה יוסף, חנה אטמה, דוד, פיינע, ישראל, וועלויל, אליהו,
יעקב, אהרן, שרה (קירשנבוים), מאסעלע, פיינעלע, אהרן
ישראל יצחק (לערמאן).
מנחם מאניש ומשפחתו, אטקה, פולה.
מענדזילבסקי נתן, דוד, חנה ובניהם.
מעסינג יעקב-הערש ומשפחתו, אליעזר.

נ

נאביצקי ראובן ומשפחתו.
נאבגעלד הערשל, גולדע, משה, יעקב, שרה, חנה.
ניידארף נימפל ומשפחתו.

ס

סאפערשטיין שלמה, רחל, דוד, חנה, דבורה.
סאקאל מענדל, פערל, יוסף, שמטיהו, שיינדל, סיטה (מרום).
סאקאלאבער יונה ומשפחתו.
סטאלאבסקי חנה.

פ

סאפאווער בצלאל, שיינדל, אברהם שמואל, משה אליהו.
סוטערמאן שמואל יעקב.
סיטקאביין זלמן, רבקה שרה, חנה, רויזע, אייויק, חיים, דוד,
פערל, אלי מאיר, הנה, רבקה, גיטל, מענדל, יוכבד, רחל.
פינגענבוים משה יוסף, חיה, משה יחיאל, משה אהרן, יעקב,
שפרה, מנחם, לאה, שלמה, ישראל, רבקה, מלכה, אברהם,
קינגזילבער אליעזר ומשפחתו.
פיינשטיין חיים יהושע ומשפחתו.
פינקעלשטיין אהרן אליעזר, יחזקאל, פישל, יעקב שלום, ומשפ'.
פישמאן לייבא, רבקה, פערל, משה, צביה, אהרן, חיה רחל,
שמעון יוסף, אהרן, גיטל, מרים, איידל.
סלאם לייביש ומשפחתו, יעקב ומשפחתו אליהו.
פערערמאן אשר, הערשל, פראול, חוה, משה, ברכה, ישראל-
יהושע, מרים, נחמה.
סעלרמאן דוד, יוסף, מענדל, פייויל, שרה, איטקה, משה, שלמה,
ישראל הערש — ומשפחותיהם.

Yizkor Book Necrology. Most yizkor books have a necrology—a list of the dead from the town. This portion is from the book for Garwolin, Poland. Listed on the fourth line of entries under the Hebrew equivalent of the letter 'M' are members of the Mokotow family, including Yechiel-Tuvia, Rachel, Dan, Moshe and his family, Leiba and Asher. Pages of Testimony indicate that most of them fled Garwolin to Lwow, where they perished.

can help you find someone.

Yizkor books are a possible link to the present—the articles were written by persons who may still be alive. If not, their children may be alive and able to provide information about your family. If a list of survivors is printed in the book or an address of the society that published the book is given, consider writing to them. First note the copyright year of the publication. If it is decades ago, there is less likelihood that the person is alive or lives currently at the address given. Telephone books of other countries are often available at major libraries in your area, or you can contact the nearest consulate or embassy for the country of interest. Consulates and embassies have on hand telephone books of the major cities in their country.

Where to Find Yizkor Books

The largest collections of yizkor books are held at Yad Vashem in Jerusalem, YIVO Institute for Jewish Research in New York, the Library of Congress in Washington, D.C., the UCLA Library in Los Angeles and the Jewish Public Library in Montreal. Substantial collections exist in large public and university libraries throughout the world, as well as in Holocaust research centers. Libraries known to have large collections of yizkor books are listed in Appendix D.

It is extremely difficult to purchase yizkor books. All but the most recently published are out of print, and it is unusual for one to come on the market—usually a Holocaust survivor has died and the family has given the books to a book wholesaler. Check with dealers in used Jewish books. The National Yiddish Book Center states they do not usually sell yizkor books to the general public but reserve their acquisitions for libraries. Two companies have developed a reputation as sellers of yizkor books; both are located in Israel—both publish catalogs: J. Robinson & Co. Booksellers; 26 Nachlat Benjamin Street; Tel Aviv. Also, Chaim Dzialowski; P.O. Box 6413; 91063 Jerusalem.

YAD VASHEM

**Martyrs' and Heroes'
Remembrance
Authority**

DAF-ED

A Page of Testimony

דף-עד

P.O.B. 3477
Jerusalem, Israel

חוק זכרון השואה והגבורה —
תשי״ג 1953
קובע בסעיף מס׳ 2:

תפקידו של יד-ושם לאסוף
אל המולדת את זכרם של כל
אלה מבני העם היהודי, שנפלו
ומסרו את נפשם, נלחמו ומרדו
באויב הנאצי ובעוזריו, ולהציב
שם וזכר להם, לקהלות,
לארגונים ולמוסדות שנתרבו בגלל
השתייכותם לעם היהודי.

(ספר החוקים מס׳ 132,
כ״ז אלול תשי״ג 28.8.53)

THE MARTYRS' AND HEROES' REMEMBRANCE LAW, 5713—1953
determines in Article No. 2 that

The task of YAD VASHEM is to gather into the homeland material regarding all those members of the Jewish people who laid down their lives, who fought and rebelled against the Nazi enemy and his collaborators, and to perpetuate their memory and that of the communities, organizations, and institutions which were destroyed because they were Jewish.

ת מ ו נ ה **Photo**	1. Family name *	שם המשפחה * .1
	2. First Name (maiden name)	השם הפרטי (שם לפני הנישואין) .2
	4. Place of birth מקום הלידה (town, country) (עיר, ארץ)	3. Date of birth תאריך הלידה
	6. Name of mother שם האם	5. Name of father שם האב

7. Name of spouse (if a wife, add maiden name)	שם בן או בת הזוג .7 (אם בת זוג נא להוסיף שם משפחתה לפני הנישואין)
8. Place of residence before the war	מקום המגורים לפני המלחמה .8
9. Places of residence during the war	מקומות המגורים במלחמה .9
10. Circumstances of death (place, date, etc.)	נסיבות המוות (זמן, מקום, וכר׳) .10

I, the undersigned .... אני, החי״מ

residing at (full address) .... הגר.ה ב (כתובת מלאה) ....

relationship to deceased .... קירבה (משפחתית או אחרת) ....

hereby beclare that this testimony is correct to the best of my knowledge.

מצהיר/ה בזה כי עדות זו נכונה לפי מיטב ידיעותי.

Signature .... חתימה

Place and date .... מקום ותאריך

"..ונתתי להם בביתי ובחומותי יד ושם...אשר לא יכרת" ישעיהו נ"ו,ה

"..even unto them will I give in mine house and within my walls a place and a name...that shall not be cut off." Isaiph, LVI,5

• נא לרשום את שמו של כל נספה על דף נפרד
* Please inscribe the nameof each victim of the Holocaust on a separate form.

Page of Testimony, English Language Version

PAGES OF TESTIMONY

Background

The major archives and documentation center for the Holocaust is Yad Vashem in Jerusalem, Israel. Since 1955, Yad Vashem has been attempting to document every one of the six million Jews murdered in the Holocaust in a manuscript collection called Pages of Testimony. To date, more than three million victims have been documented. Persons have been requested to come forward and submit, on a preprinted form, information about the victim, including name; place and year of birth; place, date and circumstances of death; occupation; names of mother, father and spouse; and, in some cases, names and ages of children. Each submitter is required to sign this Page of Testimony and to show his or her name, address and relationship to deceased. By submitting this form, the person testifies that he or she knew of the victim and the circumstances surrounding his or her death. The majority of the submitters are relatives of the deceased. Most Pages of Testimony were submitted in the 1950s when the project started. Most have been submitted by Israelis and, therefore, are written in Hebrew. In recent years, there has been an effort to increase the size of the collection significantly. Holocaust survivors are encouraged to contribute Pages now; otherwise, information that only they can provide will be lost to future generations. The emigration of a large number of Jews from the former Soviet Union has also provided an opportunity to add significantly to the collection.

Description

To make it as simple as possible for people to complete the form, it is available in many languages. The form has been redesigned a number of times through the years, but it still asks for essentially the same information:
- Family name of victim, in native language and Roman letters
- Given name of victim, in native language and Roman letters
- Name of father
- Name of mother
- Country and place of birth
- Place of permanent residency
- Occupation
- Nationality before German occupation

דף־עד

להענקת אזרחות־זכרון לחללי השואה

No *1714*	מס. תרשם:	

שם המשפחה בעברית בשפת ארץ המדג	מוקוטוב MOKOTOW
שם פרטי בעברית בשפת ארץ המדג	חיים דן CHAIM DAN
שם כנוי או שם מושאל	
שם האב	משה
שם האם	ברכה
מצב משפחתי	נשוי
תאריך הלידה	1904
מקום וארץ הלידה	פולין - דרבין
השתייך/ת לקהלה/ות	
בארץ	פולין
הנתינות בשנת 1939	פולין
המקצוע	סוחר
המקום והזמן של מותו/ה	אנ זגיר 1942-3
נסיבות המות	הרצח ע״י הנאצים (אושויץ)

חוק זכרון השואה והגבורה —

יד ושם

תשי״ג 1953

קבע בסעיף מס' 2

הפקירו של יד־ושם הוא לאסוף א ולגבו...

...נ.ה... להענקי לבני העם היהודי שנ...

אזרחות־זכרון

שמות הילדים	גיל	המקום והזמן שנספו
מאלה	4	ותג? אן הלויו
גוזה	8	

שם משפחתה לפני הנשואין ... ברכה ... שם האשה

הכתובת האחרונה הידועה של הנרשם	דרבין פולין
כתובות ידועות מזמן המלחמה	רוסיה

אני מוקוטוב משה הגר ב ת״א רח' אפקה ... כתובת מלאה ...	34
קרוב/ה מכר/ה א.ח של מוקוטוב ... רח' ...	

מצהיר/ה בזה כי העדות שמסרתי כאן על פרטיה היא נכונה ואמיתית לפי מיטב ידיעתי והכרתי.

אני מבקש/ת להעניק לנ״ל אזרחות־זכרון מטעם מדינת ישראל.

מקום ותאריך	ת״א 15.8
תאריך	11.5.55
חתימה	מוקוטוב

חתימת הפוקד

Page of Testimony for Chaim Dan Mokotow. The importance of documenting Holocaust victims through Pages of Testimony is illustrated by this document. It was completed in 1955 by Chaim's brother, Aryeh Mokotow, about nine months before Aryeh died. It is the only known documentation of the Dan's two children, Moshe and Guza. No living member of the family recalled their names.

- Places of residency during the war
- Marital status
- Number of children
- Spouse's name and age and, if wife, maiden name
- Names of children under 18, ages, places and dates of death
- Name and address of person giving testimony
- Relationship to the deceased
- Signature and date

How to Use Pages of Testimony

Pages of Testimony serve two valuable functions: They provide detailed information about the Holocaust victim, and they may offer a link to the present—to a person who either knew the victim or was familiar with the victim's fate. This link is becoming weaker as the years pass because many of the Pages of Testimony were filled out in the late 1950s, and many of the submitters are no longer alive. In this case, it becomes necessary to locate descendants of the submitters, who may be more difficult to track down and whose knowledge of the victims may be secondary.

How to Get Pages of Testimony

The Pages of Testimony are currently available only at the Hall of Names at Yad Vashem. They can be accessed in person or by mail inquiry. There is a nominal charge for each document. In response to a mail inquiry, you will be sent the documents and an invoice; there is no need to prepay. In a departure from the norm, it is usually better to get copies by mail rather than in person. If you go in person, a number of others usually are waiting to use the one microfilm reader/printer allocated to accommodate the public. Most requests are not for specific persons; therefore, it can take a fair amount of time for the operator of the machine to search through the films for each patron. Instead, write to:

Hall of Names
Yad Vashem
P.O. Box 3477
91034 Jerusalem, Israel

The handling of mail inquiries does not involve the pressure of impatient patrons waiting to be serviced, and you will probably get better service using this method. The Hall of Names will accept generic searches such as "all persons named Mokotow" or "all persons named Mokotow from Garwolin"; however, they will do generic searches only for surnames for which they have fewer than three hundred documents. The cost averages less than $2.00 per document, but rates may change based on economic conditions, and rules for quality of service may change as demand rises.

If you elect to do research in person, the current hours are 10am to 2pm Sunday through Thursday and 10am to 12:30pm on Friday. Check before you go.

INTERNATIONAL TRACING SERVICE

Background

Immediately after World War II, when refugees were scattered throughout Europe, a common collection point of information about both survivors and victims evolved into what became the International Tracing Service (ITS). This was the first attempt to identify, in an orderly manner, the fate of the millions of persons, both Jewish and non-Jewish, who were displaced or killed during World War II. To this day, data is still being discovered and accumulated by ITS which is now part of the International Committee of the Red Cross. The service now has some 40 million pieces of information at their facilities in Arolsen, Germany.

Description

The ITS maintains a master index of information relating to more than 14 million individuals. If the person was a survivor, an index card may exist from the time when the individual was in a refugee camp. It would show his name, age, place of birth, and possibly names of parents and where the person was at the time the information was recorded. When a refugee was relocated, another card would show the destination. From information acquired from death lists in cities and concentration camps, the index card would show the name of the individual, date of birth, place of birth, place of death and circumstances of death. There are also index cards created from inquiries by persons trying to determine the fate of friends or family.

How to Use These Records

There are three ways this information can be accessed, each with its own advantages and disadvantages.
- Write to the ITS directly.
- Use the Foreign Location Inquiry Service of the American Red Cross.
- Use copies of ITS records located in the archives of Yad Vashem.

Write directly. To write to the ITS directly, address your inquiry to

```
                    Da No. 17114. - Sch.J.Pole
Date   1.12.50/SL
Name  MOKOTOW , Berek                    File GCC3/62/IA/4
BD    11.3.92    BP   Warschau               Nat Polish-Jew.
Next of Kin
Source of Information    Orig.Dachau Entry Register
Last kn. Location                              Date
CC/Prison  Dachau        Arr.  3.9.40 from   KLSachsenhausen
Transf. on               to
Died on 15.1.41 ?        in   CC Dachau
Cause of death
Buried on                in
Grave                                    D. C. No.
Remarks   home address:Frankfurt a.M., Schichaustr.4
```

Index Card of Victim Information—International Tracing Service Master Index. Documentation of Berek (Bernard) Mokotow of Frankfurt am Main, who was born in Warsaw and died at Dachau.

International Tracing Service, Grosse Allee 5–9, 34444 Arolsen, Germany. The ITS will search only for specific individuals, and you must provide as much information as possible about the person. You must know the name of the individual, either the place of birth or town before the war, and an approximate age. If the name you are searching is reasonably unique, this should be sufficient for them to perform the search. If the name is common, you must provide additional information to identify the individual definitively. One major disadvantage of accessing ITS records by writing to them directly is the time it takes for a reply. It can take from six months to two years for them to determine whether they have information about an individual.

American Red Cross. A more rapid way of dealing with the ITS is through the American Red Cross (ARC). Their address is:

Foreign Location Inquiry Service
American Red Cross
18th & D Street, N.W.
Washington, DC 20066
Telephone (800) 848-9277 (U.S. and Canada only). Other telephone: (410) 764-5311; fax: (410) 764-4638.

In 1990, ARC made special arrangements with ITS to act as an intermediary. There are a number of advantages to working through ARC. They will process your form immediately and reject it if they feel you have provided

```
Date     10.5.49
Name     M O K O T O W     Rachmil          File  F 18-113
BD      25 years  BP                        Nat  Polish
Next of Kin      MOKOTOW Rywka & Henri
Source of Information      AJDC,Emigr.Serv.,Paris
Last kn. Location 33.rue au Maire.Paris 3me Date   15.2.49
CC/Prison              Arr.              lib.
Transf. on                      to
Died on                         in
Cause of death
Buried on                       in
Grave                                D.C.No
Remarks       Regist.for emigr.to Australia.
```

*Index Card of Survivor Information—International Tracing Service.
Documentation of Rachmil Mokotow, his wife, Rywka, and son, Henri, living
in Paris in 1949 shortly before they emigrated to Australia. They are
survivors from Warsaw who live today in the Melbourne area.*

insufficient information about the person you are seeking. It can take as long as six months to get a comparable rejection letter for a request sent directly to ITS. It is also claimed that the response time from ITS to ARC is faster because ARC constantly monitors its open inquiries. Another advantage is that ARC is part of an international network of Red Cross organizations and will contact its counterpart in another country if evidence indicates a survivor went to that country. A major disadvantage is that, because of the huge volume of requests it receives, ARC has been forced to limit inquiries to those from immediate relatives. Immediate relatives include brothers, sisters, children and grandchildren. The form asks for relationship to person. Writing niece, nephew, cousin or any other remote relationship, or none at all, may cause rejection of the application. You need not be an American to use the services of ARC; inquiries are accepted from persons living outside the United States.

Yad Vashem Archives. The third way to access the information is by consulting the duplicate copy of much of the ITS information located at Yad Vashem archives in Jerusalem. The facility is open to the public so you can (1) go there yourself, (2) have a friend or relative living in Israel use the facility, or (3) hire a professional researcher to do the work for you. The principal advantage of using the Yad Vashem archives is time; the records can be searched within weeks, if not days. The principal disadvantage is that

Index Card of an Inquiry—International Tracing Service. Inquiry by Hella Mokotow of Brooklyn about the fate of her mother, Gitla, of Frankfurt am Main. Her mother died in Frankfurt; her father, Bernard, died at Dachau. Hella was sent out of Germany before the war to England and arrived in the United States in April 1940 when she was 16 years of age.

the records constitute the ITS collection as of 1965. With access to records held by formerly communist countries now easing, ITS has acquired additional records of the Holocaust. Some of this new information is available at Yad Vashem, but it is not collated with the earlier ITS records.

If you elect to use a professional researcher, be sure to select someone living in Israel, preferably in Jerusalem. If you hire a professional outside of Israel, all he or she will do is contact a fellow professional in Israel to do the actual work and charge you for his or her time as well as that time actually used to do the search. A list of Israeli researchers who have done this type of research is available from this author at P.O. Box 900, Teaneck, NJ 07666. To receive a list, you must include a self-addressed stamped envelope or two international postal reply coupons, if inquiring from outside the United States.

Recommendation: Check the ITS records at Yad Vashem first. If they do not provide sufficient information, then take the more time-consuming approach of using the American Red Cross to check the complete records of ITS.

ITS Records at Yad Vashem
In addition to the master index, there is an enormous amount of material that represents the original source documents from which the master index was compiled. It is always possible that some of the information was not carried to the master index and additional information might exist in the original documentation.

Record Group ID. These records, arranged by concentration camp, include more than three million documents of individuals. The camps are: Buchenwald, Dachau, Flossenburg, Gross-Rosen, Hinzert, Liebenau, Mauthausen, Dora-Mittelbau, Natzweiler, Neider-Wewelsburg, Radom and Ravensbruck. There are also a card index of names from Italy and individual records for Gestapo offices in Frankfurt am Main, Hamburg, Koblenz and Wuerzburg.

Record Group BD. This group contains more than 295,000 pages of lists of persons at various camps. Some are in alphabetical order, most in chronological order. There are lists of arrivals, transports, sick persons, executions, deaths, some burials, survivors upon liberation, changes of status, outside work details, and others. The camps include Auschwitz, Bergen-Belsen, Buchenwald, Dachau, Drancy, Flossenburg, Gross-Rosen, Lublin-Majdanek, Malines, Mauthausen, Mittelbau-Dora, Natzweiler, Neuengamme, Papenburg, Ravensbruck, Sachsenburg, Sachsenhausen, Stutthof and Theresienstadt.

Record Group CHSA. This group concerns children survivors. There are approximately 185,000 microfilm frames of information, as well as card indexes, lists and case files.

LOCATING SURVIVORS

Background

In the course of your research, you may wish to locate persons for whom the only information you have is an obsolete address or no address at all. It is impossible to describe in a brief chapter the wealth of resources available to locate persons. If you think of the number of times you have had to put your name, address and other pertinent information on application forms, consider that each of these documents is a potential method of locating you. People appear in telephone directories, belong to organizations such as Holocaust survivor groups, contribute to Jewish charities, and are members of professional societies, to name a few. All are potential sources for locating an individual. The "Selected Bibliography" includes a number of books written about the subject.

Locating Survivors

One of the simplest techniques for locating individuals is using telephone directories. In this age of computers, commercial firms in many countries have developed consolidated telephone directories that provide a complete alphabetical list of all published telephone numbers in the country, independent of region. This allows the rapid search of an entire country's telephone subscribers for the name of an individual. Its principal disadvantage is that subscribers may request that their name not be listed. It can also be difficult to use if the person has a common name since hundreds of persons with the surname may be listed in the consolidated directory.

If you know the locality where a person once lived, find out if there is a reverse telephone directory for the area. This is a directory organized by street address rather than alphabetical order. For example, such directories exist for New York City. If the directory exists, call the neighbors of the person you are searching for. They may be able to supply you with a new address for the person or at least give you clues.

Writing a letter to "Occupant" at the person's last-known address might elicit a response from the current residents. Ask if they know the current whereabouts of the person you are seeking. Be sure to include a self-addressed stamped envelope (SASE) to make it easy for the person to

Name, Vorname und Geburtsort	geb.	Jetziger Aufenthalt	Name, Vorname und Geburtsort	geb.	Jetziger Aufenthalt
Mohr Imre (Biharnagybajom)	1920	Mittenwald	Mondzi Leon (Amleva)	1920	Feldafing
Mohr Lili (Nugyszalonta)	1921	Hassag-Altenburg	Monela Monik (Lodz)	1908	Feldafing
Mohr Romek (Bendzin)	1925	Celle	Moneon Herszel (Skalmierz)	1923	Schleißheim
Mohrenfeld Hirsz (Mlawa)	1922	Salzburg	Moneta Anna (Krakow)	1919	B.-Belsen
Mohs Mindla (Leipzig)	1898	Theresienstadt	Moneta Dora (Krakow)	1898	B.-Belsen
Mois Hildegard (Berlin)	1905	Theresienstadt	Moneta Josef (Sosnowice)	1924	Bamberg
Mois Rusa (Kastolan)	1922	Altötting	Moneta Leibusch (Sosnowice)	1896	Mittenwald
Moisoi (Director)		Obergracheim	Moneta Lola (Czenstochowa)	1925	Ainring
Moitzhaim (Charlotte (Berlin)	1866	Theresienstadt	Moneta Maier (Ksiaze Wielkie)	1902	Bamberg
Mojezcko Ewa (Lodz)	1918	Rentzmüller	Moneta Mordka (Skala)	1923	Salzburg
Mojerkiewicz Cesia (Dabrowa)		Gardelegen	Moneta Mordka (Czenstochowa)	1924	Ainring
Mojinkiewicz Chiel (Tomasow)	1923	Feldafing	Moneta Nuchcim (Wodzislaw)	1888	Mauthausen
Mojszewica Jakob (Rumancsety)	1906	Moosburg	Moneta Semek (Brzezin)	1926	Ainring
Mokoboska Frania (Warschau)	1924	Schweden	Moneta Anna (Krakau)	1919	Schweden
Mokoloczki Nachem (Lodz)	1925	Feldafing	Monheitowa Frida	1900	Bratislava
Mokotow Bronislaw (Warschau)	1916	Kempten	Monian Teresa (Saloniki)	1925	B.-Belsen
Mokovocki Ruvhen (Lodz)	1925	Feldafing	Monitz Kaszriel (Warta)	1926	Feldafing
Mokowski Josef (Lodz)	1906	Feldafing	Monitz Rafal (Lodz)	1898	Celle
Mokron Zipora Kh. (Sokolov-Pode)		Grodno	Monitz Samuel		Feldafing
Moks Rudi (Berlin) '	1917	Feldafing	Monk David (Schidlowecz)	1925	Feldafing
Mol Wilhelm (M.-Gladbach)	1897	Theresienstadt	Monk Leo	1922	Feldafing
Molan Franz	1921	Buchberg	Monk Majer (Warschau)	1919	Celle
Moldauer Jakob		Innsbruck	Monka Leo (Warschau)	1915	Feldafing
Moldowar Ludwika (Strx)	1910	B.-Belsen	Monkasch Mordkhai (Warschau)		Belostok
Moldowan Eva (Marmarosziget)	1924	Hassag-Altenburg	Monkobowski Nachum (Lodz)	1917	Schleißheim
Moldowan Leopold (Oradea mare)	1902	Feldafing	Monnatch Mordukhai (Chijec)		Grodno
Moldowan Lipot (Oradea)		Feldafing	Monowicz David (Chenice)	1919	Feldafing
Moldowan Morne (Marmarosziget)	1904	Hassag-Altenburg	Monowicz Kopel (Premjesica)	1913	Feldafing
Moldowan Nandor (Baia sprie)	1898	Feldafing	Monsta Szaja (Bendzin)	1924	Salzburg
Moldowan Roza (Gutfalva)		Feldafing	Monszajn Abram-Icek (Bendzin)	1904	Feldafing
Moldowan Zigmund (Capolnoc-Mon.)	1913	Feldafing	Montag John (Hannover)	1879	Theresienstadt
Moldowan Zigmund (Capolnok-Mon.)	1918	Feldafing	Montag Lajb (Krakow)	1905	Feldafing
Moldowan Zoltan (Debrecen)	1930	Hillersleben	Montag Leo (Zaklichin)	1905	Feldafing
Moler Alice	1912	England	Montag Leopold (Hamburg)	1880	Hamburg
Moler Moses (Tauroggen)	1904	Feldafing	Montanjes Jesina	1892	Hillersleben
Moler Richard	1906	England	Monxaz Nathan (Szydlow)	1922	Dachau
Molerich Leon (Kassel)	1918	Theresienstadt	Montbrun Lehna (Freiburg/Br.)	1894	Theresienstadt
Molicky Abram (Sosnowice)	1925	Feldafing	Montejka Eli (Saloniki)	1929	Föhrenwald
Molinaro Alfonso (Udine/Italien)	1916	Kosice	Montejka Pepi (Saloniki)	1929	Föhrenwald
Molio Alberto (Saloniki)	1905	Feldafing	Montszek Aron (Jawierni)	1924	Feldafing
Molisko Abraham (Lenischowo)	1925	Feldafing	Monya Elisabeth (Düsseldorf)	1877	Theresienstadt
Molnar Dr. Alexander		Bratislava	Monyuska Monia (Bendzin)	1923	Feldafing
Molnar Dezsö (Cluj)	1900	Feldafing	Mor Eva (Budapest)	1928	Schweden
Molnar Ferenc	1906	Bratislava	Mor Ida (Kaiserslautern)	1892	Theresienstadt
Molnar Gabor (Toplita)	1892	Feldafing	Mor Rozsi (Budapest)	1904	Schweden
Molnar Fried Helena		Bratislava	Mora David (Radom)	1911	Garmisch-Partenk.
Molnar Ilona (Zalaszanto)		Homberg	Mora Kyja (Radom)	1919	Mittenwald
Molnar Katalin (Kiskunmaja)	1924	Hassag-Altenburg	Mora Moszek (Radom)	1908	Dachau
Molnar Laszlo (Bpest)	1910	Hillersleben	Mora Moszek (Radom)	1910	Feldafing
Molnar Zuzana		Bratislava	Mora Pejsach (Radom)	1925	Mittenwald
Molochka Jankiel		Feldafing	Mora Sziva (Radom)	1919	Feldafing
Mololowacz Zuza (Maroswaszarbay)	1910	B.-Belsen	Moranski Hersz (Prusany)	1915	Feldafing
Molowan Edith (Marmarosziget)	1925	Hassag-Altenburg	Morawcowa Marie (Praha)	1903	B.-Belsen
Molsz Israel (Schaulen)	1893	Feldafing	Morawiec Moszek (Lodz)	1913	Schleißheim
Molsz Moses (Schaulen)	1897	Feldafing	Morawiecka Cela (Lodz)	1921	Landsberg
Moluchus Tarvia (Malowa)	1906	Feldafing	Morawiecka Mania (Lodz)	1908	Landsberg
Molwar Thomas (Budapest)	1921	Dachau	Morawiecka Mania (Lodz)	1927	Landsberg
Molz Hedwig (Stuttgart-Vaih.)	1893	Theresienstadt	Morawska Barbara (Lyezzea)	1924	Schweden
Monasewicz Mendel	1907	Buchberg	Morawski Emil (Linz)	1917	Bamberg
Monastyrski Boris		Riga	Morberger Elisabeth	1892	Australia
				1892	Australia

Sharit ha-platah (Lists of Survivors). Register of Polish Holocaust survivors compiled after World War II includes the name of Bronislaw (actually Bronislawa) Mokotow of Warschau (Warsaw) who was then located in Kempten, Germany. She had hidden during the war, posing as an Aryan. After the war, she emigrated to Australia.

respond. If writing to another country, instead of an SASE, go to the post office and purchase two international postal coupons and include it with your letter. The responder can redeem these coupons in exchange for cash equivalent to the cost of an air mail stamp. State in the letter that you would appreciate a response even if they know no information. You may wish to include a preprinted questionnaire to make it as simple as possible for the person to respond.

In virtually every major country in the world where Jews relocated after the Holocaust, agencies helped them with the task of settling in their new country. Each of these organizations created files of information about their clients that can be a starting point for locating survivors. When corresponding with these organizations, give as much factual information as possible about the person(s) sought—name, names of parents, name of spouse, place of birth, places lived before the war, location(s) during the war, occupation. Keep the letter brief, limiting it to information that might be useful in identifying the individual from the agencies' records. Do not write long letters describing the events in the person's life—they may be important to you, but not relevant to the searcher.

Many of these agencies have limited budgets. Therefore, to defray the cost of their responding to you, if the agency is in your country, include a legal-sized, self-addressed stamped envelope. If the agency is in another country, include two international postal coupons instead of a stamp.

Described below are institutions in various countries that can help you locate survivors.

ARGENTINA

On July 18, 1994, a terrorist bomb exploded in front of the office of the Jewish Federation (AMIA) on Pasteur Street, killing nearly one hundred persons and destroying the building. AMIA has established provisional headquarters at 632 Ayacucho Street in Buenos Aires.

AUSTRALIA

Although thousands of Holocaust survivors emigrated to Australia after World War II, there are no organized lists of those who did so. Attempts to create such documentation have met with resistance from community bodies anxious not to generate lists of names that may be used by persons carrying out some unknown future threat.

The Australian Jewish Welfare Society, which has branches in the various states of the Australian Commonwealth, has records of those they helped, but files have not been cataloged and are in storage and considered inaccessible. The two largest groups of survivors live in the area of Sydney and Melbourne.

Nazwisko _Mokałowicz_ .... Nr _1277_

Imiona _Israel_ .... Oznaczenie ....

ur. _28 II 1919_ w ....

Narodowość _Zyd._ .... Przyn. państw. ....

Zawód .... przybył _15. VIII 1942_

przeniesiony .... do ....

zmarł .... zwolniony ....

U w a g i : ....

Źródła i materiały _APMM Iol-5 s. 7_

....

LDA Lublin, zam. 794/82 n. 10 000

Nazwisko .... FAMILY NAME .... Nr File #

Imiona .... FIRST NAME .... Oznaczenie i.e. political / Type of prisoner

ur. .... DATE OF BIRTH .... w PLACE OF BIRTH

Narodowość ... NATIONALITY .... COUNTRY OF RESIDENCE / Przyn. państw.

Zawód .... OCCUPATION .... przybył DATE OF ARRIVAL

przeniesiony ... DATE OF TRANSFER ... do DESTINATION (to)

zmarł .... DATE OF DEATH .... zwolniony DISCHARGE

U w a g i : .... REMARKS ....

Źródła i materiały .... SOURCE OF REFERENCE (document number)

....

LDA Lublin, zam. 794/82 n. 10 000

*Index Card from the Archives of Majdanek Concentration Camp.
Many camps now have archives that will search their files for information
about specific individuals.*

Sydney. Australian Association of Jewish Holocaust Survivors. Address: Beth HaShoah; 148 Darlinghurst Road; Darlinghurst, 2010 Sydney, NSW, Australia. The principal purpose of this association is to serve as a support group for Holocaust survivors living in Australia. A library and archives located at the Sydney Jewish Museum answers inquiries about particular survivors at no charge.

Melbourne. A computerized search service has been created by the Jewish Welfare Society. For a fee of AU$25, they will search their records. Write to Jewish Community Services Tracing Service; 26 Alma Road; St. Kilda, Melbourne, 3182 Victoria, Australia. Telephone 525-4000; fax: 525-3737. Everyone who has ever contributed to a Jewish cause in Melbourne since 1945, or had an advertisement in the *Australian Jewish News* of Melbourne, is supposedly listed in this database.

Jewish communities that include Holocaust survivors exist in a number of other Australian communities. Make inquiries to the individuals listed below:

Adelaide. Mrs. Hilde Hines; 25 Wootoona Terrace; St. Georges, Adelaide, SA; 5064 Australia. Telephone 379-6030.

Brisbane. Morris Ochert; 3/23 Lucinda Street; Taringa, Brisbane, Queensland; 4068 Australia.

Hobart. Amelie Rauner; GPO Box 128B; Hobart, Tasmania; 7001, Australia.

Perth. Holocaust Institute; 61 Woodrow Avenue; Yokine, Perth, WA; 6060 Australia. Also, Association of Jewish Holocaust Survivors; Abe Nidorf; 8 Warralong Crescent; Mt. Lawley, Perth, WA; 6050 Australia.

AUSTRIA

Dokumentationsarchiv des Osterreichischen Widerstandes; Altes Rathaus; Wipplingerstrasse 8; A-1010 Vienna, Austria.

CANADA

Jewish Immigrant Aid Society (JIAS); 5151 Cote St. Catherine Road; Montreal, Quebec H3W 1M6. Telephone: (514) 342-9351; fax: (514) 342-8452. JIAS is a social service organization founded in 1919 to serve the needs of post-World War I Jewish immigrants who planned to settle in Canada. After World War II, it served to assist Holocaust survivors. Unfortunately, due to budget cuts, JIAS has abandoned its locator service. The organization is seeking funding that would reestablish this service.

National Archives of Canadian Jewish Congress (CJC); 1590 Docteur Penfield Avenue; Montreal, Quebec H3G 1C5. Telephone: (514) 931-7531; fax: (514) 931-0548. This organization has three major and some minor

Jerusalem **15. 6. 82** ירושלים

Your Ref. No. _____ מספרכם

Our Ref. No. 0621 **83475** מספרנו

Mr. Gary Mokotoff
507 Crest Drive
Northvale, NJ 07647
USA

Dear Sir (Madam)   א. (ג.) נ.

In reply to your communication dated **14.8.81** בתשובה לפניתך מיום

which has been addressed to *Int. Tracing Service* על שנשלחה

we have pleasure in notifying you the   הרינו להודיעך את

following addresses :   הכתובות הבאות :

(1 _____ *Moshe Mokotov (Brother of* (1

_____ *18 Rembrandt str.   Bronka)*

2) _____ *Tel Aviv* (2

_____ *Israel*

3) _____ (3

4) _____ (4

your address and message have been transmitted to the enquirer.

העברנו לנ״ל את הידיעה ממך וכן את כתובתך.

Further Information about the other persons sought will be forwarded to you only when received by us.

הודעה נוספת בדבר שאר המבוקשים תשלח לך אחרי שיעלה בידנו למצאם.

בכבוד רב

your faithfully,

Search Bureau for Missing Relatives

המדור לחיפוש קרובים

Search Bureau for Missing Relatives. *This division of the Jewish Agency is noted for its excellent record in locating persons living in Israel. An inquiry to the International Tracing Service in Germany was forwarded to the Search Bureau, which was able to locate the brother of a Holocaust victim.*

collections that include information about Holocaust survivors. The collections are described below.

Jewish Immigrant Aid Society (JIAS). There is a "catch-22" in the relationship between the CJC and JIAS. CJC will not release information included in JIAS records without approval of JIAS. JIAS says it does not have the funding to process inquiries. Persistence and patience should prevail if you suspect there is useful information in this collection. A further obstacle is privacy. The records may include personal information, such as financial conditions and social problems of the individuals. Again, persistence, patience and the ability to demonstrate a need to know might allow you to gain access to the case files.

United Jewish Relief Agencies (UJRA). Established in 1938, UJRA helped escapees, evacuees and interned refugees located in England. After the war, the group sent supplies, helped trace families of displaced persons, and brought skilled immigrants to Canada, in addition to other services. Their collections include: (1) case files of interned refugees, mainly Jewish Germans and Austrians interned in Britain in 1940 as prisoners of war; (2) War Orphans Immigration Project; (3) Skilled Labourers Immigration Project for Displaced Persons; (4) Joint Distribution Committee Refugee and Relief Program (including assistance and location services for Holocaust survivors); and (5) CJC Special Immigration Cases.

United Restitution Organization. This worldwide organization assists victims of Nazi persecution to submit claims against the German and Austrian governments. The Canadian branch was created in 1953. It holds individual case files of persons requesting help in restitution claims.

Other collections. Some landsmanshaftn and survivor association files are included in the CJC collections. Other materials of these organizations are at the Jewish Public Library in Montreal (Address: 5151 Cote St. Catherine Road; Montreal, Quebec H3W 1M6). The National Archives of CJC also has oral testimonies of survivors, as well as letters and journals of both survivors and victims.

CZECH REPUBLIC
Jewish Community of the Czech Republic; 18 Meisel Street; Prague, Czech Republic.

ENGLAND
Association of Jewish Refugees in Great Britain, Hannah Karminski House,

<ɔ1 MOKOTOWICZ		JAKOB			¢ 4149	
SE SURNAME		1. MAN	2. WOMAN		CASE NO.	

T. SURNAMES	CITY AND COUNTRY OF RESIDENCE				
MOKOLOWICZ	ASL				

CASE UNIT MEMBERS	BIRTHDATE	CY OF BIRTH	MS	REL. TO #1	ARRIVAL DATE
✓	11-9-12	Pd	M		3-25 -47
Ester STEINBERG (MN)	-10		M	W	2-13-49
Michael	-41	USA	S	S	

U. S. ADDRESS	CITY AND STATE		DATE		
2762 W 35th St	B'klyn		2-13 -49	RE 3-10-47	
				DEPT. M	

HQ UHS 12/54 MASTER CARD   WHEELDEX FORM C 41205-1A

WHEELDEX FORM C-41205-1B

INTERESTED U. S. PERSONS	ADDRESS	REL. TO #1
GINSBURG: DAVID	B'klyn	
SLIPSTEIN: ROSA	B'klyn	Sis L
MURRAY: Miriam	Los Angeles Calif	Sis L
STEINBERG: PAULINE	Los Angeles Calif	ML

OSS-REFERENCE CASES - CHANGES - ADD'L DATA

SE SURNAME	1. MAN	2. WOMAN	CASE NO.
MOKOTOWICZ	JAKOB		C 4149

HIAS Case Files. *After World War II, the Hebrew Immigrant Aid Society (HIAS) helped more than 75,000 Jewish families relocate in the United States. The organization has a Location Service that will search its files to determine if they helped specific individuals. This index card (front and back) from HIAS records shows that they helped the family of Jakob Mokotowicz who lived in Brooklyn in 1947. Routine genealogical research uncovered the information that Jacob had a daughter, Deborah, who was born in New York in 1950. The author has not yet located the family.*

9 Adamson Road, London NW3 3HX, England. Telephone 0171-483-2536.

Holocaust Educational Trust; BCM Box 7892; London WC1N 3XX, England. Telephone 0171-222-6822.

FRANCE

Amicales des Anciens Deportes Juif de France; 14 rue de Paradis; 75010 Paris, France.

ISRAEL

Search Bureau for Missing Relatives, P.O. Box 92, Jerusalem, Israel. Telephone 972+2-612471; fax: 2-202730. Shortly after World War II, the Jewish Agency, the international Jewish help organization, established a division to assist Holocaust survivors in locating relatives who might have gone to Israel either before or after the war as Holocaust survivors. Situated in Jerusalem, the division is known as the Search Bureau for Missing Relatives. The bureau maintains a database of the more than one million requests it has received since its inception. In recent years, the bureau has taken on a more general role of locating relatives in Israel independent of reason. For example, in the 1990s, much effort has been devoted to helping Russian Jews locate relatives who might have gone to Israel. The success of this organization is due primarily to the dedication of its director, Batya Unterschatz, who has been working at the task since 1972. Her commitment to her job and her access to Israeli government information has earned her an international reputation for successfully locating relatives living in Israel.

ITALY

Fondazione Centro Di Documentatzione Ebraica Contempororanea; Via Eupili 6; 20145 Milano, Italy.

NETHERLANDS

Jewish Historical Museum; POB 16737; Amsterdam 1001 RH, Holland.

Rijkarchief in Noord Holland; Kleine Houtweg 18; 2012 CH Haarlem, Holland. They have records for Dutch war orphans.

Rijksinstituut voor Gorlogsdocumentatie; Herengracht 474; 1017 CA Amsterdam, Holland. This is a war documents archive.

Stichting Joods Maatschappelijk Werk; De Lairessestraat 145–147; NL 1075 HJ Amsterdam, Holland. They have records of *Le Ezrath ha Jeled*, an organization involved with the emigration of Dutch Jews.

SOUTH AFRICA

South African Board of Deputies; P. O. Box 1180; Johannesburg 2000, South Africa.

SWEDEN

Swedish Association of Holocaust Survivors; PO Box 34036; 100-26 Stockholm, Sweden.

UNITED STATES

American Gathering of Jewish Holocaust Survivors, Suite 205, 112 West 30th Street, New York, NY 10001. Telephone (212) 239-4230; fax: (212) 279-2926. In 1982, a World Gathering of Holocaust Survivors was held in Jerusalem. One of the persons attending the event, Benjamin Meed, a survivor of the Warsaw ghetto, came back to the United States with a dream—the establishment of a national registry of all Jewish Holocaust survivors living in the United States. As of 1995, this registry includes information about some 40,000 survivors, their spouses and children. The total list is approaching 100,000 entries. Survivors included in the registry were asked to include their name before the Holocaust, where they were born, where they lived and where they were during the Holocaust. The entire computer database is accessible at the U.S. Holocaust Memorial Museum in Washington, D.C., where it is known as the Benjamin and Vladka Meed Registry of Jewish Holocaust Survivors.

The survivor portion of the registry is published in book form by the American Gathering as the *National Registry of Jewish Holocaust Survivors*. It is available at Holocaust research centers and major Jewish and Holocaust libraries throughout the world. The book is organized in three sections. Section I is an alphabetical list of survivors, which includes cross references for names before the war. Section II is arranged alphabetically by town of birth or town before the war. Section III is arranged alphabetically by place of incarceration. If a person was in more than one location during the war, there would be multiple entries, one for each location. People are listed in Sections II and III by current names as well as names before and during the war. As the database grows, the book is reissued to reflect the latest information. The organization accepts inquiries but will not divulge the address of any person on their list. Instead, staff will forward a letter written to a specific individual. If the survivor is no longer alive, contact can often be made through the children, whose names and addresses are on file.

Hebrew Immigrant Aid Society (HIAS) Location Service, 333 Seventh Avenue, New York, NY 10001. Telephone: (212) 613-1424; fax: (212) 967-

4442. HIAS is a Jewish social service organization that has helped Jewish immigrants settle within the United States since before the turn of the century. In the period after World War II, it helped no fewer than 75,000 Holocaust families who came to the U.S. HIAS has index cards for each family showing the names of all the persons in the household, ages, town of origin and names of potential contacts within the U.S. They also have case files for each family helped. The information on the index cards is publicly available; the case files themselves are most likely considered private to the individuals helped. If there is a strong need to know, there is a possibility that HIAS will provide information in the case file. HIAS requests that you provide the person's name, birth date, birth place, country of emigration and when last contact occurred. The cost is $25 per search request.

YUGOSLAVIA

Federation of Jewish Communities, Belgrade, Yugoslavia. Note: fax, do not write. Their fax number is 38+111-662-674.

LANDSMANSHAFTN SOCIETIES

A potential source of information is the Holocaust survivors themselves. They are not necessarily a good source of information about people from the town where they lived before the war. First, many individuals are reluctant to talk about their experiences because it resurfaces memories they would rather forget. Secondly, many know little more than what happened to their immediate families and perhaps the families of aunts and uncles. This is because most survivors living today were in their late teens and early twenties during the Holocaust, and they had yet to develop social relationships that would allow them to know a large number of people in their community.

The idea of landsmanshaftn societies is probably as old as the Diaspora. They are social and welfare organizations of persons who emigrated from a specific location. Landsmanshaftn became prominent in the early part of this century when large numbers of emigrants left Europe for other countries. Those societies that continued to exist at the time of World War II and after the war assisted thousands of Holocaust refugees. Most groups have discontinued operation over the past 50 years, but a few still are active.

The Council of Organizations of the UJA-Federation of New York maintains a list of active landsmanshaftn societies in the U.S. To determine if a town of interest has an active group, write to them at 130 E. 59th Street, New York, NY 10022. Telephone: (212) 836-1101.

Yad Vashem maintains a list of landsmanshaftn societies in Israel. The complete list of more than four hundred names and addresses is published in *A Guide to Jewish Genealogical Research in Israel, Revised Edition* (Teaneck, NJ: Avotaynu, 1995). Experience with the list demonstrates that it has not been maintained for years and, in a number of cases, the person listed is deceased or has moved. Where the person is deceased, quite often a family member can provide the name and address of another person who is a member of the society.

ORAL TESTIMONIES

The value of the tens of thousands of oral testimonies given by survivors for locating information about individuals is controversial. This author has consulted two persons in the Jewish genealogical community who have used them extensively. One stated that oral testimonies usually include little information about individuals. Their purpose was to describe the testifier's personal experiences during the Holocaust. Close family members may be described as "my uncle Sol" or "my sister" without specifically identifying the individual. Yet the other person stated they often contain names of family members as well as members of the community. The latter party also commented that oral testimonies are an excellent source of first-person accounts of the events that transpired in a particular town.

Members of the Jewish genealogical community are mounting a campaign to have interviewers encourage survivors to name individuals and their relationships to each other. Often, the survivor's memory is the only documentation of individuals murdered in the Holocaust, especially children, and failure to document who these people were ensures that no record will remain that they ever existed.

Bekanntmachung.

Gemäss der Anordnung des Herrn Kreishauptmanns von 7 Dezember d.J. gebe ich bekannt, dass die jüdische Bevölkerung des Kreises Warschau mit einer einmaligen Abgabe belegt wurde.

Für die Stadt Otwock wurde diese Abgabe auf

100.000 zł. festgesetzt,

Die Frist der gesammten Einzahlung der Abgabe wurde bi . zum 20 Dezember festgelegt.

Um d e richtige Verteilung und die Abfuhrung des obengenannten Betrages zuvollbringen wurde am 10 Dezember d.J. ein „besonderes Komitee" berufen in nachstehender Zusammensetzung.

Für die Durchführung der Sammlung ist das Komitee berechtigt die jüdischen Bürger der Stadt Otwock zur Mithilfe heranzuziehen.

Die Berufenen haben kein Recht sich der Mithilfe zu entziehen sind gefallls unter den strengsten Verantwortung heranzuziehen.

[illegible lines]

BÜRGERMEISTER

JAN GADOMSKI

Das Komitee

1. ARONIAK ELA
2. ... UCH CHAIM
3. ...TLIN CHONON
4. FLEISYNG BACHRIL
5. FELDMAN ...

6. FROM HERSZ
7. FRYDMZON JANKIEL
8. GRIES EFROIM
9. ...WSKA GUSTAWA
10. ...PAC... CHAIM

Obwieszc.

Na podstawie zarządzenia Pau mana z dn. 7 bm. podaję do wiado ludność narodowości żydowskiej pow. warszawskiego została obłożona jednorazową daniną.

Wysokość daniny na miasto Otwock wynosi

100.000 zł.

Termin wpłacenia całej daniny wyznaczony został do dnia 20 grudnia r. b.

Dla opowiedniego podziału i dla ściągnięcia wyżej wymienionej sumy, został powołany dn. 10 bm. „Specjalny Komitet" w składzie osób niżej wymienionych.

Dla przeprowadzenia zbiórki Komitet upoważniony jest do dokooptowania żydowskich obywateli miasta, przyczym nikt nie ma prawa, pod rygorami surowej odpowiedzialności uchylać się od tej współpracy.

[illegible lines]

BURMISTRZ

JAN GADOMSKI

... LESMAN IZAAK
12. LANDSBERG MORDKA
13. MOKOTOWSKI TOBIAS
14. ORLINSKI MORDKA
15. RUKNER EFROIM

Otwock Artifact. Visitors to the museum at Yad Vashem will see that the exhibits depict the events of the Holocaust with few individuals named. This broadside, which ordered the Jews of Otwock, Poland, to raise 100,000 zlotys, lists the committee of Jews who had the responsibility to raise the funds. One person was Tobias Mokotowski. Other records located by the author determined that he was shot in Otwock by the Germans.

CASE STUDY:
THE MOKOTOWSKIS OF
OTWOCK, POLAND

Holocaust research does not come to a successful conclusion in a matter of days. The events in my research described below actually occurred over a period of years. Furthermore, the narrative describes only my successes and not the failures. A researcher in any discipline will tell you that in any project the number of failures far exceeds the number of successes, but persistence and patience can yield results, such as occurred in the case study presented here.

When, on September 1, 1939, Germany invaded Poland, precipitating World War II, more than 50 men, women and children named Mokotowski lived in the town of Otwock, Poland, a suburb of Warsaw. When Germany surrendered in April 1945, not one of these persons remained alive. Those who did not perish as a result of the atrocities committed against the Jews in Otwock itself were deported to Treblinka on August 19, 1942, and immediately gassed to their death. How does one document such a large list of people?

Otwock Yizkor Book

This yizkor book is written in Hebrew and Yiddish. My familiarity with the two languages consists of the ability to transliterate phonetically from the Hebrew to the Roman alphabet and an understanding of some basic words in each language. I scanned the table of contents of the book, but found no person named Mokotowski. I scanned the captions of pictures, but did not find the name Mokotowski, despite the claim of an Israeli relative that there was a picture with a caption that included the name Joshua Mokotowski. The necrology portion of the book, however, revealed a wealth of information. Under the Hebrew equivalent of the letter "M" (מ) were the names of more than 50 Mokotowskis. They are listed in the book on pages 1069 and 1071 in the following manner:

Mokotowski, Esther Raizel, Bela[?] Shmuel (slaughterer) and their children
Mokotowski, Yrachmiel Yitzhak, Chava Leah
Mokotowski, Leibel, wife and children
Mokotowski, Yehoshua, wife and two daughters
Mokotowski, Pinchas, wife and their sons
Mokotowski, Yente
Mokotowski, Leizer and his daughters
Mokotowski, Itshe (daughter of Idel)
Mokotowski, Tshurna Sheindel, Aron Shmuel
Mokotowski, Tuvia, Masha
Mokotowski, Idel, wife, children and grandchildren
Mokotowski, Esther, Migdal, her husband and five children
Mokotowski, Leah, her husband and two children
Mokotowski, Leibel, his wife and four children

Each set of names appears to be a family unit. Note that the occupation of Shmuel Mokotowski is given. It seemed unreasonable to me that the book would include no information about Mokotowskis, given the number who lived in the town. I very carefully "read" every story title and subtitle. Finally, I achieved success. On page 527 was an article, written in Yiddish entitled "Mein Vater Eliezer Mokotowski" (My father Eliezer Mokotowski). The author was not named Mokotowski; the author was a woman, Sarah Landau. I had unwittingly allowed my male chauvinist bias get the best of me by assuming that all Mokotowskis would be named Mokotowski, and I had excluded married women from consideration. On page 73, as part of a story about the Jewish citizens of Otwock, I located a paragraph devoted to a man named Yitzhak Mokotowski. Since I do not understand Hebrew, I copied both articles and had them translated. Of significance was that Eliezer was born in Karczew, Poland, in 1865 and died on the 7th day of the Jewish month of Tishri (September 23) in 1936. Yitzhak Mokotowski was a food store owner. He was described as rich and short, with bushy eyebrows and a short temper.

Pages of Testimony

I sent a letter to Yad Vashem asking for copies of Pages of Testimony of all persons named Mokotow or Mokotowski. These are unusual names, and the researchers at Yad Vashem will conduct a search under that condition. Some weeks later, 23 documents arrived, including 9 relating to persons named Mokotowski from Otwock. They listed:

Pina Mokotowski, daughter of Yitzhak and Chava, born 1906, died Treblinka

Yenta Mokotowski, daughter of Yitzhak and Chava, born 1908, died Treblinka

Leibl Mokotowski, son of Yitzhak and Chava, born 1902, died Treblinka, wife Golda

Sheea (Joshua) Mokotowski, son of Yitzhak and Chava, born 1904, died Treblinka. Wife Zlata Birenbaum. Children: Aryeh, Yehoshua, Pinchas and Malka

Yenta Mokotowksi, daughter of Leibel and Rachel, born 1920, died Treblinka

Rachel Mokotowski, daughter of Bezalel and (illegible), born 1899, died Treblinka, husband Aryeh

Yitzhak Mokotowski, son of Eliezer and (illegible), born 1890, death unknown, wife Chava

Leibel Mokotowski, son of Eliezer and Idel Tsurna, born 1889, died Warsaw, wife Rachel

Leibel Mokotowski, son of Eliezer and Idel Tsurna, wife Rachel Finkelstein. Children: Yentl, Mendel, Zvi, Huza[?]

Note that the last two Pages of Testimony were for the same family. The first Page was submitted by a cousin who did not know as much information as the second person, a brother-in-law.

Two of the Pages of Testimony, the one for Yitzhak and the last one listed above were submitted on June 1, 1955, by Abraham Dov Landau, Kiryat Shalom, Israel. This document created a link between the victim and a living relative. A check of the Tel Aviv telephone book showed no person named Abraham, Dov or Sarah Landau. This was reasonable. The Page of Testimony was submitted in 1955. There was a likelihood that both parties was no longer alive.

How do you locate a person, or descendants of a person, in Israel? Answer: The Jewish Agency Search Bureau for Missing Relatives.

Search Bureau for Missing Relatives

I sent a copy of the Page of Testimony written in 1955 by Abraham Dov Landau to the Search Bureau and some weeks later, I received a response that neither Sarah nor Abraham Landau were alive, but that their son, Moshe Landau, lived in Holon. This led to the breakthrough that allowed me to document the Mokotowskis of Otwock. In January 1985, Avi Landau, son of Moshe and grandson of Abraham Dov and Sarah, came to the United States on a business trip and brought with him the complete family tree of his branch of the Mokotow family.

Holocaust Survivors

Friends and neighbors of Holocaust victims can often provide valuable information. In 1985, more than 5,000 Holocaust survivors from throughout the United States gathered in Philadelphia to remember the Holocaust. The Jewish Genealogical Society of Philadelphia participated in assisting survivors who were still trying to determine the fate of their loved ones. At the event, I met a woman from New York who told me the tragic story of how she had to abandon her six-year-old son on a street in Warsaw during World War II and was looking for advice on how to locate him today. Each survivor wore a name tag showing their name and European town of origin. She was from Otwock. After discussing her plight, I commented that I had relatives named Mokotowski from Otwock. Her face lit up. "Do you mean Yitzhak Mokotowski?" she asked. "He and his family were neighbors of mine." This meeting was a chance encounter, but other exchanges have occurred on a more formal basis. The National Registry of Jewish Holocaust Survivors located at the U.S. Holocaust Memorial Museum consists of computerized information about more than 35,000 Holocaust survivors living in the United States. While the Museum will not release addresses of persons in this database, they will forward letters.

German Records of Otwock

The archives at Yad Vashem has a number of documents relating to the fate of the Jews of Otwock. No documents in this collection offered information pertaining specifically to persons named Mokotowski; however, one interesting artifact they hold from Otwock is a broadside that was posted in Otwock shortly after the Germans occupied the town demanding the Jews raise 100,000 zlotys. The poster named 15 persons responsible for raising the money. One of the names was Tobias (Tuvia) Mokotowski.

Vital Statistics Records

Although most things Jewish were destroyed in the Holocaust, government records usually were not. It is a credit to the archivists of the world that, despite the attempts by the human race over the centuries to destroy each other, archivists have been conscientious in trying to preserve the original source material of our history. Vital statistics records for Poland, Hungary and Germany have been readily available to the public for many years. With the fall of the Iron Curtain, other countries have opened their doors to inquiries, most notably Estonia, Latvia, Lithuania, Czech Republic and Slovakia. Other countries such as Belarus, Russia, Ukraine and Moldova are still in the process of establishing links with the West for purposes of record research. Inquiries to Romanian archives generally go unanswered.

Luck

People sometimes attribute successes to luck. In Holocaust research, what seems like luck is often the product of persistence. If you try many avenues of exploration, most will be unsuccessful; the few efforts that do succeed, you may attribute to luck. I will end this case study with two stories of luck that will describe how I linked the Mokotowskis of Otwock to the main tree of the Mokotow family. The veteran genealogist will see that, in truth, it was nothing more than taking all the resources available to the researcher and piecing them together to come to a successful conclusion.

The vast majority of information I amassed about the Mokotowskis of Otwock came from the Otwock yizkor book and the recollections of living persons who had secondary information. Response from the Polish State Archives in Warsaw to my inquiry indicated that there were no vital statistics records for Otwock from the 19th century; therefore, it was not possible to go back in time on that path. It was while attending a Jewish genealogical conference in Washington, D.C., that I located the Otwock yizkor book and had translated for me the article "My Father Eliezer Mokotowski." Toward the end of the seminar, while sitting in the Hebraic division of the Library of Congress and convincing myself that I had done everything possible at the library, I recalled that the article stated that Eliezer Mokotowski had been born in Karczew. *The Shtetl Finder*, by Chester Cohen, lists about 1,200 towns in Eastern Europe where Jews had lived in the nineteenth century. To give the book more substance, the author included the names of individuals from the town who were prepublication subscribers to books written in Yiddish during that era. Under the description of Karczew was the entry: "In 1879, advanced subscribers to the book *Da'at Moshe* were. . .Yehosie Efraim Mankitow [sic]. . ." Monkitow is the Yiddish pronunciation of Mokotow. At that moment, I recalled that I had in my possession a marriage record from the town of Karczew of a Mokotow.

Some months earlier, I had devoted a full week at the LDS (Mormon) Family History Library in Salt Lake City searching the vital statistics records of the Mokotow ancestral town of Warka, located about 50 miles south of Otwock. After completing that task, in ever-widening concentric circles, I searched records of adjacent towns. This included Karczew, for which there was only one Mokotow record—a marriage record.

I had brought my LDS findings to the seminar and opened my file folder to the Karczew record. The name of the groom was Efraim, but the previous word was not Yehosie. Then I realized the registrar had gotten lazy. He had come to the end of the line when he wrote the groom's name and, not having enough room, arbitrarily hyphenated the name. The groom's name was "Szaja Efraim." According to the yizkor book article about Eliezer Mokotowski, his father's name was Yehoshua; *The Shtetl Finder* noted a Yehosie Efraim Mankitow from Karczew; the marriage record found at the LDS library had the name Szaja Efraim. Yehoshua, Yehosie, Szaja: All these names are Yiddish and Hebrew variants of the name Joshua. All the documents referred to the same man! The marriage record had the name of the groom's parents. The father's name was Iczek (Isaac). The progenitor of the Mokotow family had a son Isaac. Through an incredible set of slender threads, I had linked the Mokotowskis of Otwock to the Mokotow family tree. Sarah Landau's father, Eliezer Mokotowski, was the son of Joshua Efraim Mokotow, son of Isaac Mokotow, son of Tuvia David Mokotow.

FACILITIES WITH

COLLECTIONS OF

HOLOCAUST MATERIALS

Yad Vashem Administration Building

YAD VASHEM

Address: Yad Vashem's address is P.O. Box 3477; 91034 Jerusalem, Israel. Telephone (international dialing): 972+2-751611; fax: 2-433511

Background

Under its full name, Yad Vashem Martyrs and Heroes Remembrance Authority, this facility, located on Mount Herzl in Jerusalem, is the principal repository in the world for information about the Holocaust (*Yad vashem* means "a place and a name" and is taken from a passage in Isaiah 56:5). It was founded in 1953 to commemorate the six million Jews murdered in the Holocaust, the destruction of many of the Jewish communities, the heroism of Jews who resisted the Germans and their collaborators, and the Gentiles who risked their lives to save Jews. The mission of Yad Vashem is to gather material regarding those people and institutions who were involved in the Holocaust. The legislative act that created Yad Vashem also conferred on the Holocaust victims commemorative citizenship of the State of Israel.

Yad Vashem's hours occasionally change. In general, the research facilities are open from 9:00am to 3:00pm, Monday through Thursday, except holidays. If you plan to visit, call for a current schedule.

Tourists know Yad Vashem for its multitude of exhibit halls depicting the events of the Holocaust and for its efforts to memorialize the victims. For researchers, Yad Vashem offers a library, an archives and, most importantly, a special memorial called the Hall of Names which houses a manuscript collection called "Pages of Testimony."

Library

Located on the first floor of the administration building, the Yad Vashem library contains the world's largest collection of books and periodicals about the Holocaust. More than 80,000 volumes in 50 languages, plus thousands of periodicals, are part of its collection. The library regularly receives some 250 publications currently being published with information about the Holocaust. Many books include information specific to towns (such as yizkor books) and data specific to individuals (yizkor books and lists of victims).

Hall of Names. *The Hall of Names at Yad Vashem in Jerusalem. At the right and extending to the rear are the shelves that house more than three million Pages of Testimony that identify victims of the Holocaust.*

These lists include deportation lists, names of Holocaust survivors collected in post-World War II displaced persons camps, concentration camp registers and other similar items. The staff of the library is very helpful in assisting visitors in locating books of interest.

Archives

Officially known as the Central Archives of the Holocaust and Jewish Resistance, this repository holds more than 50 million items relating to the Holocaust. It, too, is located on the first floor of the administration building. Much of the original source material is organized by town, camp or refugee center. The collection of information was published in four volumes entitled *Guide to the Unpublished Material of the Holocaust Period*, Volumes 3–6 (1975–81). These books are arranged alphabetically and give brief descriptions of the contents of each record group. A complete list of towns identified in the four volumes is listed in Appendix B. Researchers report that very little information in these archival collections identifies individuals. Furthermore, many more acquisitions have been made by the archives since these books were published.

Two collections are worth noting here because they do contain information about individuals.

• International Tracing Service records.
• Extraordinary State Commission to Investigate German-Fascist Crimes Committed on Soviet Territory records.

International Tracing Service Records

Of all the archival records at Yad Vashem, the collection offering the greatest potential value for Holocaust research is the set of microfilms of the holdings of the International Tracing Service (ITS) in Arolsen, Germany. This resource is so valuable that it is described in depth here in its own chapter, "International Tracing Service." Yad Vashem is the only place in the world where a researcher may peruse these records. There is no on-site access to the ITS records in Arolsen, Germany. They only accept inquiries by mail.

Some 14 million file cards, one for each citation of an individual in the records, are included in the microfilms. Inquiries made either directly to ITS or through the American Red Cross must demonstrate your close kinship to the person you are researching, and you must provide details, such as date and place of birth and other data that would allow the organization to identify whether they have information on that specific person. By going in person to Yad Vashem, you can browse through the collection looking for more distant relatives or friends. When you are the active researcher, the information you have about the individual can be incomplete, and the search is limited only by the amount of time you are willing to devote to the project and whether or not other researchers at the archives want to use the microfilm readers.

Extraordinary State Commission to Investigate German-Fascist Crimes Committed on Soviet Territory

In the winter of 1942–43, as the Soviet Army was recapturing its land from the Nazi invaders, the Supreme Soviet, the ruling body of the USSR, established an Extraordinary State Commission whose function was to gather data on atrocities committed in every community that had been occupied by the Germans. The Extraordinary State Commission was organized by *oblast* (province), then *uezd* (district) and finally by town. Each town was required to document in detail the events that transpired. Because the directive came from Moscow and the bureaucratic mechanism was in place to watch over the project, no fewer than 1,400 communities complied with the directive. Many reports include not only the events and dates, but also the names of the individuals murdered or deported.

These records have recently been microfilmed. The entire report is in Russian, of course, handwritten and, therefore, sometimes difficult to read. The U.S. Holocaust Research Institute has created an index of towns referenced in the record group; it appears in Appendix C.

HOLDINGS IN THE LIBRARY THAT
INCLUDE LISTS OF VICTIMS AND SURVIVORS

The call number of the item appears in brackets [ ].

Liste alphabetique des personnes, en majorité Israélites, qui on été deportées par les convois partis du camp de rassemblement de Malines (Caserne Dossin) entre le 4 aout 1942 et le 31 juillet 1944. 3 vols. Bruxelles, 1954. [1553] Persons, mostly Jews, deported to the Malines (Caserne Dossin) concentration camp. Organized alphabetically. Includes surname, given name, maiden name, birth date, convoy number, date of departure to camp, remarks.

Mémorial de la deportation des Juifs de Belgique. Klarsfeld and Steinberg. [2°82-851] Contains lists of Jews deported from Belgium by convoy. Data includes name, date of birth, place of birth, date of deportation and destination.

Liste des Israélites libérés de camps de concentration d'Allemagne et arrivés en Belgique. Bruxelles: Aide aux Israelites Victimes de la Guerre, n.d. [2°84-558] Divided into two parts, those living in Belgium before May 10, 1940, and transits. Includes surname, given name, place and date of birth, nationality, convoy number.

Liste des Israélites domiciles en Belgique en Mai 1940 . . . transferes dans les Camps . . . de Malines, Drancy, Breendonk, et dans les prisons Belges. Deportes, evades, liberes, et decedes. 2 vols. [78-615] Organized alphabetically by surname. In French and Dutch. Includes surname, given name, place and date of birth, place of forced labor, place of internment in France, fate of victim.

Register of All Persons Saved from Anti-Jewish Persecution in Slovakia. 3 vols. Bratislava: American Joint Distribution Committee, 1945. [2°58 653] Names of all persons surviving persecution in Slovakia between March 1939 and April 1945 and who resided in Slovakia up to October 15, 1945. Includes surname, given name, birth year, present domicile, name of father, remarks.

Totenbuch Theresienstadt (Theresienstadt death book). Wien: Jüdisches Komitee für Theresienstadt und Junius Verlags, 1987. [2°87-560] Has much introductory material in German before a list of names. Organized alphabetically by surname. Includes surname, given name, birth date, convoy, death date (if known).

Terezín–Ghetto. Czechoslovak Republic Ministry for the Protection of Labour and Social Welfare, 1945 [?] [57 1241] There are two alphabetical lists. The first is of those taken directly to Terezin from their homes; the second is of those driven to Terezin by retreating Germans at the end of the war. Includes surname, given name, birth date, transport number, place where deportation originated.

Rishimot Netzulei Theresienstadt (List of Theresienstadt survivors). 2 parts. Jerusalem: American Joint Distribution Committee, n.d. [61-1178] Organized alphabetically by surname. Roman characters. Includes surname, given name only.

Gedenkbuch: Opfer der Verfolgung der Juden unter der nationalsozialistischen Gewaltherrschaft in Deutschland, 1933–1945. (Frankfurt/Main: J. Weisbecker, c1986) [2°86-713] List of 128,000 German Jews killed during the Holocaust. Shows name, last place of residence, date of birth, place of deportation and, in some cases, date of death. Because many Jews were displaced from their homes in the years prior to deportation, last place of residence was not necessarily the place of permanent residence.

Shärit Ha-Plätah Bavaria (Register of names). Munich, Bergen-Belsen, Central Jewish Committee, Central Committee of Liberated Jews in Bavaria, 1945–46. 7 vols. [2° 1446] Lists names of survivors organized alphabetically by surname. Includes surname, given name, birth date, place where located.
    Vol. I: Jews in Dachau and other camps.
    Vol. II: Buchenwald and others.
    Vol. III: Bergen-Belsen and others.
    Vol. IV: Linz and others.
    Vol. V: Feldafing and others.
    Vol. VI: Volume I revised.
    Vol. VII: Bergen-Belsen.

Sie sind nicht Vergessen. Oberrat der Israeliten Badens, Karlsruhe. Karlsruhe, Germany: Badenia, 1958. [58 2792] Lists deaths of Jews in the camps of Gurs, Noe, Recebedou and Rivesaltes alphabetically by surname. Includes surname, given name, date of death. For Noe and Recebedou, birth dates are also given.

Sche'erith Hapletah: Jewish Survivors in Celle, Germany, July 1945. Compiled by Rabbi E. Munk, 30th Army Corps, B.L.A., August 1945. [85-258] Organized by nationality, then alphabetically by surname. Separate additional list of women. Includes surname, given name, birth date, town of origin.

Deportationsbuch der von Frankfurt am Main aus gewaltsam verschickten Juden in den Jahren 1941 bis 1944. [22°85-96 Diamant, Adolf] List of Jews showing name, date of birth, place of birth and destination.

Gedenkbuch: Zum Gedächtnis der Toten zu Mahnung den Lebenden Universitätsstadt Giesen. 1987. [86-841a] On the Jews of Giessen, Germany. Alphabetical list by surname. Includes surname, given name, maiden name, birth date, birth place, death date, place of death.

Deportationsbuch der in den Jahren 1942 bis 1945 von Leipzig aus gewaltsam verschickten Juden. Frankfurt, 1991. [2°92-443 Diamant, Adolf] Organized by convoy, then alphabetically by surname. Includes surname, given name, date and place of birth, nationality, former address.

Gedenkbuch für die judischen Mitbürger aus Niedensachsen, die Opfer der nationalsozialistischen Gewaltherrschaft in Deutschland wurden. 3 vols. Hanover, 1988. [2°89-1267] Each volume is organized differently; check all three. Includes surname, given name, maiden name, birth date, birth place, death date or other fate, place of deportation.

Totenbuch Neuengamme. Dokumentation: Franz Glienke. Wiesbaden, Germany: Saaten-Vlg., 1968. [2°68-539a] Lists of those who died or "disappeared" while in the Neuengamme camp. Organized by country, then alphabetically by surname. Includes surname, given name, town of residence, birth date, date of death or disappearance. The USSR list is written in Cyrillic characters.

Die Juedischen Offer des Nationalsozialismus 1933–1945, Wiesbaden. Der Hessischen Landeshauptstadt, Wiesbaden, n.d. [22°91638] Organized alphabetically by surname. Includes surname, given name, birth date, death date and place of death, if known.

BIBΛIO MNHMHΣ (Memorial book of Greek Jews). Athens: Central Board of the Jewish Communities, 1979. [79-650] All text in Greek.

Shearit Hapleitah B'Italia: Jewish Refugees in Italy. 2 vols. Rome: Organization of Jewish Refugees in Italy, 1946. [2°84-559] Organized alphabetically by surname. Includes surname, given name, place of birth, year of birth, names of parents.

Aufstehen! Friulani nei campi di Sterminio Nazisti 1943–1945. Assoc. Nazionale ex Deportati Sezione di Udine, 1978. [79-186] Organized alphabetically by surname. In Italian. Includes surname, given name, former address, date and destination of deportation, death date.

Il libro della memoria Gli Ebrei deportati dall'Italia (1943–1945.) (Memorial book of Jews Deported from Italy, 1943–1945). Liliana Picciotto Fargior. Milan: Mursia, 1991. [91-477] Organized alphabetically by surname. In Italian. Includes surname, given name, place and date of birth, parents, spouse, final address, details of arrest, deportation, place and date of death.

Alphabetische Lijst van Zich in Nederland Beyindende Joden. Amsterdam: Centraal Registratiebureau Voor Joden, Joodsche Coordinatie-Commissie, June 1945, plus later supplements. [2°57-5785] Organized alphabetically by surname. Several supplements. Includes surname, given name, date and place of birth, present address, former address.

In Memorion: Nederlandse Oorlogsslachtoffers. Compiled by G.G. Couwenberg, edited by B.A. Slager and A.L. Wilkeshuis. 42 vols. Gravenhage, Oorlogsgravenstichting, 1961–1966. [82-183] Names of Jews deported from Holland. Includes surname, given name, date and place of birth, date and place of death.

Rishimot Hashe'arit shel Yehudei Polin. (List of Polish-Jewish survivors). n.p., n.d. [83-86] Organized by community, then alphabetically by surname. In Roman characters. Includes surname, given name, sometimes town of origin.

Surviving Jews in Czestochowa. New York: World Jewish Congress. [57-7403] Organized alphabetically by surname. Includes surname, given name, year of birth, present address.

Surviving Jews in Kielce District. New York: World Jewish Congress. [61-1640] Organized by community, then alphabetically by surname. Includes surname, given name, year of birth, present address.

Surviving Jews in Lublin. New York: World Jewish Congress, 1945. [2°61-2209] Organized alphabetically by surname. Includes surname, given name, year of birth, address in 1939, names of parents, present address in Lublin.

Getto Litzmannstadt. Adolf Diamant. Frankfurt, 1986. [87-108] Lists of Jews in the Lodz, Poland, ghetto (Lodz was renamed Litzmannstadt by the Germans during World War II). Organized by community of residence. Includes surname, given name, date and place of birth, nationality, former address.

Surviving Jews in Przemysl. New York: World Jewish Congress. [57-7404] Organized alphabetically by surname. Includes surname, given name, year of birth, present address.

```
     12.8.bis
     1.9.41 Wilna-Stadt    425 Juden, 19 Jüdinnen, 8 Kommunist.
                           9 Kommunistinnen                              461
     2.9.41      "     "   864 Juden, 2019 Jüdinnen,
                           817 Judenkinder
                           (Sonderaktion, weil von Juden auf
                           deutsche Soldaten geschossen wurde)    3 700

     12.9.41 Wilna-Stadt  993 Juden,1670 Jüdinn.771 J.-Kind.     3 334
     17.9.41     "     "  337  "    687  "   247       "          1 271
                          und 4 lit.Kommunisten
     20.9.41 Nemencine    128 Juden, 176 Jüdinn. 99       "          403
     22.9.41 Novo-Wilejka 468  "   , 495  "   196       "         1 159
     24.9.41 Riesa        512  "    744  "   511       "         1 767
     25.9.41 Jahiunai     215  "    229  "   131       "           575
     27.9.41 Eysisky      989  "   1636  "   821       "         3 446
     30.9.41 Trakai       366  "    483  "   597       "         1 446
     4.10.41 Wilna-Stadt  432  "   1115  "   436       "         1 983
     6.10.41 Semilieki    213  "    359  "   390       "           962
     9.10.41 Svencieny   1169  "   1840  "   717       "         3 726
     16.10.41 Wilna-Stadt 382  "    507  "   257       "         1 146
     21.10.41    "     "  718  "   1063  "   586       "         2 367
     25.10.41    "     "   -   "   1766  "   812       "         2 578
     27.10.41    "     "  946  "    184  "    73       "         1 203
     30.10.41    "     "  382  "    789  "   362       "         1 533
     6.11.41     "     "  340  "    749  "   252       "         1 341
     19.11.41    "     "   76  "     77  "    18       "           171
     19.11.41    "     "    6 Kriegsgefangene, 8 Polen              14
     20.11.41    "     "    3        "                               3
     25.11.41    "     "    9 Juden, 46 Jüdinnen, 8 J.-Kinder,      64
                           1 Pole wegen Waffenbesitz u.Besitz
                           von anderem Kriegsgerät


     Teilkommando des EK.3
        in Minck
     von 28.9.-17.10.41:

                Plescnitsa,
                Bicholin,
                Soak,
                Dobor,
                Ugda         620 Juden,1285 Jüdinnen,1126 J.-Kind.
                             und 19 Kommunisten                  3 050
                                                            _____

                                                             133_346
```

Einsatzgruppen Report. More than one million Jews were killed by special mobile killing squads of the German SS (Einsatzgruppen) who followed the regular German army in its invasion of the Soviet Union. This document, taken from the records of a unit operating in the area of Vilna (Vilnius, Lithuania), shows the counts of the day-by-day killing of Jewish men (Juden), Jewish women (Jüdinn.), and Jewish children (J.-Kind.), as well as communists (Kommunisten), Poles (Polen) and prisoners of war (Kriegsgefangene).

List of Names of the Surviving Jews in [and from] Siedlce [Poland]
Compiled by Do Komitetu Zydowskiego w Siedlach (Jewish Committee of
Siedlach), n.d. [10391] In alphabetical order by surname. Includes a list of
Siedlce survivors in Soviet Russia with their addresses. Includes surname,
given name, year of birth, names of parents.

Vernietigingskamp Sobibor. Schelvis, Jules. [94-406] Background material
in Dutch 1–309, transport lists 310–542. Organized by date of convoy, then
alphabetically by surname. Includes surname, given name, birth date.

List of Jews Who Have Arrived in Sweden May 1st–June 25, 1945. Stockholm: Jewish Congregation in Stockholm. [2°84-565] Organized by
nationality, then alphabetically by surname. Includes surname, given name,
birth date and place of birth, last domicile, and "sends greetings to" (name
and last known address).

About Jews Liberated from German Concentration Camps Arrived [sic] *in
Sweden in 1945: List No. 1 (Supplements Follow)*. Stockholm: World Jewish
Congress and Jewish Agency for Palestine Rescue Committee, 1946. [61-
1645] Organized by nationality of victims, then alphabetically by surname.
Includes surname, given name, birth date, town of origin.

Sepher Hanitzcha Lezecher Kedoshei Rovna (Book for the perpetuation of
the memory of the martyrs of Rovno.) [86-467] Organized alphabetically by
surname. In Hebrew. Typed. Includes surname, given name of submitter,
surname and given name of persons being memorialized, their relationship
to the submitter.

The Babi Yar Book of Remembrance, Joseph Vinakurov, Shimon Kipnis and
Nora Levin, eds. Philadelphia Committee for the Babi Yar Book of Remembrance, 1983. [83-375] In Russian, English, and Yiddish. Includes surname,
given name, age at time of death.

List of Survivious [sic] *Jews in Yugoslavia, 1946*. 2 vols. Belgrade: Union of
Jewish Communities in Yugoslavia, 1946 [2°84-564] Organized by town of
residence, then alphabetically by surname. Includes surname, given name,
year and town of birth.

Surviving Jews in Jugoslavia as of June 1945. New York: World Jewish
Congress. [84-560] Lists for Belgrade printed separately later. Organized by
community, then alphabetically by surname. Includes surname, given name,
year of birth, place of birth, occupation, present address in Yugoslavia.

RECORD GROUPS IN THE ARCHIVES THAT
INCLUDE LISTS OF VICTIMS AND SURVIVORS
Source: A Guide to Jewish Genealogical Research in Israel, 2nd edition

This section is divided into two groups. The first list below includes records considered to have a high degree of information about individuals. The second list does not have as high a proportion of relevant records, but does include items that may be helpful to some. Each entry is preceded by a record group (RG) number. The numbers in parentheses denote running meters of shelf space taken up by the records.

Most Relevant

RG 0-37   Displaced Persons Collection, 1944–50 (15m). Lists of various materials, as well as lists of displaced persons from many places. Arranged according to name of DP camp or place of prewar residence.

RG 0-42   Registers of Holocaust Victims, 1955– (2m). Recorded by place, town or camp.

RG 0-50   Underground Archive of the Theresienstadt Ghetto 1939–46 (7.5m). List of deportees.

RG 0-70   Bergen-Belsen Archives (J. Rosensaft Collection), Displaced Persons Camp, 1945–51 (4m).

RG M-26   World Jewish Congress, Relatives Research Department, Stockholm, 1945–46 (18m).

RG M-7   "Relico," Committee for Relief of the War-Stricken Jewish Population, World Jewish Congress, Geneva, 1939–47 (40m). Alphabetical.

RG M-18   Joint Distribution Committee Central Location Index of the Relatives Research Department, 1944–48. (20m). Kept in 20 boxes. Good information on some; not arranged in order. Samples of contents include: Series 2, L-Z, Mail clearinghouse responses; Series 7, H-J, Mail and telephone clearance responses; Box 6, Alphabetical index; special inquiry for Germany—only agency index number; National Council of Jewish Women—index for Germany by last-known address and date of birth; special inquiries for Austria—alphabetical index, but no information other than agency index number; special inquiries for most other European countries.

RG M-7   International Tracing Service at Arolsen, Germany, 1945–
          (40m). Alphabetical by surname. Most important genealogical
          resource; as of 1995, this is the only copy that exists outside of
          Arolsen.

RG R-5   Card index to Citizenship Denials of German Jews (Ausbuerger-
          ungskartei).

Items on Microfilm

JM/10517 YIVO Institute for Jewish Research. Records on displaced
10570   persons.

JM/10675- Central State Archives—Slovakia. Card index of Jews deported
10694   from Slovakia, 1944.

JM/10645- Central State Archives—Poland. Card index of Radom ghetto.
10714

JM/10722- Personal files of prisoners in Stutthof concentration camp—
10945   primarily Hungarian Jews.

JM/11073 Personal files of prisoners in Stutthof concentration camp—
11126   primarily Hungarian Jews.

JM/11138 *Israelitische Kultusgemeinde zu Leipzig-Mitgliederkartei-und*
11146   *Transportkertei.*

Somewhat Useful

Oral/Written Testimonies

There are eyewitness accounts of survivors and others, arranged according
to locality. They are written in a variety of languages, almost none are in
English. Rescue committees may be searched by town names, list of refugees, birth dates and places of liberation. Yad Vashem holds a number of
personal archives that might yield useful information; only those that can
be identified geographically by their titles are included below. (See the
discussion of the value of these testimonies in the chapter on "Oral
Testimonies.")

RG 0-1   Dr. K.J. Ball-Kaduri Collection of Testimonies and Reports of
          German Jewry. "*Was nicht im den Archiven Steht,*" 1944–65
          (2m).

RG 0-2   Wiener Library Collection of Testimonies, London, 1933–84
          (1m).

RG 0-3   Testimonies Department of the Yad Vashem Archives, 1954–84 (29m).

RG 0-6   Collection on Poland. Material from various sources on the Holocaust of Polish Jewry, 1939–44 (4m).

Documents on Judenrät in Warsaw, Czestochowa, Lublin, Lodz and various places, 1934–44, files No. 1–20.

Council for Jewish Aid, "ZEGOTA" (Rada Pomocy Zydom), Warsaw, 1942–45 (0.3m), file No. 48.

RG 0-7   Collection of Czechoslovakian material from various sources on the Holocaust of the Jews of Czechoslovakia, 1939–48 (1.3m).

RG 0-8   Collection on Germany, 1933–48 (5m). National Jewish Organizations: "Reichsvertretung," "Hilfsverein," "Reichsvereinigung Reichsbund Juedischer Frontsoldaten," 1933–43, files no. 1–20.

Jewish School at Herrlingen. Collection of documents of Hugo Rosenthal Jishuvi, 1933–39, files no. 59–66.

RG 0-9   Collection on France. Material from various sources on the destruction of French Jewry, 1940–48 (6m).

RG 0-10   Collection of documents on the destruction of Yugoslav Jewry, 1940– (2m).

Documentation on the mass murder in Sabac, October 1941. One file.

RG 0-11   Collection of documents on the Holocaust of Romanian Jewry, 1924–52.

Jewish organizations in Romania, 1942–47, files no. 1–48.

Anti-Jewish legislation and anti-Semitic documentation from non-Jewish sources, 1939–45, files no. 49–71.

RG 0-12   Testimonies of Polish refugees taken in Eretz Yisrael, I. Perelman collection, 1943–44. (0.2m).

RG 0-13   Collection of documents on the destruction of Bulgarian Jewry, 1942– (0.6m).

RG 0-15   Collection on Hungary, Part I. Documents on the destruction of Hungarian Jewry, 1936–39 (2m).

Collection on Hungary, Part II. Collection of testimonies taken in Budapest immediately after the liberation, by the documentation division of the Jewish Agency, 1944–46 (2.2m).

RG 0-16   Jewish Historical Commission in Poland, collection of testimonies and diaries, 1944–46 (2.2m).

RG 0-20   M. Lowenthal collection, 1945–47 (0.2m). Department for Jewish Restitution in Germany. Headquarters of the U.S. Forces, U.S. Occupation Zone in Germany.

RG 0-21   Dr. M. Weichert collection; Jewish welfare, J.U.S. in the general government, 1939–45 (1m).

RG 0-26   Collection on North Africa, 1933– (0.2m).

RG 0-27   Collection on Denmark, 1941– (0.2m).

RG 0-28   Arvid Elstoft collection on the underground movement in Denmark, 1943–45 (1m).

RG 0-29   Collection of documents on the Holocaust of Belgian Jewry, 1940 (1m).

RG 0-30   Collection of documents on the Holocaust of Austrian Jewry, 1938 (1.5m).

RG 0-31   Collection of documents on the Holocaust of Italian Jewry, 1940 (0.7m).

RG 0-33   Collection of written testimonies, diaries and memoirs, 1930– (16m).

Diary of the Chairman of the Judenrät in Warsaw, Adam Czerniakow, September 6, 1939–July 23, 1942, File 1090.

RG 0-35   Collection of documents on Jewish refugees in Switzerland, 1936–50 (0.3m).

RG 0-36   David Boder collection of testimonies, 1946– (4m). Interviews with displaced persons.

RG 0-52   Collection on Jewish German communities, 1933– (9m).

RG 0-58   State of Israel Ministry of Defense committee for granting anti-
           Nazi fighter's decoration, 1967–68 (2m).

           Requests to receive anti-Nazi fighters decorations.

RG 0-59   Collection of testimonies and documents on the participation of
           Czechoslovak Jewry in the war against Nazi Germany, 1969–75
           (0.5m).

RG 0-64   Dr. Lichtenstein collection, 1950–74 (1m).

RG 0-67   Beit Berl Archives—Rescue committee in Constantinople, 1942–
           45 (0.2m).

RG 0-67   Collection of testimonies from the International Gathering of
           Holocaust Survivors, 1982 (1m). Includes names and addresses
           of those attending, listed alphabetically according to then-
           present country of residence.

RG 0-71   Collection of testimonies on Lithuania (Kuniuchovski).

RG M-1   Central Historical Commission at the Central Committee of
           Liberated Jews at the U.S. Zone, Munich, 1930–45 (20m).

           Office of the Central Historical Commission in Munich, 1946–48
           (0.2m) (SR M-1/B).

           Collection of testimonies, 1945–48 (4m) (SR M-1/E).

           Documentation of the Dachau concentration camp, 1940–45
           (2.5m) (SR M-1/D).

           Nazi documentation—Munich municipality, 1930–36 (3.5m) (SR
           M-1/DN).

           Nazi documentation, the German Academy of Science, 1929–43
           (6 files) (SR M-1/DNA).

           Questionnaires of the Regional Councils (*Landraete*), 1946–48
           (542 questionnaires) (SR M-1/L).

           Collection of Displaced Persons, 1946–48 (67 files) (SR M-1/P).

Handwritten Yiddish testimonies.

Children's Collection, 1945–48 (673 questionnaires) (SR M-1/PC).

RG M-2   Archives of the office of Dr. I. Schwarzbart, member of the Polish National Council in Exile, London, 1939–57 (20m).

Dr. I. Schwarzbart's diary, January 13, 1940–December 3, 1947 (161 files) (FL M-2/744-759).

RG M-4   Rescue Council of the Jewish Agency for Palestine, bulletins, 1940–47 (1.5m).

RG M-5   Documentation Center of the Central Union of Jewish Communities in Bratislava, destruction of Slovak Jewry, 1939–48 (5m).

Central Jewish Office (U.Z.), 1940–43 (19 files) (FL M-5/1-19).

RG M-20   Relico—Archives of A. Silberschein, Geneva, 1939–48 (11m).

Records from the archives of Joseph Thon, 1939–40 (11 files) (SR M-20/233-243).

RG M-22   Belgian Jews' Council (Comite Juif Belge), London, 1944–45 (0.3m).

RG M-23   Aid Council for Jewish Refugees from Germany, Benna Kaufmann-Basel, 1933–48 (0.5m).

RG M-25   Hebrew National Movement in France, 1941–42 (0.3m).

RG M-28   American Joint Distribution Committee Krakow, correspondence with various institutions, 1938–45 (0.6m).

RG M-32   "Compensation Treuhandstelle"—documentation on forced labor of concentration camp inmates in Krupp, Siemens and Rheinmetall, 1944–70 (1.5m).

RG M-34   Card Index—Hungarian Labor Battalions.

RG M-35   Russian Central State Archives records of the Anti-Fascist Committee. Index in Cyrillic alphabet.

RG M-37   District State Archive Lviv.

RG M-38   District State Archive Odessa.

RG P-16   Archives of Rachel Auerbach, Warsaw ghetto, 1942–73 (4.5m).

RG P-17   Archives of J. Fuksman, western Byelorussia, 1945–48 (1.5m).

RG P-18   Archives of S. Kaczerginski, Vilna partisans, 1944–52 (0.3m).

RG P-20   Zerach Warhaftig personal archives: Rescue through Shanghai, 1940–47 (1.5m).

JM/1599-   Jewish Historical Institute Warsaw, 1939–43 (15,000 microfilm
1686   frames).

           Warsaw ghetto underground archives (Ringelblum archives).

           Aeltestenrat in Litzmannstadt (Lodz), 1939–44 (14,500 frames).

           J.U.S. Jewish welfare in the Generalgouvernement, 1940–43 (22,500 frames).

           Litzmannstadt (Lodz) ghetto administration, 1940–44 (123,000 frames).

           Gestapo in France, documents on the confiscation of Jewish property, 1940–44 (23,000 frames).

JM/3684   Records from the files of KDS Radom, 1939–44.
3687

JM/3536   Records of the regional commissions for investigations of Nazi crimes in Krakow, Radom, Warsaw and Wroclaw, 1945–49.

JM/501–   Documentation Center of Contemporary Jewry, Paris, 1940–45
722   (170,000 frames).
JM/3590-
3598

JM/1211-   Jewish State Museum, Prague, 1939–45 (4,200 frames).
1212
JM/2692-
2694

JM/3402-   Center of Contemporary Jewish Documentation Milan,
3373   1922–55 (30 rolls).

JM/3724   Collection of documents on the history of the Jews in Hungary,
-3793   holdings of the State Archive, Budapest, (211 rolls).
JM/3802
-3931

JM/1687   Archives of the Jewish community, Rome, 1919–52 (32 -1695;
JM/1703– rolls).
1725

JM/1177-   Kibbutz Haarzi Holocaust Archives.
1188

JM/730-   Finance Department, Bamberg; files on Jewish property,
750   1933–45 (22,000 frames).

JM/2798   Collection of documents on the Kloga-Estonia concentration
2800   camp.

JM/1198   Collection on Sweden and Norway, 1940– (10,000 frames).
JM/1215-
1219
JM/2617

JM/1770-   Belgian Association for Refugee Emigration, "Belhicem,"
1773   1933–46 (43,000 frames).
JM/1791-
1897
JM/2740-
2782

JM/10188- Public Records Office, London; records pertaining to the fate of
10247   Jews during the Holocaust.

JM/10464- Zentrales Staatsarchive, Potsdam.
10546

JM/10990- Central State Archives, Slovakia.
11050

U.S. Holocaust Memorial Museum, Washington, D.C.

U.S. HOLOCAUST RESEARCH INSTITUTE

Address: 100 Raoul Wallenberg Place, SW; Washington, DC 20024-2150. Telephone: (202) 488-6115; fax: (202) 479-9726. Internet: research@ ushmm.org.

As the scholarly division of the United States Holocaust Memorial Museum, the U.S. Holocaust Research Institute is one of the most significant Holocaust resource sites to have developed in decades. A rigorous acquisition program has made it one of the major sites in the world today.

The Research Institute's stated purpose is to serve as an international resource for the development of research on the Holocaust and related issues. Research libraries and archives have been the domain of scholars for centuries, and, at most facilities, laypersons are treated with disdain, if not hostility. The Research Institute was conceived originally as an institution to foster research by scholars. It has found, however, that the vast majority of its visitors and supporters are interested in more personal subjects—that is, the fate of their families and communities in the Holocaust. Consequently, the institute has adjusted to this new demand, and its staff is accustomed to dealing with people whose familiarity with research is limited to using the card catalogue at their local libraries.

The Research Institute, located on the fifth floor of the museum, is open seven days a week from 10am to 5pm and requires no ticket for admission. Staffing is minimal on weekends, and visitors should not expect extensive assistance at this time. Seven departments comprise the institute: the Library, Archives, Registry of Jewish Holocaust Survivors, Photo Archive, Oral History Department and Archive, Film and Video Archive, and Academic Programs Department. The first three departments may be of primary interest to Holocaust researchers, although any department may offer something of value to a particular researcher.

Library

The library is quickly accumulating one of the world's foremost collections of printed material on the Holocaust. At present, its collection numbers roughly 25,000 books and journals. Organized according to the U.S. Library of Congress system, it is an open-shelf library that permits readers to

Markovits, Kato 006873 see Carmela Zelkowitz.
Markovits, Laszlo 060780 see Leslie Markley.
Markovits, ? 011390.
Markovitz, Aron 045143 Svalava.
Markovitz, Arya 047672.
Markovitz, Edward 011390.
Markovitz, Elizabeth 097597 see Elisabeth Fischer.
Markovitz, Ida 045143 Svalava.
Markovitz, Regina 010113 see Regina Reitzer.
Markovitz, Sari 055239 see Shary Farkas.
Markovitz, Zita 047672 see Zita Weber.
Markow, Edith Loffler 005460 (Edith Loffler).
Markowice, Mania 008710 (Mania Kowicz) Tomaszow.
Markowicz, Abe 039089.
Markowicz, Bella 015447 (Bella Solarz) Lodz; Auschwitz,
  Lodz, Neu Kolln, Ravensbruck.
Markowicz, Chil 004733 see Charles Markowitz.
Markowicz, Feivel 039109 see Philip Markowicz.
Markowicz, Harry 010555 Berlin, Antwerpen; Bruxelles.
Markowicz, Ida 008395 see Ida Henig.
Markowicz, Manfred 039077 see Manfred J Marko.
Markowicz, Mania 008710 see Mary Shampaner.
Markowicz, Marja 010555 Berlin; Bruxelles.
Markowicz, Minia 033536 see Minnie Heber.
Markowicz, Nathan 015447 (Nota Markowicz) Lodz;
  Auschwitz, Dachau, Kaufering, Lodz.
Markowicz, Nota 015447 see Nathan Markowicz.
Markowicz, Philip 039109 (Feivel Markowicz) Przerab;
  Auschwitz, Flossenburg, Gor, Lodz.
Markowicz, Rosa 004386 see Rose Schwarz.
Markowicz, Ruth 039109 (Rywka Ruchel Fajerman) Bedzin;
  Gelenau, Langenbielau.
Markowielki, Moniek 007093 see Martin Marks.
Markowitch, Hermina 097545 see Hermina Levi.
Markowitsch, Rolf 039062 see Ralph H Mark.
Markowitz, ? 039096.
Markowitz, Channa 006730 see Anna Hollander.
Markowitz, Charles 004733 (Chil Markowicz) Lodz;
  Auschwitz, Buchenwald, Dachau, Janikowa, Lodz, Poznan,
  Stuttgart.
Markowitz, Clara 008146 see Clara Mermelstein.
Markowitz, Erwin 007450 (Ignac Markowitz) Uzgorod, Velki
  Berezny; Chust, Erdely, Mauthausen, Mukachevo, Nagy
  Banya, Ujverbasz.
Markowitz, Erwin 006043 (Ignac Markovic) Uzgorod, Velki
  Berezny; Chust, Mauthausen, Mukachevo, Nagbanya, Sighet,
  Ujverbasz.
Markowitz, Esther 008962 (Ester Moskovics) Velyatin;
  Auschwitz, Bydgoszcz, Chust, Tovn.
Markowitz, Frances 009801 (Fruma Warzecha) Tomaszow
  Mazowiecki; Auschwitz, Blizyn, Tereizen, Wilischthal.
Markowitz, Frank 099530.
Markowitz, Golda 015823 see Goldie Weiss.
Markowitz, Gucia 004733 (Gitly Kochman) Bedzin; Bergen
  Belsen, Koyzalc.
Markowitz, H. 012517 Lodz.
Markowitz, Herman 077919 (Herman Markovic) Nizne
  Nemecke; Bucza Kosseg, Gunskirchen, Horty Liget, Joseva,
  Mauthausen, Sarospatak.
Markowitz, Hinda 009686 Ciechanow.
Markowitz, Ignac 007450 see Erwin Markowitz.
Markowitz, Irvin 009801 Tomaszow Mazowiecki; Ebensee.
Markowitz, Isaac 008962 (Isaac Markovics) Sinevir; Auschwitz,
  Chust, Mauthausen.
Markowitz, Israel 005027.
Markowitz, Kopel 006144 (Kopel Markiewitz) Lodz; Dora.
Markowitz, Lajzer 039118 see Leon Markowitz.

Markowitz, Leo 039096.
Markowitz, Leon 039118 (Lajzer Markowitz) Wielun;
  Czestochowa, Lodz.
Markowitz, Max 047672 Svalava; Auschwitz, Mauthausen,
  Mukachevo.
Markowitz, Mayer 039105.
Markowitz, Molle 039105.
Markowitz, Rachel 039118 (Rachela Zusman) Ozorkow;
  Auschwitz, Lodz.
Markowitz, Regina Kremer 099530.
Markowitz, Ruth 012517 (Ruth Halpern) Lodz; Auschwitz,
  Bergen Belsen, Hamburg.
Markowitz, Ruzena 039094 (Ruzeba Skinivuts) Nagy Dovrony;
  Auschwitz, Freidetal, Sunaten, Uzgorod.
Markowitz, Sam 039114.
Markowitz, Thereza 054369 see Thereza Zeman.
Markowitz, Tobie 007450 (Tobie Weiss) Kerecke; Auschwitz,
  Birkenau, Hamburg, Perto, Reichenbach, Sweden.
Markowitz, Tobie 006043 (Terez Weiss) Kerecke; Auschwitz.
Markowski, Alan 039055 see Alan Mark.
Markowski, Jack 049584 see Jack Marcus.
Markowski, Joseph 038799 see Joseph Markowsky.
Markowski, Leib 049584 Kolo.
Markowski, Sprinea 049584 Kolo.
Markowsky, Joseph 038799 (Joseph Markowski) Lodz;
  Auschwitz, Dachau, Lodz.
Marks, Bernard 038799 (Ber Marowsli) Lodz; Auschwitz,
  Dachau, Lodz.
Marks, Fanny 097460 (Fanny Lemberger) Paris.
Marks, Harry 013329 (Hersh Chaim Purzycki) Mlawa; Buna,
  Mlawa.
Marks, Helen Solomon 060807 (Helene Salomon) Antwerpen;
  Antwerpen, Bruxelles, Liege.
Marks, Joanna 007020.
Marks, Martin 007093 (Moniek Markowielki) Bedzin; Bergen
  Belsen, Bunzlau, Markstadt, Ottmuth.
Marks, Nathan 011830 (Naftali Mokotow) Warszawa.
Marks, Paula 007093 (Pola Rajchman) Ozorkow; Auschwitz,
  Bergen Belsen, Lodz, Milhausen, Ravensbruck.
Marks, Rose 013329 (Rose Litwak) Radom, Lodz;
  Czestochowa, Lodz.
Marks, Silvia 011830 (Silvia Edelsburg) Lublin; Kassel.
Markus, Amalie 054275.
Markus, Armin 010891 Wien.
Markus, Charlotte 010908 (Charlotte de Haas) Bad Pymont;
  Sweden.
Markus, Dezso 099137 see David Marcus.
Markus, Hedwig Amalie 010891 (Hedwig Gellert) Wien.
Markus, Helmut 010908 Koblenz.
Markus, Lind 006901 see Lind Mark.
Markus, Lola 040578 see Lena Obar.
Markus, Paula 024662 see Paula Ebstein.
Markus, Tamas 054320.
Markuse, Leah 039127.
Markuse, Oscar 099587.
Markuse, Oskar 039127.
Markush, Catherine A. 053326 Budapest.
Markushamer, Hadassah 099781 see Helen Hirschbein.
Markusz, Valeria 099755 see Valeria Davy.
Markuze, Hela 029000 see Helen Dymant.
Marmor, Genia 053505 Chrzanow; Bergen Belsen, Grunberg.
Marmor, Ilona 026168 see Eleanore Berger.
Marmor, Maria 031799 see Mary R Glucksman.
Marmor, Rachel 036699 see Rosa Kramer.
Marmor, Tauba 043709 see Toby Sharf.
Marmorek, Dr Erich 078782 see Eric S Marmorek.
Marmorek, Eric S. 078782 (Dr Erich Marmorek) Wien;

National Registry of Jewish Holocaust Survivors. The Benjamin and Vladka Meed Registry of Jewish Holocaust Survivors located at the U.S. Holocaust Memorial Museum in Washington, DC, maintains information about 100,000 survivors and their families who live primarily in the United States and Canada. The survivor portion of the database is published in book form. Shown here is a page from the book that includes Nathan Marks, born Naftali Mokotow, who lived in Warsaw before the war.

browse through its volumes. The computerized reference system, which also includes the holdings of the archives and the Oral History Department, is far more detailed than that of most institutions with larger collections. Since the scope of the library is more limited than that of a university library, for example, it has been possible to cross-index to a much greater degree than one might expect elsewhere.

Consider the subject "Dachau" This library's catalog has 15 subheadings (compared to 6 in the Library of Congress), and 119 holdings are listed under the 15 subheadings. The reference system is relatively user friendly, allowing one to explore subjects in a variety of ways, e.g., Holocaust-Jewish-Ukraine-Galicia-Galicia Eastern. The library follows the Library of Congress methodology in determining locations. For example, what was once Galicia is now part of Ukraine; materials are listed under "Ukraine." The fact that a particular book might have been written during the period when Galicia was a province of the Austro-Hungarian Empire does not affect its classification.

For a researcher seeking specific names, but without much specific information—for example, the fate of the Cohn family from Posen—the search can be difficult, but sometimes rewarding. In this example, one would consult the reference system to see what materials exist specifically on Posen and the fate of its Jewish population. Since most of the Jews from Posen were sent to Auschwitz, one might consult reference works on Auschwitz, consult archives and registry materials, and perhaps even peruse the books on survivors or persons deported from Western Europe, where many Poles had fled prior to 1939.

Archives

Because the library and archives share and staff the same reference desk, a visitor may be served by either a librarian or an archivist. There are some more fundamental differences between the two divisions, however, the most obvious of which is the open stack library system versus the need to request access to materials from the archives. The latter holds records (mostly on microfilm) on all aspects of the Holocaust, but with special concentration on Eastern Europe and the former Soviet Union.

Existing holdings include material on the deportation of Jews from Romania, Gestapo and *Einsatzgruppen* (Nazi mobile killing units in the Soviet Union) activities, concentration camps, etc. Although a major effort has been made to organize and identify the contents of the material, and much of it includes information on individuals, names have not yet been indexed. In a very few cases, the catalog lists names (e.g., under the heading "Dusseldorf-Gestapo," one finds 807 family names, but in almost all other cases, the only names that appear in the catalog are those of authors or persons who are the subjects of books).

Researchers must examine the materials to determine if a certain name appears. Particular attention should be paid to the collection of records that document the fate of the Romanian Jewish community, including material from Transnistria. This collection is probably the most extensive available anywhere outside of Romania and is essential for anyone researching this subject.

Registry of Jewish Holocaust Survivors

Unlike other sections of the Research Institute, individuals are the focus of the Benjamin and Vladka Meed Registry of Jewish Holocaust Survivors. This registry is the successor to the National Registry of Jewish Holocaust Survivors developed by the American Gathering of Jewish Holocaust Survivors, and it continues to help survivors search for relatives and friends through voluntary registration of survivors and their families. Visitors may access roughly 85,000 names through a computer system, and the registry assists those who wish to contact these survivors. The registry also collects references to survivors who are not registered (e.g., the names of 50,000 Polish survivors and various lists of persons living in displaced persons camps after World War II), but these names have not yet been computerized.

HOLDINGS FOUND IN THE LIBRARY THAT INCLUDE LISTS OF VICTIMS AND SURVIVORS

It is recommended that you look in the library catalog for a more detailed description of the materials listed below. Call numbers after the items are in brackets [ ].

Sharit ha-platah Bavaria. 1945) Names of Jews scattered throughout the many camps in Bavaria. 5 vols. [810.J4 S42 1945]

National Registry of Jewish Holocaust Survivors. 1995. List of some 35,000 Holocaust survivors living in the United States and Canada. [D 810.J4 N275 1991]

Die Opfer der nationalsozialistischen Judenverfolgung in Baden-Württemberg 1933-1945: ein Gedenkbuch. [DS 135.G42 B2 O63 1969]

Binder, Cornelia, and Michael Mence. *Last traces = Letzte Spuren: Last traces of German Jews in the Landkreis of Bad Kissingen = von Deutschen jüdischen.* [DS 135.G42 F572 KIS B56 1992]

Szerkesztette, Carmilly, and Mózes Weinberger. *A Kolozevári zsidóság emlékkönyve* (Memorial volume for the Jews of Cluj-Kolozsvár). New York: Sepher-Hermon, 1970. Text in Hungarian, Hebrew and English. [DS

135.R72 CLU K6 1970]

Sharit ha-platah: an extensive list of survivors of Nazi tyranny published so that the lost may be found and the dead brought back to life. Munich: Central Committee of Liberated Jews in Bavaria, 1946) [D 810.J4 S42 1946]

Diamant, Adolf. *Deportationsbuch der von Frankfurt am Main aus gewaltsam verschickten Juden in den Jahren 1941 bis 1944.* Frankfurt am Main: Jüdische Gemeinde Frankfurt am Main, 1984) [DS 135.G42 H52 FRA D36 1984]

Diamant, Adolf. *Deportationsbuch der in den Jahren 1942 bis 1945 von Leipzig aus gewaltsam verschickten Juden.* Frankfurt am Main: Selbstverlag, 1991) [DS 135.G42 S32 LEI D47 1991]

Drexler, Siegmund, Siegmund Kalinski and Hans Mausbach. *Ärztliches Schicksal unter der Verfolgung, 1933-1945 in Frankfurt am Main und Offenbach: eine Denkschrift.* Frankfurt am Main: Verlag für Akademische Schriften, 1990) [DS 135.G42 H52 FRA D755 1990]

Die Juden in Bamberg. Bamberg?: Gesellschaft für Christlich-Jüdische Zusammenarbeit?, 1962?) [DS 135.G42 F5752 BAMB F75 1962]

Gedenkbuch: Opfer der Verfolgung der Juden unter der national-sozialistischen Gewaltherrschaft in Deutschland, 1933-1945. Frankfurt/Main: J. Weisbecker, c1986) List of 128,000 German Jews murdered in the Holocaust. Includes person's name (including maiden name of married women), place of deportation, birth date and, in some instances, place and date of death. [D 810.J4 G32 1986, Vol. 1; D 810.J4 G32 1986, vol. 2]

Die jüdischen Opfer des Nationalsozialismus in Hamburg. Hamburg: Staatsarchiv Hamburg, 1965) [DS 135.G42 H155 J83 1965b]

Hepp, Michael. *Die Ausbürgerung deutscher Staatsangehöriger 1933-45 nach den im Reichsanzeiger veröffentlichten Listen* (Expatriation lists as published in the "Reichsanzeiger" 1933-45). [DD 256.8.E9 A88 1985-1988]

Die Landauer Judengemeinde: ein Abriss ihrer Geschichte. Landau/Pfalz: Stadtarchiv, 1969) [DS 135.G42 P42 LAN H47 1969]

Totenbuch Theresienstadt I: Deportierte aus Österreich. Wien: Jüdisches Komitee für Theresienstadt, 1971) [D 805.5.C9 TER T68 1971]

Klarsfeld, Serge. *Memorial to the Jews Deported from France, 1942-1944*

(English-language version). New York: Beate Klarsfeld Foundation, c1983) [DS 135.F83 K53 1983]

Klarsfeld, Serge, and Maxime Steinberg. *Mémorial de la déportation des juifs de Belgique*. Bruxelles: Union des déportés juifs en Belgique et filles et fils de la déporation; New York: Beate Klarsfeld Foundation, 1982) [DS 135.B4 M35 1982]

Klarsfeld, Serge. *Documents concerning the destruction of the Jews of Grodno 1941-1944*. New York: Beate Klarsfeld Foundation, 1985?) [DS 135.S72 B92 GRO D63 1985]

Kleinert, Beate, and Wolfgang Prinz. *Namen und Schicksale der Juden Kassels, 1933-1945: ein Gedenkbuch*. Kassel: Magistrat der Stadt Kassel, Stadtarchiv, 1986. [DS 135.G42 H52 KAS K54 1986]

Kliner-Lintzen, Martina and Siegfried Pape. "——*vergessen kann man das nicht": Wittener Jüdinnen und Juden unter dem Nationalsozialismus*. [DS 135.G42 N62 WIT K5 1991]

Klukowski, Zygmunt. *Diary from the years of occupation, 1939-44*. Translated from Polish by George Klukowski. Urbana: University of Illinois Press, c1993) [**KLUKOWSKI .AU 1993]

Kolonomos, Zamila, and Vera Veskovilk-Vangeli. *Evreite vo Makedonija vo Vtorata svetska vojna, 1941-1945: zbornik na dokumenti* (Jews in Macedonia during the Second World War, 1941-1945). Skopje: Makedonska akademija na naukite i umetnosti, 1986) Vol. 2 only. [DS 135.M23 K65 1986]

Minninger, Monika, Joachim Meynert and Friedhelm Schäffer. *Antisemitisch Verfolgte registriert in Bielefeld, 1933-45: Eine Dokumentation jüdischer Einzelschicksale*. Bielefeld, Germany: Stadtarchiv Bielefeld, 1985) [DS 135.G42 N62 BIE M45 1985]

Mohn, Joseph. *Der Leidensweg unter dem Hakenkreuz*. Bad Buchau, Germany: die Stadt, 1970) [DS 135.G42 B22 BUCH M6 1970]

Morris, Henry. *Våre Falne: 1939-1945/utgitt av den norske stat*. Oslo: Grondahl, 1949-1951) [D 763.N6 V27 1949-51 Vols. 1–4]

Sie sind nicht vergessen: Bericht über die letzten Ruhestätten der am 22. Oktober 1940 nach Südfrankreich deportierten badischen Jüden. Karlsruhe, Germany: der Oberrat der Israeliten Badens, 1958) [DS 135.G42 B2 S43 1958]

Olszewicz, Bolesław. *Lista strat kultury polskiej, 1. IX. 1939-1. III. 1946.* Warszawa: C. Arct, 1947) May be a list of non-Jews only. [D 804.G4 O58 1947]

Romano, Jatsa. *Jevreji Jugoslavije 1941-1945, tzrtve genocida i utcesnici.* Beograd: Savez jevrejskih optstina Jugoslavije, 1980) Text in Serbo-Croatian. [DS 135.Y8 R66 1980]

Totenliste Hamburger Widerstandskämpfer und Verfolgter, 1933-1945. Hamburg: Vereinigte Arbeitsgemeinschaft der Naziverfolgten e. V. <VAN>, 1968) [D 810.U6 GER T77 1968]

Schäfer-Richter, Uta, and Jörg Klein. *Die jüdischen Bürger im Kreis Göttingen, 1933-1945: Ein Gedenkbuch.* Göttingen, Germany: Wallstein, c1992) [DS 135.G42 N42 GOT S33 1992]

Czuperska-Sliwicka, Anna. *Cztery lata ostrego dyłzuru: wspomnienia z Pawiaka, 1940-1944.* Warszawa: Czytelnik, 1965) [**SLIWICKA .AU 1965]

Sliwicki, Zygmunt. *Meldunek z Pawiaka.* Warszawa: Panstwowe Wydawn. Naukowe, 1974) [D 805.5 .P6 PAW S55 1974]

Totenbuch Theresienstadt: Damit sie nicht vergessen werden. Wien: Junius, c1987) [D 805.5.C9 TER T68 1987]

Krefelder Juden. Bonn: Röhrscheid, 1980) [DS 135.G42 N62 KRE K73 1980]

Counted remnant: register of the Jewish survivors in Budapest. Budapest: World Jewish Congress: Jewish Agency for Palestine, 1946) [DS 135.H9 C68 1946] Includes about 68,000 names.

Wulman, Leon. *The martyrdom of Jewish physicians in Poland.* New York: published for Medical Alliance-Association of Jewish Physicians from Poland by Exposition Press, c1963) An alphabetical necrology of Jewish physicians martyred during the German occupation of Poland. Includes bibliographies. [DS 135.P6 W85 1963]

Zugic, Tomislav, and Miodrag Milic. *Jugosloveni u koncentracionom logoru Ausvic 1941-1945.* Beograd: ISI, 1989. Text in Serbo-Croatian (Roman). [D 805.5.P6 AUS Z84 1989]

RECORD GROUPS IN THE ARCHIVES THAT INCLUDE LISTS OF VICTIMS AND SURVIVORS

Records of Nazi concentration camps, 1939–1945. Includes information about various concentration and labor camps in Europe from 1939 to 1945. The bulk of the collection consists of transport lists of prisoners who were moved between major concentration camps. These lists provide information about the place and date of birth, occupation, religion, and identification number of the prisoners. In some cases, the date of death is also given. There is data from Auschwitz, Dachau, Dora-Mittelbau, Ellrich, Flossenburg, Gross-Rosen, Lodz, Mauthausen, Natzwiller, Neuengamme, Ravensbruck, Riga and Sachsenhausen. It is necessary to go to the archives to determine the nature of the material available for each of the camps. [RG-04.006M]

Extraordinary State Commission to Investigate German-Fascist Crimes Committed on Soviet Territory. An enormous collection (27 reels) of information resulting from the investigation of German war crimes by the Soviet government. Included are materials about victims, crimes against persons, and perpetrators. Types of documents include name lists of victims, interrogations of eyewitnesses and signed depositions. Organized by town within Soviet *oblast* (province). Appendix C lists the towns included in the commission reports. All the information is in Russian. [RG-22.002M]

Amsterdam City Archives, Selected Records. Consists of various documents relating to the Jewish community in Amsterdam during the Holocaust. [RG-41.001*01]

Auschwitz Concentration Camp Häftlingspersonalbogen (Prisoner Registration Forms). Information on 5,423 male and 331 female prisoners who arrived during the period May 1942–October 1944. Each form includes information about a particular inmate, such as date of birth, place of birth, marital status, date of arrest, date of entry into the camp, nationality, occupation, religion, race and physical appearance. Also included is information about escapes by prisoners and information about divisions of the Reichssicherheitshauptamt making arrests of Jews to be sent to Auschwitz. [RG-04.031M]

Auschwitz Death Book. Compiled in September 1942. The death book provides prisoner identification numbers, native cities, names of parents, names of the attending physicians, and alleged causes of death. [RG-04.007*01]

Bergen-Belsen Concentration Camp, Selected Records from the

American Field Service Archives and Museum. Consists of a variety of documents relating to the work of the American Field Service (C and D Platoons) at Bergen-Belsen concentration camp after liberation. Includes lists. [RG-04.038*01]

Berlin. Consists of a copy of a transport list of the names and addresses of Jews and Gypsies deported from Berlin to Auschwitz on May 5, 1943. [RG-07.008*02]

Bytom in Upper Silesia. Lists of 982 Jews evacuated from Bytom. [RG-15.030*01]

Chisinau (Chernovtsy). Name lists, situation reports, other material. Includes information about the internment of Romanian Jews in several ghettos in Romania and Bessarabia; administration of the Chisinau ghetto (including census information); the ghetto in Balti; the ghetto in Soroca; activities of the police in the Chisinau ghetto; disposal of Jewish property; deportations of Jews from Bessarabia; Jews placed in internment camps; and executions of Romanian Jews. [RG-54.001M]

Cleveland, Ohio, Survivors. Includes information about 287 Jewish Holocaust survivors. Also includes information about the family members of the Cleveland survivors who perished in the Holocaust. [RG-02.024]

Cyprus. Concerns the experiences of Frederick Wohl and his family during the evacuation of Jews from Cyprus and their travels to Israel and southern Africa. The accession also includes a list of names and addresses of those Jews evacuated from Cyprus to Tel Aviv in June 1941. [RG-03.009*01]

Dachau. Includes testimonies and articles relating to the liberation of Dachau concentration camp. [RG-09.005*09]

Dachau. See first entry at the beginning of this section.

Dolgoye (Dolha), Ukraine. Provides historical background on the Jewish community of Dolha (also known as Dovhoje); also includes name lists of Jewish residents, with personal details and indication of their fate during the Holocaust. [RG-03.013*01]

Dora-Mittelbau. See first entry at the beginning of this section.

Dunaberg. Includes information about the establishment of a kitchen for laborers from Dunaberg, rationing of food for Jewish laborers, food for Salaspils prisoners working for area businesses and the acquisition of vegetables for the city hospital in Riga. [RG-18.002M*03]

Ebensee. Contains name lists of displaced persons, grouped by nationality, remaining in Ebensee concentration camp after liberation. Lists of Polish displaced persons make up the bulk of the collection. [RG-19.027]

Ellrich. See first entry at the beginning of this section.

Flossenburg. Includes testimonies, articles and letters relating to the liberation of Flossenburg concentration camp. [RG-09.005*12]

Flossenburg. See first entry at the beginning of this section.

Flossenburg, Records Relating to the Liberation of and the 90th U.S. Infantry Division Correspondence. [RG-09.021*01]

Gomel Oblast Archive, Selected Records. Includes name lists. Documents relating to the activities of various oblast government offices in the vicinity of Gomel. Among many items is the liquidation of the ghetto at Monastyrek. [RG-53.005M]

Gorinchem, Netherlands. Photocopies of correspondence and name lists relating to the fate of Jews in Gorinchem, Netherlands, during Nazi occupation. [RG-03.014*01]

Grodno. Commissar (Amtskommissar) for Civil Administration of Belostok Region. Selected records from the Grodno Oblast Archive lists and other material. Includes census lists for Grodno and vicinity. [RG-53.004M]

Gross-Rosen. See first entry at the beginning of this section.

Kaluszyn, Poland. Michael Kishel's memoir of the Holocaust and memoir of the role of his father in the Judenrat in Kaluszyn, Poland. [RG-02.067*01]

Kloster-Indersdorf Displaced Persons Children's Center. Includes name lists, photographs and other material. [RG-19.034]

Krakow. Records for the Institut für Deutsche Ostarbeit. Includes population statistics for Krakow, Poland, through the years; birth statistics for several Polish towns and villages. [RG-15.010M1]

Krakow, Records of the Generalgouvernement. Contains information about activities of the Generalgouvernement and its officials in Krakow from circa 1939 to circa 1945. Also included is information about the administration of prisons in Krakow and Rzeszow; establishment of a separate Jewish section in Krakow; and treatment of prisoners of war. [RG-15.026M]

Latvia. Includes information about confiscation of school, sanatorium, and hospital facilities for use by occupation forces and actions for the evacuation of refugees by transport. Information about the following towns: Riga, Liebau, Daugavpils, Jelgava, Madona, Cesis, Valmiera, Valkas, Tukuma, Bauskas, Ilukste, Aizputes. [RG-18.002M*07]

Latvia. Ledgers, situation reports, lists of the SD-Sicherheitspolizei in Latvia from 1942 to 1943. [RG-18.002M*85]

Latvia. Includes information about confiscation of private and public property in several Latvian cities by the Wehrmacht, seizure of homes and furnishings of Jews after their removal to the Riga ghetto, and regulations for Jews in the labor force. Also included are lists of names and addresses of those Jewish families whose homes and property were seized by the Wehrmacht. [RG-18.002M*52]

Lodz. See first entry at the beginning of this section.

Lviv. Consists of copies of Lemberg Ukrainian police documents concerning the fate of Ukrainian Jews. Among the topics mentioned are matters of Jewish property, attempts of Jews to bribe the Lemberg police and Jewish housing. [RG-31.005*01]

Lviv. Includes information about the German occupation of Lviv, the establishment of the Lvov ghetto, and Jews involved in public work programs and industry. [RG-31.003M]

Majdanek. Includes information about the Majdanek killing center near Lublin, Poland; included are a transport list of Polish Jews who arrived in May 1942 and fragments of lists of Jews of various nationalities who died at the camp during the period May to September 1942. [RG-04.003*01]

Mauthausen. See first entry at the beginning of this section.

Mauthausen. Includes testimonies and letters relating to the liberation of the three Gusen subcamps of Mauthausen. [RG-09.005*18]

Mauthausen. Includes testimonies and letters relating to the liberation of the three Gusen subcamps of Mauthausen. [RG-09.005*27]

Mauthausen publications. Copies of two issues of "Hier Cauchemar Aujourd'hui Espoir: Bulletin interieur d'information et de liaison de l'Amicale des Deportes Politique de Mauthausen." List of French deportees who perished at Mauthausen. Also includes information about Gusen, a subcamp of Mauthausen. [RG-04.010*01]

Melnica, Records Relating to the Jewish Community of. [RG-03.017*01]

Mogilev. Consists of microfilmed documents relating to the activities of various Mogilev city administration offices and German occupation agencies in the Mogilev area during World War II. [RG-53.006M]

Natzwiller. See first entry at the beginning of this section.

Neuengamme. See first entry at the beginning of this section.

Nordhausen. Includes testimonies, letters, and other materials relating to the liberation of the Nordhausen (also known as Dora-Mittelbau) concentration camp. [RG-09.005*31]

Ohrdruf. Includes testimonies, letters, and other materials relating to the liberation of Ohrdruf concentration camp. [RG-09.005*32]

Prague Military-Historical Institute. Selected documents from the Military-Historical Institute. Description is not specific, but said to include name lists. Subject list includes mention of Buchenwald, Flossenburg, Mauthausen, Gross-Rosen, Ravensbruck, Terezin, Dachau and Chelmno. [RG-48.004M]

Ravensbruck. See first entry at the beginning of this section.

Ravensbruck. Includes documents related to the distribution of labor in the camp, names of kommandos and overseers, and transports. [RG-04.017*01]

Riga. See first entry at the beginning of this section.

Riga Prison Release Forms, Statements, Lists. Includes discharge forms for prisoners released from the Zentralgefängnis in Riga. [RG-18.002M*83]

Riga area. Includes information about rationing and food amounts for persons in prisons and concentration camps, apparently in the area of Riga,

Latvia. [RG-18.002M*01]

Riga. Includes information about the prison canteen (Gemeinschaft Termgefängnis) in Riga. [RG-18.002M*02]

Sachsenhausen. See first entry at the beginning of this section.

Schindler, Oskar. Consists of letters, photographs, and articles relating to the life of Oskar Schindler and his efforts as a righteous Gentile during the Holocaust. Included in the materials is a copy of a list, dated April 18, 1945, of Jewish inmates of Brünnlitz, a subcamp of Gross-Rosen in Czechoslovakia that was associated with Oskar Schindler's munitions factory. [RG-20.003*01]

Shanghai. Includes testimony and newsletters relating to the life of John and Harriet Isaack as members of the Jewish refugee community in Shanghai, China; the reunion of the Shanghai Jewish community in San Francisco, California, in 1980. [RG-03.011*01]

Soviet Union, Records Relating to Nazi Occupation. Includes information about killing in Lithuania during Nazi occupation; killing in retaliation for sabotage; activities of Einsatzgruppe A from October 1941 to January 1942; mass shootings of Soviet citizens; Soviet prisoners of war; creation of ghettos; operation "Hornung," the annihilation of Jews in Slutsk (Minsk Oblast); killing of Soviet citizens in retaliation for partisan activities; interrogation of Kiev inhabitants concerning the massacre at Babi Yar; operation "Swamp Fever" near Minsk; operation "Magic Flute" in Minsk; operation "Kottbus" in Byelorussia; and operation "Herman" conducted in the occupied territory of Grodno and Minsk. Central State Archive of the October Revolution and Social Construction of the White Russian SSR. [RG-22.001*01]

Terezin. Dr. Karl Loewenstein's account of events in Terezin during his imprisonment. [RG-02.048]

Ukraine. Includes numerous items of information about the German occupation of the Ukraine. Also included are name lists of Reichskommiss-ariat personnel, construction workers in the eastern oblasts, bishops of the Orthodox Church and persons killed in various villages and oblasts of the Ukraine. [RG-31.002M]

Wels, Austria. Consists of a copy of a list of names of concentration camp inmates who died at Wels, Austria, mostly in May 1945. [RG-17.001*01]

Wisznice, Poland. Includes photocopies of a register of inhabitants' names from the Wisznice ghetto and photographs of the Wisznice ghetto from circa 1939 to 1943. [RG-05.006*01]

Yugoslavian records. Consists of copies of documents concerning Yugoslavia during World War II. Included are documents relating to Banjica, Jasenovac and Zemun concentration camps. [RG-49.002]

YIVO INSTITUTE
FOR JEWISH RESEARCH

Address: 555 West 57th Street, Suite 1100; New York, NY 10019. Telephone: (212) 535-6700; fax: (212) 734-1062.

As a major world-class institution dedicated to the preservation of Eastern European heritage, YIVO Institute has an extensive collection of Holocaust period material. Included are some 6,000 volumes published in Germany during the period 1933–45; thousands of handwritten eyewitness accounts by survivors; 150 titles from publications printed by Jewish displaced persons held in camps in Germany, Austria and Italy; an extensive yizkor book collection—one of the largest in the world; and records and documents from the Warsaw, Lodz and Vilna ghettos.

HOLDINGS IN THE LIBRARY THAT
INCLUDE LISTS OF VICTIMS AND SURVIVORS

The call number of the item appears in brackets [ ].

Register of Jewish Survivors: List of Jews Rescued in Different European Countries. vol. 1. (Jerusalem: Jewish Agency for Palestine, Search Bureau for Missing Relatives, 1945). These lists are in no way as comprehensive as their titles imply. The total number of persons named in all the lists is 60,000. [3/22766A]
1. Jewish women liberated in the Bergen-Belsen camp.
2. List of Polish Jews liberated from the Bergen-Belsen camp.
3. List of Jews liberated from the Buchenwald camp.
4. Surviving Jews from European extermination camps.
5. Jewish women released from the Rentzmohler camp (Germany).
6. List of foreign Jews in Rome.
7. List of Jewish survivors in Milan.
8. List of Polish Jews liberated from the Bergen-Belsen camp.
9. List of Polish Jews liberated from the Dachau camp.
10. List of Jews (mainly Polish) liberated from the Dora (Nordhausen) camp.
11. List of Polish-Jewish survivors at the Buchenwald camp.

12. List of Jews of Polish nationality who arrived in Sweden.
13. List of surviving Polish Jews (London list).
14. List of Jews surviving in Poland (Bucharest list).
15. Second list of Jews surviving in Poland (compiled in Cracow).
16. List of surviving children in Poland.
17. List of Polish nationals (mostly Jews) in the Bergen-Belsen camp.
18. List of Jewish survivors in Eastern European towns.
19. Lists of Jewish women from Hungary and Transylvania.
20. List of Hungarian and Transylvanian Jews liberated from German camps.
21. Jews from Budapest in Northern Italy.
22. List of Jewish survivors found in Gyor (Hungary).
23. List of Czechoslovakian Nationals (mostly Jewish) registered in the Bergen-Belsen camp.
24. List of Czechoslovakian Nationals (mostly Jewish) registered in the Bergen-Belsen camp.
25. List of Czechoslovakian Nationals (mostly Jewish) registered in the Bergen-Belsen camp on May 9, 1945.
26. List of Czechoslovakian Jews who arrived in Italy and Sweden.
27. List of repatriated Czechoslovakian nationals registered at the repatriation office in Kosice.
28. Lists of Yugoslavian-Jewish survivors.
29. List of Jews found surviving in Holland.
30. List of Jewish survivors who arrived in Amsterdam from concentration camps.
31. List of Dutch-Jewish survivors who arrived in Sweden.
32. List of Jewish survivors in some Italian cities.
33. List of Jewish survivors liberated from the Salzwedel camp.
34. List of Jewish survivors found in Theresienstadt on May 10, 1945.

Register of Jewish Survivors: List of Jews in Poland, vol. 2. (Jerusalem: Jewish Agency for Palestine, Search Bureau for Missing Relatives, 1945) Includes about 58,000 names. [3/22766A]

Jewish Agency for Palestine. Accession list of the bulletin "To Those Near and Far" (Lakarov velarahok). Nos. 1–50, 28 June 1945–2 July 1946. (Jerusalem: Jewish Agency, 1946) 55 pp. [3/22777]

List officielle des decedes des camps de concentration. Nos. 1, 2, 3, 5 (Paris: Ministere des Anciens Combattants et Victimes de Guerre). Includes information from Mauthausen, Neuengamme, prison de Breslau, Auschwitz, Flossenburg. [3/22775]

Lists of Holocaust survivors and victims. (New York: World Jewish

Congress, 1945–46) Arranged chronologically. [uncataloged]

Sharit Ha-platah. [Lists of survivors] 5 vols. Germany, 1945. vol. 1, Bergen-Belsen; vol. 2, Buchenwald and others; vol. 3, Bergen-Belsen and others; vol. 4, Linz and others; vol. 5, Feldafing and others. (Munich, Central Committee of Liberated Jews in Bavaria, 1946) [3/22769]

Service d'Evacuation et de Regroupement des Enfants et Familles Juifs S.E.R. Bruxelles. List of liberated Jews in Brussels, Belgium. [3/22777B]

Relief Committee of Jews from Czechoslovakia. London. Aid for communications between displaced Jews resident in the Czechoslovak Republic in 1938 and persons then resident in Great Britain and the British Empire, Spain, Sweden, etc. [3/22777F]

Register of all persons saved from anti-Jewish persecution in Slovakia. 3 vols. (Bratislava: American Joint Distribution Committee, 1945?) [3/22767]

Totenbuch Theresientstadt. (Wien: Jewish Committee for Theresienstadt) [9/80702]

List of saved persons Terezin-Ghetto. (Prague: Czechoslovakian Ministry for the Protection of Labor and Social Welfare, 1945) 541 pp. [3/22772]

List of persons liberated at Terezin in early May 1945 and list of children at Terezin. Bulletin no. 15, July/August 1945 (New York: Czechoslovak Jewish Committee) [3/22777E]

Memorial to the Jews Deported from France, 1942–1944. New York: Beate Klarsfeld Foundation, 1983. [9/76780]

Gedenkbuch: Opfer der Verfolgung der Juden unter der National-sozialistichen Gewaltherrschaft in Deutschland 1933–1945. Koblenz: Bundesarchiv, 1986. [9/80818]

Die Toten von Dachau, Deutsche und Osterreicher. Ein Gedenk- und Nachschlagewerk. (Munchen: Generalanwaltschaft für die Wiedergut-machung.) German and Austrian victims from Dachau. [3/45499]

Lists of Polish Jews who perished in Dachau and lists of Polish Jews who were transferred from Dachau to other camps. [uncatalogued]

Jewish displaced persons at Furth, Germany, November 15, 1945. Typescript.

People found in Hamburg. October 1945. World Jewish Congress, British Section. 18 pp. [3/22777K]

Union des Israelites Sefaradis de France. Liste complète des rescapés Thessaloniciens rentrés dans leurs foyers (In *Bulletin d'Ozer Dalim*, no. 1, June, 1946). Greek Jews. [3/22777D]

Counted remnant: Register of the Jewish survivors in Budapest. (Budapest: World Jewish Congress Hungarian Section, 1946) 319 pp. [3/22766]

Organization of Jewish Refugees in Italy. Office for Statistics and Information. Jewish Refugees in Italy. 3 vols. [3/22773]

List of Jews residing in Riga. This list was brought from Riga by redactor Wafe Goldberg (New York); it had been received on his visit to Russia. (Stockholm: World Jewish Congress Swedish Section.) 60 pp. [3/2277C]

List of Lithuanian Jews who survived the Nazi tyranny and are now in Lithuania, France, Italy, Sweden, Palestine. (New York: American Federation for Lithuanian Jews, 1946) 52 pp. [3/22770]

List of Jewish refugees from the Baltic States. (New York: World Jewish Congress) [3/67011]

Alphabetische lijst van zich in Nederland bevindende Joden. June, 1945. (Eindhoven, Holland: Centraal Registratiebureau voor Joden. [3/22777A]

Surviving Jews in Czestochowa. (New York: World Jewish Congress Division for Displaced Persons) 43 pp. [3/22768]

Surviving Jews in Lublin. The list was submitted by the Central Jewish Committee in Poland. (New York: World Jewish Congress Division for Displaced Persons) 16 pp. [3/22777H]

Nazi Victims of Piotrkow Trybunalski in New York. List of survivors. [15/9823]

Surviving Jews in Warsaw as of June 5th, 1945. (New York: World Jewish Congress Division for Displaced Persons, 1945) 15 pp. [3/22777G]

Warszewer Landsmanszaftn in der US Zone in Dajczland. Liste fun di lebngeblibene Warszewer jidn in der US Zone in Dajczland. München, 1948. 96 pp. Warsaw landsmanshaftn society in the U.S. Zone in Germany. [3/22767A]

Jews liberated from German concentration camps arrived in Sweden in 1945. List no. 1, Stockholm, 1945. 158 pp. List no. 2, 28 pp. Stockholm, 1946. (World Jewish Congress Svenska Sectionen) [3/22774]

Mosaiska Församlingen (Stockholm). Registrerings-avdelningen. List no. 10 of Jews who arrived in Sweden after June 26 (group 2). List of refugees arrived June/July 1946 in Sweden. List of refugees who arrived August 1946. [Uncataloged]

Surviving Jews in Jugoslavia as of June 1945. (New York: World Jewish Congress Division for Displaced Persons) 58 pp. [3/22771]

RECORD GROUPS IN THE ARCHIVES THAT INCLUDE LISTS OF VICTIMS AND SURVIVORS

The archives contains collections of many organizations that helped pre-war refugees and postwar survivors or accumulated documentation about internees during the Holocaust. Where reference is made to case files, the data may not be available to the public for privacy reasons.

American Jewish Committee. An organization founded in 1906 to defend Jewish civil rights and religious rights. This collection appears to have little information about specific Holocaust victims or survivors. A subrecord group, RG 347.10.12, is an alphabetical file of persons that AJC dealt with from 1933–62. [RG 347]

American Jewish Joint Distribution Committee. Although this organization's primary function is to help Jews in trouble, the holdings of YIVO for the Holocaust period do not include lists of individuals helped during that period. [RG 335]

American ORT Federation. A vocational training organization. Includes files on displaced persons camps, 1945–50, that might name individuals, but there are no lists of individuals. [RG 380]

American OSE Committee. A worldwide child care and health organization. Includes lists of survivors. Most of the material consists of business correspondence and reports from areas where they operated. [RG 494]

Displaced Persons Camps and Centers. Some 300,000 pages on microfilm about the day-to-day activities in displaced persons camps. Some lists. The collection is subdivided by country. In order to find information about an individual, it is necessary to know the name or location of the camp where the individual was located. Camps in Austria [RG 294.4] include Admont, Bad Gastein, Bad Ischel, Bindermichel, Ebelsberg, Ebensee, Enns, Hallen, Klagenfurt, Kleinmunchen, Mauthausen, Ranshofn, Saalfelder, Steyr, Wegscheid (Tyler) and Wells. Camps in Germany [RG 294.2] include a large collection for Feldafing and Fohrenwald. Other German camps are Amberg, Augsburg, Bad Reichenhall, Bamberg, Berchtesgaden, Deggendorf, Eggenfelden, Eschwege, Frankfurt am Main, Fritzlar, Fulda, Gauting, Giebelstadt, Gersfeld, Hasenecke, Heidelberg, Heidenheim, Hofgeismar, Kassel, Krailing-Planegg, Lampertheim, Landau, Landsberg, Munich, Neu Freiman, Neu-Ulm, Plattling, Pocking-Waldstadt, Poppendorf, Regensburg, Rochelle, Schwabach, Schwaebisch Hall, Straubing, Stuttgart, Tirschenreuth, Vilseck, Wetzlar, Windsheim, Zeilsheim and Ziegenheim. Camps in Italy [RG 294.3] include Adriatica, Bari, Barietta, Camp Sangallia, Chiari, Cine Citta, Cremona, Ferramonti, Grugliasco, Milan, Rivoli, Santa Maria di Bani, Santa Cesarea, Scuola Cadorna and Trani. [RG 294]

Eyewitness Accounts of the Holocaust Period. Personal accounts relating to ghettos, labor and internment camps, Jews in hiding, Jewish partisans and underground fighters. Some 2,000 accounts in three series. Indexed. [RG 104]

German-Jewish Children's Aid. Activities involved in receiving and placing of refugee children from 1933–50s. Thousands of case files. [RG 249]

Hebrew Immigrant Aid Society (HIAS). HIAS is a Jewish social service organization that has helped Jewish immigrants settle within the United States since before the turn of the century. In the period after World War II, it helped no fewer than 75,000 Holocaust families who came to the U.S. This collection includes index cards for each family that give the names of all the persons in the household, ages, town of origin and names of potential contacts within the U.S. They also have case files for each family helped. [RG 245]

Kehillat Haharedim. In French, known as the Association des Israelites Pratiquants. In the period after the war, there is correspondence about their effort to locate Jewish children hidden in French-Christian homes and efforts to return them to a Jewish environment. Letters from children. Lists of refugees and internees. Lists of deportees. [RG 340]

Landsmanshaftn Archives. YIVO has a large collection of records of landsmanshaftn societies within the U.S. Those that were active during the Holocaust period and thereafter invariably describe the activities to help rescue landsmen in Europe and after the war to assist the survivors. A list of many of the societies is published in *A Guide to YIVO's Landsmanshaftn*

Archive. New York: YIVO Institute for Jewish Research, 1986. [Many Record Groups]

National Council of Jewish Women, Search Department. From 1946 to the 1950s, this organization helped Jewish survivors who were trying to locate American relatives. [RG 618]

National Refugee Service. Includes case files of persons fleeing Nazi persecution 1938–46. Refugees from Hungary, Italy, Czechoslovakia, Spain and Danzig. [RG 248]

Rue Amelot. A French underground organization providing aid to refugees, internees and children. Reports from Beaune-La-Rolande, Pithiviers, Troyes, Compeigne, Poitiers and other locations. Correspondence from internees, people hiding Jewish children and children being hidden. [RG 343]

Shanghai Collection. Documents of the day-to-day life of the Jews in the ghetto during the Japanese occupation. [RG 243]

Territorial Collection. A collection of mixed provenance consisting of miscellaneous materials from many countries. The inventory includes the following items: Alphabetical list of Jews who were in the Malines internment camp; Theresienstadt birth and death records; fragmentary documents from French internment camps; lists of Dutch deportees; communication with internees of Westerbork; records of the Dutch Red Cross, including lists of survivors; and lists of Polish survivors. [RG 116]

Union Generale des Israelites de France (UGIF). Official administrative body representing the Jews of France established by the Vichy government. Census of the Jews of France in 1941 (excluding Paris). File of 65,000 Jews who registered in 1940 as required by law (not alphabetized). Lists, correspondence, etc. for Drancy, Ost, Austerlitz, Levitan, Bassano, Compeigne, Pithiviers, Beaune-la-Rolande, La Lande and Rivesaltes. [RG 210]

United Service for New Americans (USNA). Case files of refugees helped by this organization, 1946–55. [RG 246]

Name	Place	Birth	Death/Status	Camp
Mohr, Frieda	München	16.12.82	15.10.43	Theresienstadt
Mohr, Frieda	München	03.10.98	verschollen	Riga
Mohr, Fritz	Schweinfurt (1)	18.07.00	für tot erklärt	Sobibor
Mohr, Gertrud, geb. Neufeld	Berlin	28.08.78	verschollen	Auschwitz
Mohr, Gustav S.	Berlin	05.02.56	16.01.43	Theresienstadt
Mohr, Henriette, geb. Zellner	Berlin	11.12.73	verschollen	Minsk
Mohr, Josef	Berlin	16.10.76	verschollen	Auschwitz
Mohr, Kurt	Berlin	16.09.91	verschollen	Auschwitz
Mohr, Louis	Würzburg	20.03.72	11.02.44	Theresienstadt
Mohr, Louise, geb. Davids	Düsseldorf	11.08.97	verschollen	Auschwitz
Mohr, Mathilde, geb. Katz	Ludwigshafen/Rhein	14.07.77	verschollen	Gurs
Mohr, Mathilde, geb. Rosenfeld	Würzburg	27.06.74	26.02.43	Theresienstadt
Mohr, Otto	Germersheim (1)	18.05.96	24.09.42	Auschwitz
Mohr, Paul	Reutlingen	06.04.97	verschollen	Welzheim
Mohr, Salomon	München	21.07.58	20.09.42	Theresienstadt
Mohr, Sara	München	18.01.66	22.12.42	Theresienstadt
Mohr, Selma, geb. Angress	Nürnberg	23.01.83	verschollen	Riga
Mohr, Selma, geb. Walter	Berlin	29.06.98	verschollen	Auschwitz
Mohr, Therese, geb. Gutmann	Freiburg	20.03.72	04.12.42	Theresienstadt
Mohr, Wilhelmine	Germersheim (1)	15.06.91	verschollen	Auschwitz
Mohrenwitz, Abraham	Wiesbaden	26.06.54	09.05.42	Freitod
Mohrenwitz, Bettina, geb. Hoechheimer	Schweinfurt	06.03.77	verschollen	Izbica
Mokatow, Berek	Frankfurt am Main	11.03.92	15.04.41	Dachau
Mokotoff, Gitta, geb. Liebermann	Frankfurt am Main	09.04.99	25.09.42	Freitod
Mokotoff, Israel	Frankfurt am Main	17.12.62	17.01.43	Theresienstadt
Mokrauer, Alfred	Berlin	26.04.76	verschollen	Minsk
Mokrauer, Elfriede, geb. Glaser	Berlin	28.04.82	verschollen	Minsk
Mokrauer, Fanny, geb. Loewenstaedt	Frankfurt am Main	16.08.75	verschollen	Litzmannstadt/Lodz
Mokrauer, Gertrud	Berlin	07.08.04	verschollen	Minsk
Mokrauer, Hans	Berlin	03.01.16	verschollen	Minsk
Mokrauer, Lotte	Frankfurt am Main	18.11.01	verschollen	Litzmannstadt/Lodz
Mokrauer, Lucie, geb. Cohn	Berlin	15.08.81	verschollen	Minsk
Mokrauer, Margarete	Berlin	24.05.07	verschollen	Minsk
Mokrauer, Martha, geb. Oppenheim	Frankfurt am Main	30.07.91	16.04.45	Bergen-Belsen
Mokrauer, Siegfried	Berlin	08.10.06	verschollen	Riga
Mokry, Jacob	Berlin	18.07.79	02.01.44	Auschwitz
Mokry, Johanna, geb. Turszynski	Berlin	11.11.76	verschollen	Auschwitz
Moldauer, Gerda, geb. Stoppelmann	Oldenburg (1)	07.08.12	für tot erklärt	Auschwitz
Moll, Amalie	Aachen	28.07.71	verschollen	Minsk
Moll, Bernhard	Berlin	14.04.95	verschollen	Auschwitz
Moll, Berta, geb. Schwersenzer	Berlin	21.07.91	verschollen	Riga
Moll, Ernst	Rheydt	14.02.99	verschollen	Riga
Moll, Guenther	Berlin	20.07.25	verschollen	Riga
Moll, Hermann	Aachen	18.06.65	verschollen	Minsk
Moll, Johanette, geb. Meyer	Berlin	11.02.06	verschollen	Auschwitz
Moll, Johanna, geb. Holz	Berlin	11.12.67	29.11.41	Litzmannstadt/Lodz
Moll, Josefine, geb. Wolff	Düsseldorf	18.02.64	07.07.43	Theresienstadt
Moll, Juliana, geb. Harff	Kirchberg bei Jülich	15.08.67	22.12.42	Theresienstadt
Moll, Julie	Berlin	20.08.00	06.02.42	Litzmannstadt/Lodz
Moll, Julie G.	Aachen	14.10.06	für tot erklärt	Auschwitz
Moll, Lina	Rheydt	11.03.90	verschollen	Riga
Moll, Melanie, geb. Speier	Berlin	25.04.80	verschollen	Trawniki
Moll, Rosalie	Rheydt	29.10.87	verschollen	Riga
Moll, Wilhelmine	Aachen	19.04.68	verschollen	Minsk
Molling, Kurt	Berlin	23.03.92	00.06.43	Theresienstadt
Moltke, Klara	Berlin	05.12.71	verschollen	Minsk
Moltmann, Elise, geb. Rosenzweig	Berlin	26.11.65	verschollen	Theresienstadt
Mombert, Ernst	Gießen	09.07.11	verschollen	Auschwitz
Mombert, Karl	Frankfurt am Main	30.03.76	29.12.41	Litzmannstadt/Lodz
Monach, Martin	Berlin	28.11.98	verschollen	Riga
Monas, Martha, geb. Leven	Krefeld (1)	27.07.83	für tot erklärt	Sobibor
Monasch, Berta	Badenweiler	20.01.86	verschollen	Gurs
Monasch, Charlotte	Badenweiler	14.07.82	verschollen	Gurs
Monasch, Claire, geb. Moritz	Bielefeld (1)	25.08.06	für tot erklärt	Auschwitz
Monasch, Denny	Berlin	28.10.39	verschollen	Riga
Monasch, Edith, geb. Robinsky	Berlin	18.09.07	verschollen	Auschwitz
Monasch, Erich	Berlin	13.08.97	verschollen	Mittelbau-Dora
Monasch, Gertrud	Hamburg	29.11.78	verschollen	Litzmannstadt/Lodz
Monasch, Gertrud	Badenweiler	01.02.92	verschollen	Gurs
Monasch, Herbert	Köln (1)	24.12.20	04.01.45	Dachau
Monasch, Kaethe, geb. Wolff	Berlin	29.08.79	verschollen	Auschwitz
Monasch, Karl	Berlin	03.11.07	verschollen	Riga

Gedenkbuch. *A two-volume list of more than 128,000 German Jews murdered in the Holocaust identifies three persons named Mokotow: a husband and wife, Berek (Bernard) and Gitla, and Israel. The daughter of the couple was sent out of Germany before the war and now lives in New York State.*

LEO BAECK INSTITUTE

Address: 129 East 73rd Street; New York, NY 10021. Telephone: (212) 744-6400; fax: (212) 988-1305.

Founded in 1955 in Jerusalem, the Leo Baeck Institute is dedicated to collecting, recording and preserving the rich history of the Jewish communities in German-speaking countries from the 17th century to the Holocaust period. The facility in New York is a major research center that includes a library and archives. The library holds more than 60,000 volumes. Its archives includes family and communal records and other collections relating to German-speaking Jews. In addition to the books and records listed below, there is an extensive photograph collection from the Holocaust period (1933–45), which provides a visual record of the persecution, destruction and resettlement of Jews during that period.

HOLDINGS IN THE LIBRARY THAT
INCLUDE LISTS OF VICTIMS AND SURVIVORS

Call numbers of items in brackets [ ].

Albertz, Heinrich, and Klaus Wedemeier. *Initiativkreis Gedenkfahrt nach Minsk.* (Bremen: Edition Temmen, 1991). Jews deported from Bremen. [DS135 G4 B655 D4 1991]

Althausen, Oskar, and Erhard Roy Wiehn. *Oktoberdeportation 1940: Die sogenannte "Abschiebung" der badischen und saarpfaelzischen Juden in das franzoesische Internierungslager Gurs und andere Vorstationen von Auschwitz.* Deportations from Baden and Palatinate regions. [D810 J4 O43]

Diamant, Adolf. *Deportationsbuch der von Frankurt am Main aus gewaltsam berschickten Juden in den Jahren 1941 bis 1944.* (Frankfurt am Main: Juedische Gemeinde, 1984) [Ref. DS135 G4 F7 D5]

Eerste lijst der teruggevonden Joden. Comprises lists of Dutch and French Jews found in liberated areas and a list of German, Dutch and Czech survivors from Theresienstadt who arrived in Switzerland. [x MfW S267]

Gedenkbuch: Opfer der Verfolgung der Juden unter der nationalsozialistischen Gewaltherrschaft in Deutschland, 1933-1945. (Frankfurt/Main: J. Weisbecker, c1986) List of 128,000 German Jews killed during the Holocaust. Shows name, last place of residence, date of birth, place of deportation and, in some cases, date of death. Because many Jews were displaced from their homes in the years prior to deportation, last place of residence is not necessarily the usual place of permanent residence. [Ref. DS135 G33 G38]

Gedenkbuch zum tragischen Schicksal unserer juedischen Mitbuerger. (Hagen:Germany 1961) Includes lists of Jewish citizens of Hagen, Germany, killed during the Holocaust and list of emigrants with their new addresses. [qDS135 G4 H273 G4]

Klarsfeld, Serge. *Memorial to the Jews Deported from France 1942-1944.* Lists some 70,000 Jews deported from France. [qD810 J4 K53]

Ludwig, Max, and Hans Bernd Oppenheimer. *Aus dem Tagebuch des Hans O. Dokuments und Berischte ueber die Deportation und den Untergang der Heidelberger Juden.* List of Jews deported from the city and Landkries of Heidelberg to France. [D810 J4 L83]

RECORD GROUPS IN THE ARCHIVES THAT INCLUDE LISTS OF VICTIMS AND SURVIVORS

Accession numbers are given in brackets [ ].

Augsburg. Deportation list (November 1941–February 1945) of about 400 names. [AR 990]

Baden. Gestapo list of Jews living in Baden. Part of the Adolf Loebel Collection. [AR 4185]

Beuthen (Bytom, Poland). List of Jews deported May 1942. [AR 543]

Bielefeld. Last list of Jewish residents and of deportation. [AR 7248] Rabbi Hans Kronheim collection includes lists of deportees and survivors. [AR 3156]

Bingen. List of deported Jews. [AR 3240]

Bornheim. Brochure of exhibition "Juden in Bornheim," which took place in 1989 includes a list of Jewish victims (1933–45). [AR 5993]

Bremen. List of deportations (1942). List of 574 Jews who were killed during the Nazi regime. [AR 146] Max Markreich collection includes lists of inhabitants and lists of Jews deported to Minsk. Records of German-Jewish refugee organizations. [MF 422, MF 248(5), MF 432]

Buttenwiesen. Deportation lists. [AR 5170]

Fürth. List of Jews, emigration and deportation, by names and destination (1940–43). [AR 994]

Geilenkirchen. List of deported Jews killed in the Holocaust. [AR 5383]

Germany (General). A manuscript by Gertrude Schneider includes a list of transports from Germany to Riga. [AR 3348]

Gleiwitz (Gliwice, Poland) Deportation list. [AR 151, AR 5089]

Hamburg. The Max Plaut collection includes lists of Jews interned in Theresienstadt, Lodz, Auschwitz, Vittel and elsewhere. [AR 7094]

Koblenz. Deportation lists of the Gestapo (1942). [AR 5473, AR 7085]

Koenigsberg. List of Jews deported from Koenigsberg to Theresienstadt. [AR 1815]

Konstanz. List of Jews deported in 1940. [AR 2166]

Landau. List of Jews from Landau (approximately 100 names). [AR 3017]

Nördlingen. Deportation list. List of former members of community. [AR 4881]

Leipzig. Photocopy of deportation list of Jews from Leipzig to Buchenwald after Kristalnacht (November 11, 1938). [AR 2167] List of Jews of Leipzig from the 1930s. Inventory 7 includes deportation list of 1940s. The institute has a rich collection of material about Leipzig during the Holocaust period that might include information other than lists about individuals.

Meinershagen. Deportation list. [AR 5208]

Nuremberg. List of surviving Jews in Nuremburg (1945); addresses of former residents; lists of Jews deported from Nuremburg including destination (1941–44). [AR 1706]

Oberaula. List of victims. [AR 4570]

Offenbach. Deportation lists from Offenbach and Landkreis Offenbach including the towns of Dietesheim, Heusenstamm, Klein-Auheim, Mühlheim, Hainstadt, Seligenstadt, Sprendlingen and Weiskirchen. [AR 144]

Palatinate area. Deportation lists from the early 1940s. [AR 2039, AR 3041, AR 5850]

Papenburg. List of names, members of the Jewish community from the earliest time to 1942. [AR 5620]

Regensburg. List of Jews deported to Theresienstadt in 1942. [AR 1425]

Siegburg. List of Jewish residents (1933-42); immigration and deportation lists. [AR 3077]

Wertheim (Baden). Lists of Jews in Wertheim before and during the Nazi period. [AR 2929]

Würzburg. Deportation and survivor lists; list of Würzburg Jews in United States. [AR 3788]

ADDITIONAL U.S. FACILITIES

SIMON WIESENTHAL CENTER LIBRARY AND ARCHIVES

Address: 9760 W. Pico Blvd.; Los Angeles, CA 90035-4792. Telephone: (310) 553-9036; fax (310) 277-5558. Internet: simonwie@class.org.

This facility is totally immersed in all aspects of Holocaust remembrance and education, only a portion of which is devoted to preserving records that document the Holocaust. The center's outreach and education agenda includes programs presented in hundreds of communities throughout the United States, Canada and Europe, in which people can interact with Holocaust survivors, scholars and other eyewitnesses to the Holocaust. The media department has produced a number of films on the Holocaust. Beit-Hashoah—Museum of Tolerance—located adjacent to the center, is an eight-level, 165,000 square foot educational complex designed to challenge visitors to confront bigotry and racism. The center has an international reputation for fighting anti-Semitism and Holocaust revisionism and for pursuing Nazi war criminals.

Their library and archives include some 25,000 books and periodicals on the Holocaust, anti-Semitism, racism and related issues. Books and collections that include lists of survivors or victims at the Simon Wiesenthal Center Library and Archives include the following:

Aid for Communication between Displaced Jews Resident in the Czechoslovak Republic in 1938. London: Relief Committee of Jews from Czechoslovakia, n.d.

Biographisches Handbuch der Deutschsprachigen Emigration nach 1933. 3 vols. Muenchen: K.G. Saur, 1980.

Die Toten von Dachau: Deutscher und Oesterriecher: Ein Gedenk und Nachschlagwerk. Muenchen, 1949.

Fargion, Liliana Picciotto. *Il Libro della Memoria: Gli Ebrei Deportati dall'Itlaia (1943–1945):* Ricerca del Centro di Documentazione Ebraica Contemporanea. Milano: Mursia, 1991.

Surname	Name	Date	Place
MAOUS	DINAH	29.06.11	LA ROCHELLE
MAOUS	ROGER	21.05.05	MONTMORENCY
MARCHINA	BELLA	06.05.80	ALGER
MARCUS	ISAAC	31.05.93	PARIS
MARCUS	LOUISE	02.07.02	PARIS
MARKOVITCH	NATHAN	30.06.88	PETROKOFF
MARKOVITCH	REBECCA	14.06.88	GACENOW
MARTER	ANDRE	28.04.22	MARSEILLE
MARTER	DANIELLE	27.04.76	MARSEILLE
MARTER	DENISE	16.04.28	MARSEILLE
MARTER	JULIE	21.03.98	MARSEILLE
MARTER	LUCIEN	23.08.97	MARSEILLE
MARTY	ESTHER	11.08.72	BORDEAUX
MARX	ALICE	19.10.90	BIESHEIM
MARX	CELINE	11.02.80	BIESHEIM
MARX	FRIEDA	07.06.08	BROHL
MARX	JEANINE	20.03.11	
MARX	RAYMOND	17.09.03	CHAYANGES
MASLIAH	BOHOR	04.61	MAGNESIE
MASLIAH	LOUNA	80	MAGNESIE
MAUER	MARIE	05.06.08	St LOUIS
MAYER	ADRIEN	28.02.79	PARIS
MAYER	BERTHE	28.10.67	MENWILLER
MAYER	MAX	24.01.67	BRATISLAVA
MAZALTO	BEATRICE	08.01.29	PARIS
MAZALTO	DOUDOU	10.06.01	
MAZALTO	SUZANNE	02.02.25	
MEISSELS	BERNARD	19.10.07	NAGYVARAD
MALAMED	ISAAC	14.05.78	SMYRNE
MELAMED	REGINE	26.12.12	
MENIOUCK	CHAIM	19.05.95	ODESSA
MERMELSTEIN	FRIEDA	06.03.12	VARSOVIE
MERMELSTEIN	MARCEL	14.01.37	ANVERS
MERMELSTEIN	PAULETTE	10.01.34	ANVERS
MESSERER	BERTA	29.12.02	
MESSERI	MARIE	04.01.04	ISTAMBOUL
MESTRANO	ESTREA	20.06.80	ISTAMBOUL
MESTRANO	JACOB	10.05.76	ISTAMBOUL
MESTRANO	KADINA	07.03.04	AIDEN
MESTRANO	VIDAL	03.03.06	ISTAMBOUL
METZGER	ALICE	03.03.84	VESOUL
METZGER	AUGUSTE	21.06.78	WITTERSHEIM
METZGER	BLANCHE	10.01.84	MOMMENHEIM
METZGER	ELISE	06.10.84	BENGENDORF
METZGER	HORTENSE	06.11.81	SCHIRR-OFFEN
METZGER	JACQUELINE	03.06.24	MOMMENHEIM
METZGER	MATHILDE	15.12.86	RINGENDORF
MEYER	JACOB	07.02.58	ROSSELM
MEYER	JULIETTE	23.08.73	SEFFUIS LE BAS
MEYER	PAULETTE	08.11.10	DOLE
MEYER	ROSE	10.10.71	GUEBWILLER
MEYNIER	LEON	20.05.09	LE LARDIN
MILHAUD	RENE	09.04.91	NIMES
MILHAUD	SIMONE	01.06.03	MARSEILLE
MILHAUD	SARAH	01.11.94	MARSEILLE
MIZRAHI	RACHEL	97	
MOEL	DANIEL	08.11.98	CONSTANTINOPLE
MOKOTOVITCH	REBECCA	01.12.23	PARIS
MOKOTOVITCH	JEAN	27.08.26	
MONATLIK	JEAN	28.10.10	VARSOVIE
MONSZAJN	DORA	28.02.10	
MORGENSTERN	JACQUELINE	26.05.32	PARIS
MORGENSTERN	KARL	06.10.03	GERNAVTI
MORGENSTERN	SUZANNE	19.02.07	PARIS
MOSSE	ANDRE	07.08.06	MARSEILLE
MOSSE	FRANCOISE	18.12.14	
MOSZKOWICZ	ABRAM	27.03.00	LODZ
MOSZKOWSKA	MARIE	14.07.01	VARSOVIE
MOYSE	GEORGES	03.08.77	PARIS
MULLER	CLAUDE	10.03.31	
MULLER	RICHARD	15.02.36	PARIS
MULLER	SUZANNE	13.04.08	PARIS
MUTTERER	FANNY	12.11.69	PARIS
NADEL	SABINA	03.03.11	LACZA
NOCHIMOWSKI	NICOLE	06.06.36	PARIS
NOCHIMOWSKI	JOSEPH	03.08.99	LULZA
NOCHIMOWSKI	RACHEL	26.12.06	PARIS
NORDMANN	HARIETTE	20.06.41	PARIS
NORDMANN	LENA	20.03.10	PABSAINIZ
NORDMANN	LUCIE	30.11.63	ST. JULIEN
OBADIA	AARON	29.06.94	MARSEILLE
OBADIA	ALICE	24.04.91	MOSTAGANEM
OBADIA	GILBERT	30.11.31	MARSEILLE
OJALVO	ESTHER	14.10.77	ISTAMBOUL
OJALVO	LOUISE	14.04.00	PARIS
OKONOWSKI	GOLDA	28.05.79	VAMOUKIE
OKSENBERG	FRADLA	01.04.02	
ORLANDE	HENRIETTE	07.03.20	PARIS
ORMIERES	ESTHER	06.10.76	BORDEAUX
OSSIA	HENRI	24.11.02	SOBKOW
OUJEVOLK	ELIANE	30.08.24	PARIS
OUJEVOLK	LEA	17.07.91	BUCAREST
OUVRARD	OLGA	01.06.83	BESANÇON
OVADIA	JOSEPH	07.03.32	CONSTANTINOPLE
OWYSZER	GITLA	01.12.09	MORGY
OWYSZER	LEON	22.12.43	PARIS
PAKULA	CHAJA	24.11.96	RAWA MARZOWIEZ
PAKULA	MOSZEK	16.02.99	MAZOWICK
PAKULA	TAUBA	22.04.24	
PALATCHI	ISAAC	15.04.98	ISTAMBOUL
PALIVODA	ESTHER	16.06.87	VARSOVIE
PALIVODA	FERNAND	05.02.26	
PALIVODA	JEANNE	15.01.17	PARIS
PALIVODA	MOCHEK	02.10.82	VARSOVIE
PALIVODA	HERSCHLEK	12.04.01	
PARDO	JULIA	01.01.81	SMYRNE
PARIENTE	FANNY	10.04.86	ALGER
PARIENTE	JOSEPH	09 05 86	CONSTANTINE
PELTA	MARIE	28 01 08	
PENECKI	WOLF	22 02 07	SIEDLACE
PERAIRE	ELISA	17 09 64	BAYONNE
PERLMUTTER	IRENE	07 02 22	
PETER-FALVI	MICHEL	1? 02 1?	
PETILON	BEILA	24 06 34	MARSEILLE
PETILON	LEONNA	09	SALONIQUE
PETILON	SYLVAIN	24 06 31	GRENOBLE
PICARD	ANDRE	05 10 22	PONTAMOUSSON
PICARD	FANNY	25 08 28	REMILLY
PICARD	JEAN	17 04 30	REMILLY
PICARD	JOSEPH	20 10 93	BUDING
PICARD	JULES	31 12 75	
PICARD	MAURICE	22 05 31	METZ
PICK	ALFRED	28 08 98	SCHLAVA
PINO	JACQUELINE	11 07 35	PARIS
PINO	MAURICE	15 09 07	ISTAMBOUL
PINO	SUZANNE	01 08 05	ISTAMBOUL
PITERMAN	CHASZA	15 05 10	BIALA
PITERMAN	GILBERTE	28 02 35	LE HAVRE
PITERMAN	SAUL	15 06 10	
PLATO	EMILIE	09 10 93	HAMBOURG
PLATO	SIMON	30 03 88	THOM
PLAUT	ALFRED	11 09 82	DELLE
POLLACK	BENOIT	01 10 33	SAVERNE
POLLACK	JULIE	27 06 96	ROSENWILLER
POLLACK	SIMONE	10 05 29	SCHIRMECK
POMERANZ	SIEGFRIED	01 01 11	CERNAUTI
PRASZKER	FRANCINE	15 09 30	PARIS
PRASZKER	ITA	19 04 96	LODZ
PRASZKER	LAZARD	24 05 32	PARIS
PRASZKER	WOLF	15 09 93	LODZ
PRESSBURGER	MILTON	13 06 07	REXINGEN
PRZEPIORKA	ITA	16 09 03	
PUNSKY	ABRAHAM	20 05 02	MINSK
PUNSKY	ALLEGRE	15 10 13	SALONIQUE
PUNSKY	BERTHE	01 02 37	MARSEILLE
PUNSKY	ESTHER	06 10 35	MARSEILLE
PUNSKY	JACQUELINE	23 11 42	MARSEILLE
PUNSKY	RENEE	28 05 39	MARSEILLE

Memorial to the Jews Deported from France. Serge Klarsfeld used captured German lists in this remarkable work to document more than 70,000 Jews deported from France, primarily to Auschwitz. The book also includes the names of persons who died in French internment camps. This page, from Convoy #74, which departed Drancy, France, on May 20, 1944, includes a brother and sister, Jean and Rebecca Mokotovitch. He survived the Holocaust and lives in France. She died at Bergen-Belsen 35 days after the camp was liberated.

Franco, Hizkia M. *The Jewish Martyrs of Rhodes and Cos.* Harare, Zimbabwe: HarperCollins, 1994.

Gedenkbuch: Opfer der Verfolgung der Juden unter der Nationalsozialistichen Gewaltherrschaft in Deutschland, 1933–1945. Koblenz, Germany: Bundesarchiv, 1986.

Klarsfeld, Serge and Maxime Steinberg. *Memorial de la Deportation des Juifs de Belgique.* Bruxelles: Union des Deports Juifs en Belgique et filles et fils de la Deportation; New York: Beate and Serge Klarsfeld Foundation, 1982.

Klarsfeld, Serge, ed. *Memorial to the Jews Deported from France, 1942–44.* New York: Beate Klarsfeld Foundation, 1983.

La-karov vela-rahok: June 28, 1945–September 17, 1947. Tel Aviv: Jewish Agency. (Microfilm reel) Includes many lists of survivors.

Laloum, Jean. "La Deportation des Juifs Natifs d'Algerie." in *Le Monde Juif* 129 (Janvier-Mars 1988): 33–48.

Liberated Jews Arriving in Sweden in 1945. Malmo, Sweden: Henry Luttrup & Co., 1946.

Names of the Deported Jews from Hajdu County, Hungary. New York: Beate and Serge Klarsfeld Foundation, 1991.

Names of the Jewish Victims of Hungarian Labor Battalions. 2 vols. New York: Beate and Serge Klarsfeld Foundation, 1991.

National Registry of Jewish Holocaust Survivors. Washington, D.C.: American Gathering of Jewish Holocaust Survivors in cooperation with the United States Holocaust Memorial Council, 1993.

Premiere List des Juifs Liberes. Bruxelles: S.E.R., n.d.

Register of Jewish Survivors. 2 vol. Jerusalem: Jewish Agency for Palestine, 1945.

Schneider, Gertrude. *Transports from the Reich to the Riga Ghetto in Journey into Terror: Story of the Riga Ghetto.* New York: Ark House, 1979, 155–75.

Surviving Jews in Yugoslavia as of June 1945. New York: World Jewish Congress, n.d.

Surviving Jews in Lublin. New York: World Jewish Congress, n.d.

Survivors in Lithuania, Italy, France, Sweden, Palestine, Germany. New York: American Federation for Lithuanian Jews, n.d.

Totenbuch Theresienstadt. Wien: Juedisches Komitee fuer Theresienstadt, 1971.

Vinokurov, Joseph, Shimon Kipnis and Nora Levin, eds. *The Babi Yar Book of Remembrance: Dedicated to the Memory of the Victims of the Babi Yar Mass Killings in 1941*. Philadelphia: Committee for the Babi Yar Book of Remembrance, 1983.

World Gathering of Jewish Holocaust Survivors (June 14–18, 1981) List of participants.

U.S. NATIONAL ARCHIVES

Address: Pennsylvania Avenue at 8th Street NW; Washington, DC 20408. Telephone: (202) 501-5402.

The U.S. National Archives has more than 200 rolls of microfilm of entry registers, questionnaires, transport lists, death books and postwar personnel records from various concentration camps. They are part of the Collection of Seized Enemy Records, 1941– (Record Group 242). A duplicate copy of these microfilms is available at the Branch Regional Archives located in New York at 201 Varick Street. Telephone: (212) 337-1300. These rolls of microfilm are a donation of the Jewish Genealogical Society, Inc.

Berlin. Gestapo Transport Lists from Berlin.

Buchenwald. Entry questionnaires, primarily of male inmates, in alphabetical order. Information includes name, birth date, religion, occupation, nationality, race, names of parents (including mother's maiden name), number of children, name of spouse and physical attributes. If a person died or was transferred to another location, it was noted on the form. These records also include questionnaires filled out by the prisoners after liberation. They are interspersed with the concentration camp question-naires and include birth date, nationality, religion, home address, occupa-tion, date of arrest, places of detention and planned destination after leaving

Buchenwald.

Buchenwald. Register of deaths from December 2, 1942, through December 31, 1943, and from October 15, 1994, through April 19, 1945.

Buchenwald. Numerical registers of inmates; transport lists to Buchenwald; death lists. All are in chronological order.

Dachau. *Listes internationales Dachau.* Alphabetical list prepared by the U.S. Army. Some portions are missing or out of order. Each entry includes name of person, birth date, birth place, nationality, registration number, date of arrival and date of death at Dachau, or name of camp where person was liberated.

Dachau. Registers of inmates who were assigned numbers 1–37575, 13501–79577 and 79290–147536. Entries are chronological. Includes inmate's name, birth date, birth place, date of transfer to Dachau and place of deportation.

Dachau. Dachau Book of Arrivals and Departures. Chronological list for period December 1, 1941, to December 1, 1943.

Bergen-Belsen. Death certificates issued January–April 1945. Names of parents and birth dates are included.

Constanz (Feldkirch) Hospital. Alphabetical card files of patients during the period May–July 1945.

Gross-Rosen. Inmate lists from 1943-45.

Mauthausen. Inmate personnel cards in alphabetical order. Death lists in chronological order. Numerical register of inmates. List of Belgian Jews in Mauthausen. List of deaths by nationality, in alphabetical order showing birth date, birth place and death date. List of survivors and discharged persons in alphabetical order. Information includes birth date, birth place and names of spouses.

Mittlebau (Sangerhausen). Death books, mostly Belgian and French, from November–December 1944.

Natzweiler. Lists in alphabetical order of inmates.

Sandbostel. Lists of inmates by nationality.

LIBRARY OF CONGRESS

Address: Adams Building—Hebraic Section; 110 Second St. SE; Washington, DC 20540. Telephone: (202)707-5422; fax: (202) 707-1724.

Bar Sheked, Gavriel. *Nevek—Shemot—Names*. Jerusalem: Yad Vashem, 1990. Hungarian registers of dead. [DS135.H9 N48 1992]

Benjamin, Yigael. *They were our friends: a memorial for members of the Hachsharot and the Hehalutz underground in Holland murdered in the Holocaust*. Jerusalem: Association of Former Members of the Hachsharot and the Hehalutz underground in Holland, 1990. [DS135.N4 B45 1990]

Binder, Cornelia, and Michael Mence. *Last traces of German Jews in the Landkreis of Bad Kissingen*. [DS135.G4 B159134 1992]

Brand, Mechtild. *Geachtet—geachtet: aus dem Leben Hammer Juden in diesem Jahrhundert*. Hamm: Stadt Hamm, 1991.

Diamant, Adolf. *Deportationsbuch der von Frankfurt am Main aus gewaltsam verschickten Juden in den Jahren 1941 bis 1944*. Frankfurt am Main: Jüdische Gemeinde Frankfurt am Main, 1984. [DS135.G4 F625 1984]

Diamant, Adolf. *Deportationsbuch der in den Jahren 1942 bis 1945 von Leipzig aus gewaltsam verschickten Juden*. Frankfurt am Main: Selbstverlag, 1991. [Aquisition in progress.]

Diamant, Adolf. *Getto Litzmannstadt*. Frankfurt, 1986. Lists of Jews in the Lodz, Poland, ghetto (Lodz was renamed Litzmannstadt by the Germans during World War II). Organized by community of residence. Includes surname, given name, date and place of birth, nationality, former address. [DS135.P62 L6433 1986]

Drexler, Siegmund, Siegmund Kalinski and Hans Mausbach. *Ärztliches Schicksal unter der Verfolgung, 1933-1945 in Frankfurt am Main und Offenbach: eine Denkschrift*. Frankfurt am Main: Verlag für Akademische Schriften, 1990. [MLCM 93/10559 (R)]

Handler-Lachmann, and Ulrich Schutt. *"Unbekannt verzogen" oder "weggemacht": Schicksale der Juden im alten Landkreis Marburg: 1933-1945*. Marburg: Hitzeroth, c 1992. [DS135.G4 M3454 1992]

Hepp, Michael. *Die Ausbürgerung deutscher Staatsangehöriger 1933-45 nach den im Reichsanzeiger veröffentlichten Listen* (Expatriation lists as published in the "Reichsanzeiger" 1933-45) [CS614 .A94 1985]

Herausgeber, Mary Steinhauser, and Dokumentationarchiv den Osterreichischen Widerstandes. *Totenbuch Theresienstadt: damit sie nicht vergessen werden.* [D805.C9 T68 1987]

Klarsfeld, Serge, and Maxime Steinberg. *Mémorial de la déportation des juifs de Belgique.* Bruxelles: Union des déportés juifs en Belgique et filles et fils de la déporation. New York: Beate Klarsfeld Foundation, 1982. [DS135. B4 M46 1982]

Klarsfeld, Serge. *Memorial to the Jews Deported from France, 1942-1944.* (English-language version) New York: Beate Klarsfeld Foundation, 1983. [DS135.F83 K4313 1983] List of about 70,000 Jews deported from France. Listed by date train convoy left France.

Klarsfeld, Serge. *Documents concerning the destruction of the Jews of Grodno 1941-1944* New York: Beate Klarsfeld Foundation, 1985? [DS135.R93 G733 1985]

Klarsfeld, Serge. *Additif au Mémorial de la déportation des juifs de France; Le proces de Cologne.* Paris: Les Fils et filles des deportes juifs de France. [DS135.F83 K42 1988]

Kleinert, Beate, and Wolfgang Prinz. *Namen und Schicksale der Juden Kassels, 1933-1945: ein Gedenkbuch* Kassel: Magistrat der Stadt Kassel, Stadtarchiv, 1986. [DS135.G4 K375 1986]

Kliner-Lintzen, Martina and Siegfried Pape. "——*vergessen kann man das nicht": Wittener Jüdinnen und Juden unter dem Nationalsozialismus.* [DS135.G4 W5755 1991]

Klukowski, Zygmunt. *Diary from the years of occupation, 1939-44.* Translated from Polish by George Klukowski. Urbana: University of Illinois Press, c1993. [D802.P62 Z3413 1993]

Knauss, Erwin. *Die Jüdische Bevölkerung Giessens: 1933–1945; Dokumentation.* Wiesbaden: Kommission fur die Geschichte der Juden in Hessen, 1974. [DS135.G4 G534]

Kolonomos, Zamila, and Vera Veskovilk-Vangeli. *Evreite vo Makedonija vo Vtorata svetska vojna, 1941-1945: zbornik na dokumenti* (Jews in Macedonia during the Second World War, 1941-1945) Skopje: Makedonska akademija na naukite i umetnosti, 1986. [D810.J4 K675 1986]

Meirtchak, Benjamin. *Jewish Military Casulaties in the Polish Armies in World War II.* Tel Aviv: World Federation of Jewish Fighters, Partisans annd Camp Inmates and Association of Jewish War Veterans of the Polish Armies in Israel, 1994. [DS135.P63 A1514 1994]

Minninger, Monika, and Joachim Meynert, Friedhelm Schaffer. *Antisemitisch Verfolgte registriert in Bielefeld, 1933-45: Eine Dokumentation jüdischer Einzelschicksale.* Bielefeld, Germany: Stadtarchiv Bielefeld, 1985. [DS135.G4 B5255 1985]

Mohn, Joseph. *Der Leidensweg unter dem Hakenkreuz.* Bad Buchau, Germany: die Stadt, 1970. [DD901.B96 M6]

Romano, Jatsa. *Jevreji Jugoslavije 1941-1945, tzrtve genocida i utcesnici.* Beograd: Savez jevrejskih optstina Jugoslavije, 1980. Text in Serbo-Croatian. [D810.J4 R647 1980]

Schäfer-Richter, Uta, and Jörg Klein. *Die jüdischen Bürger im Kreis Göttingen, 1933-1945: Ein Gedenkbuch* Göttingen, Germany: Wallstein, c1992. [DS135.G5 A1587 1992]

Szerkesztette, Carmilly, and Mózes Weinberger. *A Kolozevári zsidóság emlékkönyve* (Memorial volume for the Jews of Cluj-Kolozsvár). New York: Sepher-Hermon, 1970. Text in Hungarian, Hebrew and English. [Acquisition in progress.]

Szots, E. *Lili Mihaly naploja: a II. vilaghaboryu bonyhadi aldozatai.* Bonyhad: Volgysegi Muzeum, 1992. [DB955.6.L55 A3 1992]

Wulman, Leon and Joseph Tenenbaum. *The martyrdom of Jewish physicians in Poland.* New York: published for Medical Alliance-Association of Jewish Physicians from Poland by Exposition Press, c1963. An alphabetical necrology of Jewish physicians martyred during the German occupation of Poland. Includes bibliographies. [R536 .F3]

About Jews Liberated from German Concentration Camps Arrived [sic] *in Sweden in 1945: List No. 1 (Supplements Follow).* Stockholm: World Jewish Congress and Jewish Agency for Palestine Rescue Committee, 1946. Organized by nationality of victims, then alphabetically by surname. Includes surname, given name, birth date, town of origin. [D810.J4 A24 1946]

Die Jüdischen Opfer des Nationalsozialismus in Hamburg. Hamburg: Staatsarchiv Hamburg, 1965. [DS135.G4 H366 1965]

Die Landauer Judengemeinde: ein Abriss ihrer Geschichte. Landau/Pfalz: Stadtarchiv, 1969. [Acquistion in progress.]

Die Opfer der nationalsozialistischen Judenverfolgung in Baden-Württemberg 1933-1945: ein Gedenkbuch. [CD1373.B33 A3 Heft 20 1969]

Die Juden in Bamberg. Bamberg?: Gesellschaft für Christlich-Jüdische Zusammenarbeit? 1962? [MLCS 85/3452 (D)]

Es geht tatsächlich nach Minsk: Texte und MAterialien zur Erinnerung an die Deportation von Bremer Juden am 18.11.1941 in das Vernichtungslager Minsk. Bremen: Bremen Staatsarchiv Bremen, 1992. [DS135.G4 B7937 1992]

Gedenkbuch: Opfer der Verfolgung der Juden unter der national-sozialistischen Gewaltherrschaft in Deutschland, 1933-1945. Frankfurt/Main: J. Weisbecker, c1986. List of 128,000 German Jews murdered in the Holocaust. Includes person's name (including maiden name of married women), place of deportation, birth date and, in some instances, place and date of death. [D804.3 .G43 1986]

Il libro della memoria Gli Ebrei deportati dall'Italia (1943–1945). (Memorial book of Jews Deported from Italy, 1943–1945). Liliana Picciotto Fargior. Milan: Mursia, 1991. Organized alphabetically by surname. In Italian. Includes surname, given name, place and date of birth, parents, spouse, final address, details of arrest, deportation, place and date of death. [DS135.I8 P53 1991]

Krefelder Juden. Bonn: Röhrscheid, 1980. [DD901.K9 K68]

Les 955 fusilles du Mont Valerian (1941–1944): parmi lesquels 163 Juifs. Paris: Documentation reunie et publiee par l'association Les Fils et filles des deportes juifs de France. [D804.G4 A17 1988]

Liste officielle des decedes des camps de concentration. Ministere des anciens combattants et victimes de guerre. [D797.A2 F82]

National Registry of Jewish Holocaust Survivors. New York: American Gathering of Jewish Holocaust Survivors, 1993. List of some 35,000 Holocaust survivors living in the United States and Canada. [D804.3 .N37 1993]

Norsk fangeleksikon, Grinifangene. Oslo: J.W. Cappelen. Grini concentration camp. [D805.N6 G5]

Quislings honsegard, Berg interneringsleir. Oslo: I kommisjon A. Cammer-meyer, 1948. [D805.N6 H13]

Register of Jewish Survivors: List of Jews Rescued in Different European Countries. vol. 1. Jerusalem: Jewish Agency for Palestine, Search Bureau for Missing Relatives, 1945. These lists are in no way as comprehensive as their titles imply. The total number of persons named in all the lists is 60,000. [D810.J4 J315 (Hebr)]

Sharit ha-platah. An extensive list of survivors of Nazi tyranny published so that the lost may be found and the dead brought back to life. Munich: Central Committee of Liberated Jews in Bavaria, 1946. [D810.J4 C42]

Sie sind nicht vergessen: therausgeben vom Oberrat der Israeliten Badens. Karlsruhe, Germany: der Oberrat der Israeliten Badens, 1958. [MLCS 87/167 (D)]

Terezín–Ghetto. Czechoslovak Republic Ministry for the Protection of Labour and Social Welfare, 1945. There are two alphabetical lists. The first is of those taken directly to Terezin from their homes; the second is of those driven to Terezin by retreating Germans at the end of the war. Includes surname, given name, birth date, transport number, place where deportation originated. [D805.C9 A55]

The Babi Yar Book of Remembrance, Joseph Vinakurov, Shimon Kipnis and Nora Levin, eds. Philadelphia Committee for the Babi Yar Book of Remembrance, 1983. In Russian, English, and Yiddish. Includes surname, given name, age at time of death. [D810.J4 K59 1983]

Totenbuch Neuengamme. Dokumentation: Franz Glienke. Wiesbaden, Germany: Saaten-Vlg., 1968. Lists of those who died or "disappeared" while in the Neuengamme camp. Organized by country, then alphabetically by surname. Includes surname, given name, town of residence, birth date, date of death or disappearance. The USSR list is written in Cyrillic characters. [D797.A2 T68]

Totenbuch Theresienstadt I: Deportierte aus Österreich. Wien: Jüdisches Komitee für Theresienstadt, 1971. [D805.C9 J84]

Totenliste Hamburger Widerstandskämpfer und Verfolgter, 1933-1945. Hamburg: Vereinigte Arbeitsgemeinschaft der Naziverfolgten e. V. <VAN>,

1968. [DD256.3 .T68]

Vare falne, 1939–1945. Oslo: Den Norske stat. [D797.N6 V3]

Vivlio mnemes (Memorial book of Greek Jews). Athens: Central Board of the Jewish Communities, 1979. All text in Greek. [DS135.G7 V58 1979]

Wspomnienia wiezniow Pawiaka. Warszawa: Ludowa Spoldzielnia Wydawnicza, 1964. [D805.P7 P6]

LISTE DE DÉCÉDÉS DE BERGEN-BELSEN APRÈS LA LIBÉRATION

(FEMMES).

NOMS ET PRÉNOMS.	DOMICILE.	DATE de naissance	LIEU DE NAISSANCE.
AUSSEL Marguerite.........	....	....	....
BARON Gisèle.............	Chenu (Sarthe)............	9. 7.07	CHENU....................
BAUDRY Yvonne...........	Toulouse..................	26. 4.22	....
BENNAROS Anette..........	Paris.....................	16. 2.20	....
BERGER Bella.............	....	....	....
BERRIER Jeanne ou Janine...	Vic-le-Comte..............	17. 7.01	....
COUSSON ou GOUSSON Honorine.	Quincey (Vienne)..........	20.12.95	....
DARQUES Alice............	Pas-de-Calais.............	12. 5.02	....
DUBOIS Yvonne...........	....	10. 2.17	AUTUN....................
FREIBERG Sala............	....	....	....
FRENID Madeleine..........	....	....	....
GELBSKY Marie............	....	....	....
GOGEAU Françoise.........	....	....	....
GOLDBERG Rose...........	....	20. 4.18	GRENOBLE...............
GOLDENBERG Annie........	Paris.....................	18. 2.95	....
GULLIANO Henriette........	....	....	....
HAUTIER Marie............	Bregnac (Dordogne)........	21.12.02	....
HIBON Prudence...........	Nord.....................	7.10.95	....
JORDAN Ida..............	Juan-les-Pins.............	8. 4.12	....
LACHOT Marie-Louise.......	Côte-d'Or.................	10.10.99	....
LEBLANC Geneviève........	Aubusson.................	5. 6.08	....
MARCHILE Muguette........	....	....	....
MARTIN Gabrielle..........	Lyon-Bretteau.............	19. 6.04	....
MASERAUX Françoise.......	....	....	....
MATTAU ou MAZEAU Jeanne.	Dordogne.................	11. 3.24	....
MIRIVOL Marie............	....	....	....
MOKOTOVICZ Rebecca......	46, rue des Marais, Paris..	1.12.23	_April 24, 1945_
NOURRY (Dʳ) Anne-Marie	15, rue Émile-Duclaux, Paris.	....	....
NUSSBAUM Élisabeth........			
PAYEN Léa...............	Dury.....................	21. 6.99	....
PHILIPPE Yvonne...........	Nîmes....................	7. 3.05	....
PITOIS Louise.............	Ille-et-Vilaine.............	20.10.04	....
POLIN Hélène.............	....	30 ans	....
ROSSEL Irène.............	....	21. 6.99	....
ROTTEULIEZ Marthe........	....	....	....
LABETTE Janette...........	Orléans..................	31.12.19	....
SABOTSKY Françoise........	....	....	....
SALMON Elsa.............	Lyon.....................	10. 8.26	....
SCHENKMANN TL.......	....	15. 4.04	....
SECHE	....	6. 2.20	....

List of Deceased Persons at Bergen-Belsen after the Liberation. *During and after the war, numerous lists were compiled of victims and survivors. The largest collection of these lists has been collated into the Master Index of the International Tracing Service in Arolsen, Germany. This list shown above identifies women who died at Bergen-Belsen concentration camp after it was liberated. It includes Rebecca (Rivka) Mokotovicz, who died at age 22. She was deported with her brother, Jean, from Paris about a year earlier. He survived and lives in France.*

FACILITIES OUTSIDE THE UNITED STATES

There are collections throughout the world of Holocaust-related material.

ARCHIVES OF THE JEWISH HISTORICAL INSTITUTE WARSAW, POLAND

Address: Archiwum Zydowskiego Instytutu Historycznego; ul. Tiomackie 3/5; 00-090 Warszawa, Poland.

This facility has numerous collections on the Jewish presence in Poland from the 17th century until today. Shortly after World War II, the archives assisted in the prosecution of Nazi war criminals and consequently collected much Holocaust-related data, including information about individuals. Not all the collections are indexed.

Although the Archives of the Jewish Historical Institute is a government-sponsored institution and inquiries are processed at no cost, contributions are accepted, but not required, and are used to further the work of the institute. Checks should be made payable to the Jewish Historical Institute Association and sent to the above address.

Among its Holocaust-related holdings, which include lists of persons, are the following (shelf space in meters is indicated):

RG 201. Death Records of Jews in the Warsaw Ghetto, 1939–41, 1.3m.

RG 203. Underground Materials, 1939–45. 210 items, 1m.

RG 204. Underground Archive of the Bialystok Ghetto (so-called Tannenbaum Archive), 1939–42. 76 items, .2m.

RG 205. Lodz Ghetto, 1939–45. 147 items, 1.5m.

RG 206. Personal Records from the Krakow Ghetto, 1940–41.

RG 207. Records from the Hassag-Pelzer (Czestochowa) Labor Camp, 1940–42, 1m.

RG 208. Records of Jewish War Prisoners in the Lublin Camp at 7 Lipowa Street, 1939–45, 2.5m.

RG 209. Literary Works, 1939–43. 485 items, 1.5m.

RG 210. American Jewish Joint Distribution Committee (AJJDC), 1939–41, 2.1m.

RG 211. Jewish Self-Help Organization (JJUS),1939–42, 7m.

RG 212. Jewish Councils in Bedzin, Czestochowa, Falenica, Jaslo, Jedrzejow, Konskie, Krakow, Lodz, Lublin, Lwow, Radom, Staszow, Warsaw and Wloszczowa, 1940–43, 2.2m.

RG 213. Maps, Plans, Regulations, Proclamations, 20th century, 1,200 items.

RG 214. German Documents, 1939–45, 1.2m.

RG 215. Photocopies of Materials in Jewish Historical Institute Collection, .5m.

RG 216 and 217. Trials of German War Criminals, 1945, 2m.

RG 218. Camps, 1940–45. 237 items, 1.7m.

RG 221. SIPO and S.D.—FRANCE: Personal papers of French Jews who had valuables and money confiscated, 1939–41, .3m.

RG 222. Photographic collection, 20th century, approximately 17,000 photographs of specific locations, deportation and executions. Virtually no individual photos.

RG 303. Education Division of the Central Committee of the Jews in Poland. Includes individual registration records for children in various postwar orphanages and children's homes and personal records from Jewish postwar schools throughout Poland.

RG 333. Postwar Zionist Organizations. Assorted records of various Zionist groups in Poland after the war. Those who know of a specific Zionist affiliation of a survivor might find these records useful.

RG 337. Executions. Excerpted testimonies from civil courts about group and mass executions of Jews, where and how they happened. Some testimonies provide names; most describe circumstances. Indexed by place of execution.

RG 340. List of Polish-Jewish Survivors. List compiled in 1946–47 by the Central Committee of Jews in Poland of all Polish Jews known to have survived, regardless of their postwar location. Registration was voluntary, so some survivors may not appear. This list, in near-alphabetical, soundex-like order, is available in the archives and summarizes a 150,000 card file from which individual cards can be called up and photocopied. (A soundex is a method of clustering names by how they sound rather than alphabetically.) The list provides name, registration number, names of parents, year of birth, and addresses in 1939 and 1947.

Survivor Lists for Bergen-Belsen, Theresienstadt; Displaced persons' camps, namely, Buchberg, Dachau, Feldafing, Freiman, Garmish, Landsberg, Mittenwald, Neustift, Pasing, Penzing, Shleisheim, St. Ottelia; list of Polish Jews in DP camps; Polish-Jewish children receiving postwar cash assistance from foreign donors; Jews who fled to Sweden in 1945; survivors of Miedzyrec, Poland; Italian Jews known to have been deported; alphabetical list of all Jews deported from Radom province to Nazi camps.

Deportation list from Krakow, 1940–41, giving name, date of birth, address.

Signatures of 300 inmates on receipts from the Oskar Schindler DEF Emalia factory.

Microfilms of some holdings were made by Yad Vashem and are housed in its archives in Jerusalem, where they are available to researchers.

Ringelblum Archives. Seemingly endless amounts of material about the fate of communities and individuals. Cataloged in only a limited manner and difficult to search.

ORGANIZATION OF FORMER RESIDENTS OF LODZ IN ISRAEL (OFRLI)

Address: 158 Dizengoff Street; 63461 Tel Aviv, Israel. Telephone: (international) 972+3-524-1833; fax: 972+3-523-8126

This group has computerized information about more than 200,000 individuals from Lodz and its environs. The source is German records of the Lodz ghetto for the period February 1940–August 1944, and Lodz cemetery records for 1895–1944. During the Holocaust, the Judenrat—the Jewish-run, German-controlled government—in Lodz kept detailed records of the population of the ghetto, including the names of individuals by street address and daily death reports. These records survived the war, and a copy exists at Yad Vashem.

In the late 1980s, microfilms of the register were purchased by OFRLI and deposited in the Yad Vashem archives in Jerusalem. With resources provided by OFRLI, the Yad Vashem archives created a computerized database of all the information, alphabetized by surname and given name. Information includes birth dates and, in some cases, dates of deportation and death. Although it charges no fee for responding to inquiries, contributions are welcomed and are used to further the work of the organization.

CONCENTRATION CAMPS WITH ARCHIVES THAT RESPOND TO INQUIRIES

A number of concentration camps have survived World War II as archives or museums, as well as sites for tourists to visit. Those noted below contain archives which respond to mail inquiries:

Auschwitz   Panstwowe Muzeum
       POB 32-603
       Oswiecim #5, Poland

Buchenwald   Nationale Mahn und Gedenkstatte Buchenwald
       Direktion - Haus 5

0-5301 Weimar-Buchenwald, Germany

Dachau	KZ-Gedenkstätte Alte Römerstraße 75 85221 Dachau, Germany
Majdanek	Majdanek Panstwowega Muzeum Majdanek Droga Mexcennikow Majdenka 67 20-325 Lublin, Poland
Mauthausen	Mauthausen Museum Archive Bundesminiterium fur Inners Postfach 100 1014 Wien, Austria
Neuengamme	KZ-Gedenkstatte Neuengamme Dokumenthaus Aussenstelle des Museums fur Hamburgische Geschichte Neungammer Heerweg 2050 Hamburg 80, Germany
Ravensbruck	Mahn und Gedenkstatte Ravensbruck Strasse de Nationen 1 1432 Furstenberg/H, Germany
Sachsenhausen	National Mahn und Gedenkstatte Sachsenhausen 1400 Oranienburg, Germany

PERSONS DEPORTED FROM FRANCE

Ministere des anciens combattants
Delegation a la Memoire et a l'Information Historique
37, rue de Bellechasse
75007 Paris, France

This organization maintains a computer database of persons deported from France who perished during the Holocaust. This author's one inquiry produced no information beyond what is published in the book by Serge Klarsfled, *Memorial to the Jews Deported from France* (New York: Beate Klarsfeld Foundation, 1983).

APPENDIXES

APPENDIX A
TOWNS WITH PUBLISHED YIZKOR BOOKS
Source: Yad Vashem

The towns for which yizkor books have been published to date are listed below. They are shown with their contemporary names in the countries as they exist today. For example, Vilnius (Vilna), Kaunas (Kovno), Warszawa (Warsaw), Lviv (Lwow). For some towns, more than one book has been published. The most complete annotated bibliography of yizkor books is maintained by the Jewish Genealogical Society; P.O. Box 6398; New York, NY 10128. It was developed by Zachary Baker, head librarian of YIVO Institute for Jewish Studies. The list can be purchased from JGS for $5.00.

List of Country Abbreviations

Aus.	Austria	Ger.	Germany	Neth.	Netherlands
Bel.	Belarus	Hun.	Hungary	Pol.	Poland
Belg.	Belgium	It.	Italy	Rom.	Romania
Croat.	Croatia	Lat.	Latvia	Slov.	Slovakia
Cz.	Czech Republic	Lith.	Lithuania	Ukr.	Ukraine
Fr.	France	Mold.	Moldova	Yug.	Yugoslavia

Towns with Published Yizkor Books

Adutiskis, Lith.
Aleksandriya, Ukr.
Aleksandrow Lodzki, Pol.
Alsfeld, Ger.
Altenstadt, Ger.
Amersfoort, Neth.
Amsterdam, Neth.
Andernach, Ger.
Andrychow, Pol.
Annopol (Lublin), Pol.
Antopol, Bel.
Antwerp, Belg.
Apeldoorn, Neth.
Apolda, Ger.
Arnsberg, Ger.
Arolsen, Ger.
Artsiz, Ukr.

Asen, Neth.
Augustow, Pol.
Babenhausen, Ger.
Baczki, Pol.
Bad Kissingen, Ger.
Bad Kreuznach, Ger.
Bad Mergentheim, Ger.
Bad Nauheim, Ger.
Bad Segeberg, Ger.
Baden Baden, Ger.
Baden, Ger.
Badenweiler, Ger.
Baia Mare, Rom.
Bakalarzewo, Pol.
Baligrod, Pol.
Balin, Ukr.
Balmazujvaros, Hun.
Bamberg, Ger.

Bar, Pol.
Baranovichi, Bel.
Baranovka, Ukr.
Baranowo, Pol.
Baremel, Ukr.
Baryluv, Ukr.
Bathmen, Neth.
Beclean, Rom.
Bedzin, Pol.
Belchatow, Pol.
Belgorod Dnestrovskiy, Ukr.
Belitsa, Bel.
Beltsy, Rom.
Belz, Ukr.
Bendery, Mold.
Bendorf, Ger.
Bensheim, Ger.

Beregovo, Ukr.
Berestechko, Ukr.
Bereza, Bel.
Berezhany, Ukr.
Berezno, Ukr.
Bergen Enkheim, Ger.
Bergen, Ger.
Bergheim, Ger.
Berlin, Ger.
Bernecebarati, Hun.
Bershad, Ukr.
Beuel, Ger.
Biala Podlaska, Pol.
Biala Rawska, Pol.
Bialystok, Pol.
Biecz, Pol.
Bielefeld, Ger.
Bielsk Podlaski, Pol.
Bielsko Biala, Pol.
Biezun, Pol.
Bilgoraj, Pol.
Bistrita, Rom.
Bitola, Yug.
Bivolari, Rom.
Bledow, Pol.
Bobrka, Ukr.
Bobruysk, Bel.
Bolekhov, Ukr.
Bolimow, Pol.
Bonn, Ger.
Bonyhad, Hun.
Borculo, Neth.
Borislav, Ukr.
Borken, Ger.
Bornheim, Ger.
Borsa Maramures,
    Rom.
Borshchev, Ukr.
Bransk, Pol.
Braslav, Bel.
Bratislava, Slov.
Braunschweig, Ger.
Bremerhaven, Ger.
Brest, Bel.
Brezova pod Bradlom,
    Slov.

Brichany, Mold.
Bricheva, Mold.
Brilon, Ger.
Brody, Ukr.
Bronka, Ukr.
Bronkhorst, Neth.
Broshnev Osada, Ukr.
Bruhl, Ger.
Brzesc Kujawski, Pol.
Brzesko, Pol.
Brzeziny, Pol.
Brzeznica, Pol.
Brzozow, Pol.
Buchach, Ukr.
Buchau, Ger.
Budanov, Ukr.
Budapest, Hun.
Bukachevtsy, Ukr.
Bukowsko, Pol.
Burshtyn, Ukr.
Busko Zdroj, Pol.
Buttenhausen, Ger.
Butzbach, Ger.
Bychawa, Pol.
Byten, Bel.
Cakovec, Croat.
Celle, Ger.
Charsznica, Pol.
Chelm, Pol.
Chemnitz, Ger.
Chernovtsy, Ukr.
Chervonoarmeisk, Ukr.
Chmielnik, Pol.
Chodecz, Pol.
Chortkov, Ukr.
Chorzele, Pol.
Chrzanow, Pol.
Ciechanow, Pol.
Ciechanowiec, Pol.
Ciechocinek, Pol.
Cieszanow, Pol.
Cluj, Rom.
Cmielow, Pol.
Coburg, Ger.
Coesfeld, Ger.
Csenger, Hun.

Culemborg, Neth.
Cuxhaven, Ger.
Czarnkow, Pol.
Czarny Dunajec, Pol.
Czerwin, Pol.
Czestochowa, Pol.
Czyzew, Pol.
Dabrowa Gornicza, Pol.
Darmstadt, Ger.
Daugavpils, Lat.
David Gorodok, Bel.
Debica, Pol.
Deblin, Pol.
Debrecen, Hun.
Dej, Rom.
Delmenhorst, Ger.
Delyatichi, Bel.
Demidovka, Ukr.
Derechin, Bel.
Derecske, Hun.
Derevna, Bel.
Derevno, Bel.
Deventer, Neth.
Dieburg, Ger.
Diepenven, Neth.
Dieveniskes, Lith.
Disna, Bel.
Dmitrov, Ukr.
Dnepropetrovsk, Ukr.
Dobromil, Ukr.
Dobrzyn nad Wisla, Pol.
Doesburg, Neth.
Dokshitsy, Bel.
Dolginovo, Bel.
Dolgoye, Ukr.
Dolinka, Slov.
Dorohoi, Rom.
Dorsten, Ger.
Dregelypalank, Hun.
Dresden, Ger.
Drogichin, Bel.
Drogobych, Ukr.
Drohiczyn, Pol.
Drozdin, Ukr.
Druya, Bel.
Druysk, Bel.

Druzhkopol, Ukr.
Dubetsko, Pol.
Dubienka, Pol.
Dubinovo, Bel.
Dubno, Ukr.
Dubossary, Mold.
Dubrovitsa, Ukr.
Dubrovnik, Yug.
Duisburg, Ger.
Dukla, Pol.
Dukstas, Lith.
Dumbraveny, Mold.
Dunajska Streda, Slov.
Dunilovichi, Bel.
Duren, Ger.
Dusetos, Lith.
Dyatlovo, Bel.
Dynow, Pol.
Dzerzhinsk, Bel.
Dzialoszyce, Pol.
Dzikow Stary, Pol.
Egen, Ger.
Eger, Hun.
Einbeck, Ger.
Eisenach, Ger.
Eisenstadt, Aus.
Eisiskes, Lith.
Eitorf, Ger.
Emmerich, Ger.
Esens, Ger.
Essen, Ger.
Falenica, Pol.
Fehergyarmat, Hun.
Feuchtwangen, Ger.
Filipow, Pol.
Frampol, Pol.
Frankfurt am Main,
  Ger.
Freiburg im Breisgau,
  Ger.
Freudenthal, Ger.
Friesenheim, Ger.
Fritzlar, Ger.
Fulda, Ger.
Gailingen, Ger.
Gardelegen, Ger.

Gargzdai, Lith.
Garwolin, Pol.
Gaukonigshofen, Ger.
Gdansk, Pol.
Geldern, Ger.
Gemund, Ger.
Gemunden, Ger.
Gennep, Neth.
Genoa, It.
Gescher, Ger.
Gevelsberg, Ger.
Gherla, Rom.
Giessen, Ger.
Glebokie, Bel.
Glinyany, Ukr.
Glogow, Pol.
Glussk, Bel.
Gniewoszow, Pol.
Gniezno, Pol.
Golshany, Bel.
Golub Dobrzyn, Pol.
Golynka, Bel.
Gomel, Bel.
Goniadz, Pol.
Goppingen, Ger.
Gora Kalwaria, Pol.
Gorinchem, Neth.
Gorlice, Pol.
Gorodenka, Ukr.
Gorodnitsa, Ukr.
Gorodno, Bel.
Gorodok (near Lviv),
  Ukr.
Gorokhov, Ukr.
Goryngrad, Ukr.
Goshcha, Ukr.
Gostynin, Pol.
Gotha, Ger.
Gottingen, Ger.
Goworowo, Pol.
Gran, Pol.
Grodek, Pol.
Grodno, Bel.
Grodzisk Wielkopolsk,
  Pol.
Grojec, Pol.

Grossgerau, Ger.
Grosskrotzenburg, Ger.
Grozovo, Bel.
Gusyatin, Ukr.
Gutersloh, Ger.
Gvardeyskoye, Ukr.
Gwozdziec, Pol.
Gyerk, Hun.
Gymnich, Ger.
Hachenburg, Ger.
Hadamar, Ger.
Hagen, Ger.
Haigerloch, Ger.
Hajdunanas, Hun.
Hajdusamson, Hun.
Haldensleben, Ger.
Halle, Ger.
Halmeu, Rom.
Hamburg, Ger.
Hamm, Ger.
Hannover, Ger.
Heidelberg, Ger.
Heilbronn, Ger.
Heino, Neth.
Hengelo, Neth.
Heppenheim an der
  Bergstrasse, Ger.
Herford, Ger.
Hessen, Ger.
Hochheim, Ger.
Hochst im Odenwald,
  Ger.
Hofgeismar, Ger.
Hollabrunn, Aus.
Holten, Neth.
Hont, Hun.
Horodlo, Pol.
Horvati, Hun.
Hrubieszow, Pol.
Huedin, Rom.
Hungen, Ger.
Ignatovka, Bel.
Iklad, Hun.
Ileanda, Rom.
Illingen, Ger.
Ilya, Bel.

Indura, Bel.
Ingolstadt, Ger.
Iody, Bel.
Iody, Pol.
Iserlohn, Ger.
Ivano Frankovsk, Ukr.
Ivanovka (near
Terebovlya), Ukr.
Ivanovka, Ukr.
Ivanovo, Bel.
Ivatsevichi, Bel.
Ivenets, Bel.
Ivye, Bel.
Jablonka, Pol.
Jadow, Pol.
Jaroslaw, Pol.
Jaslo, Pol.
Jaunjelgava, Lat.
Jebenhausen, Ger.
Jedrzejow, Pol.
Jedwabne, Pol.
Jeleniewo, Pol.
Jieznas, Lith.
Jonava, Lith.
Jordanow, Pol.
Jozefow, Pol.
Jurbarkas, Lith.
Kadzidlo, Pol.
Kalarash, Mold.
Kaliningrad, USSR
Kalisz, Pol.
Kaltinenai, Lith.
Kalush, Ukr.
Kaluszyn, Pol.
Kalvarija, Lith.
Kamen, Bel.
Kamen Kashirskiy,
Ukr.
Kamenets, Bel.
Kamenets Podolskiy,
Ukr.
Kamennyy Brod, Ukr.
Kamiensk, Pol.
Kapreshty, Mold.
Karcag, Hun.
Karczew, Pol.

Kassel, Ger.
Kaunas, Lith.
Kazimierz Dolny, Pol.
Kedainiai, Lith.
Kemence, Hun.
Keretski, Ukr.
Kettwig, Ger.
Kezmarok, Slov.
Khmelnitskiy, Ukr.
Khorostkov, Ukr.
Khotin, Ukr.
Kielce, Pol.
Kiernozia, Pol.
Kiliya, Ukr.
Kirchen, Ger.
Kishinev, Mold.
Kisvarda, Hun.
Kitay Gorod, Ukr.
Klagenfurt, Ger.
Kletsk, Bel.
Klobuck, Pol.
Knyazhnychi, Ukr.
Koblenz, Ger.
Kobrin, Bel.
Kobylnik, Bel.
Kock, Pol.
Kokeszi, Hun.
Kolbuszowa, Pol.
Kolin, Cz.
Koln, Ger.
Kolno, Pol.
Kolo, Pol.
Kolomyya, Ukr.
Kolonie Zoludzk, Pol.
Kolonja Synajska, Bel.
Komarno (near Lviv),
Ukr.
Konigstein, Ger.
Konigswinter, Ger.
Konin, Pol.
Konstanz, Ger.
Konyar, Hun.
Kopin, Ukr.
Koprzywnica, Pol.
Kopyl, Bel.
Korbach, Ger.

Korczyna, Pol.
Korelichi, Bel.
Korets, Ukr.
Kosice, Slov.
Kosov, Ukr.
Kossovo, Bel.
Kostopol, Ukr.
Kosyno, Ger.
Kowal, Pol.
Kozhan Gorodok, Bel.
Kozienice, Pol.
Kozlovshchina, Bel.
Kozyany, Bel.
Krakovets, Ukr.
Krakow, Pol.
Krasnapole, Pol.
Krasnik, Pol.
Krasnobrod, Pol.
Krasnystaw, Pol.
Krefeld, Ger.
Krekenava, Lith.
Kremenets, Ukr.
Krems an der Donau,
Aus.
Kremyanitsa, Bel.
Krivichi, Bel.
Kronach, Ger.
Kroscienko (near Nowy
Targ), Pol.
Kroscienko, Pol.
Krosniewice, Pol.
Krynki, Pol.
Krzepice, Pol.
Ksiaz Wielki, Pol.
Kubanovo, Hun.
Kunow, Pol.
Kurenets, Bel.
Kurow, Pol.
Kushnitsa, Ukr.
Kutno, Pol.
Kuty, Ukr.
Kybartai, Lith.
Laasphe, Ger.
Lackenbach, Aus.
Ladenburg, Ger.
Lahr, Ger.

Lakhva, Bel.
Lambsheim, Ger.
Lancut, Pol.
Landau, Ger.
Langenbrucken, Ger.
Lanovtsy, Ukr.
Lapichi, Bel.
Lask, Pol.
Laskarzew, Pol.
Lechenich, Ger.
Leczyca, Pol.
Leeuwarden, Neth.
Leipzig, Ger.
Lenin, Bel.
Leonpol, Bel.
Leovo, Mold.
Lesko, Pol.
Lezajsk, Pol.
Libicovo, Ukr.
Lichtenstein
Lida, Bel.
Linkmenys, Lith.
Linz am Rhein, Ger.
Lipkany, Mold.
Lipnishki, Bel.
Lipno, Pol.
Lippstadt, Ger.
Lisicovo, Ukr.
Lodz, Pol.
Lokachi, Ukr.
Lomza, Pol.
Lopatin, Ukr.
Losice, Pol.
Lowicz, Pol.
Lozansky, Ukr.
Lubartow, Pol.
Lubcza, Pol.
Lublin, Pol.
Lubraniec, Pol.
Luckenwalde, Ger.
Ludwigsburg, Ger.
Lukow, Pol.
Lunen, Ger.
Luninets, Bel.
Lutowiska, Pol.
Lutsk, Ukr.

Luxembourg
Lviv, Ukr.
Lyakhovichi, Bel.
Lynki, Bel.
Lyntupy, Bel.
Lyskovo, Bel.
Lyszkowice, Pol.
Lyuban, Bel.
Lyuboml, Ukr.
Lyubonichi, Bel.
Maastricht, Neth.
Macedonia, Neth.
Mad, Hun.
Mainz, Ger.
Makow Mazowiecki,
 Pol.
Makow Podhalanski,
 Pol.
Malchow, Ger.
Malech, Bel.
Malsch, Ger.
Mannheim, Ger.
Marghita, Rom.
Maribor, Yug.
Marijampole, Lith.
Markuleshty, Mold.
Markuszow, Pol.
Medenice, Ukr.
Melnitsa Podolskaya,
 Ukr.
Memmingen, Ger.
Menden, Ger.
Meppel, Neth.
Merkine, Lith.
Merkulovichi, Bel.
Merzig, Ger.
Mezhirichi, Ukr.
Michalovce, Slov.
Michelstadt, Ger.
Miechow, Pol.
Miedzyrzec Podlaski,
 Pol.
Mielec, Pol.
Mikepercs, Hun.
Mikulintsy, Ukr.
Mikulov, Cz.

Milosna, Pol.
Mingolsheim, Ger.
Minkovtsy, Ukr.
Minsk, Bel.
Minsk Mazowiecki, Pol.
Miory, Bel.
Mir, Bel.
Miskolc, Hun.
Mitburger, Ger.
Mizoch, Ukr.
Mlawa, Pol.
Mlinov, Ukr.
Mlynary, Ger.
Moers, Ger.
Mogielnica, Pol.
Moisling, Ger.
Molchad, Bel.
Monastyriska, Ukr.
Montabaur, Ger.
Motol, Bel.
Mszczonow, Pol.
Mukachevo, Ukr.
Mullheim, Ger.
Munchen, Ger.
Munster, Ger.
Murava, Ukr.
Myjava, Slov.
Myslenice, Pol.
Myszyniec, Pol.
Nadarzyn, Pol.
Nadvornaya, Ukr.
Nagykallo, Hun.
Naliboki, Bel.
Narayev, Ukr.
Nasaud, Rom.
Naujasis Daugeliskis,
 Lith.
Neheim Husten, Ger.
Nemirov, Ukr.
Nesterov, Ukr.
Nesvizh, Bel.
Neumark, Ger.
Neuss, Ger.
Neuwied, Ger.
Niederwerrn, Ger.
Nikolayev (Lwow), Ukr.

Nikolayevka
 Novorossiyskaya,
 Ukr.
Nikolayevka, Ukr.
Nimes, Fr.
Nonnenweier, Ger.
Nordhorn, Ger.
Northeim, Ger.
Nottuln, Ger.
Novograd Volynskiy,
 Ukr.
Novogrudok, Bel.
Novoseltsy, Ukr.
Novoukrainka, Ukr.
Novyy Dvor, Bel.
Novyy Vitkov, Ukr.
Nowe Miasto, Pol.
Nowogrod, Pol.
Nowy Dwor, Pol.
Nowy Korczyn, Ger.
Nowy Sacz, Pol.
Nowy Targ, Pol.
Nowy Zagorz, Pol.
Nurnberg, Ger.
Nyiregyhaza, Hun.
Ober Ramstadt, Ger.
Oberhausen, Ger.
Odessa, Ukr.
Offenbach am Main,
 Ger.
Offenburg, Ger.
Okuniew, Pol.
Oldenburg, Ger.
Olkusz, Pol.
Olst, Neth.
Olyka, Ukr.
Opatow, Pol.
Opsa, Bel.
Oradea, Rom.
Orgeyev, Mold.
Orlova, Cz.
Oshmyany, Bel.
Osiek, Pol.
Osipovichi, Bel.
Osnabruck, Ger.
Osterode am Harz,

Ger.
Ostrog, Ukr.
Ostrolenka, Pol.
Ostrow Lubelski, Pol.
Ostrow Mazowiecka,
 Pol.
Ostrowiec Swietokrzyski,
 Pol.
Ostrowik, Pol.
Ostryna, Bel.
Oswiecim, Pol.
Otwock, Pol.
Overijssel, Neth.
Ozarow, Pol.
Ozernyany, Ukr.
Ozeryany, Ukr.
Ozorkow, Pol.
Pabianice, Pol.
Pabrade, Lith.
Paderborn, Ger.
Paks, Hun.
Papa, Hun.
Papenburg, Ger.
Parafyanovo, Bel.
Parichi, Bel.
Parysow, Pol.
Passau, Ger.
Perocseny, Hun.
Pforzheim, Ger.
Piaski, Bel.
Piatnica, Pol.
Piestany, Slov.
Pilawa, Pol.
Pinczow, Pol.
Pinsk, Bel.
Piotrkow Trybunalski,
 Pol.
Pirot, Yug.
Plawno, Pol.
Plock, Pol.
Plonsk, Pol.
Plyussy, Pol.
Pochayev, Ukr.
Podgaytsy, Ukr.
Podvolochisk, Ukr.
Pogost, Bel.

Pogost Zagorodskiy,
 Bel.
Polaniec, Pol.
Poligon, Lith.
Polonnoye, Ukr.
Popowa, Pol.
Porcsalma, Hun.
Porozovo, Bel.
Postavy, Bel.
Praga, Pol.
Preselany, Hun.
Pruszkow, Pol.
Pruzhany, Bel.
Przasnysz, Pol.
Przeclaw, Pol.
Przedborz, Pol.
Przedecz, Pol.
Przemysl, Pol.
Przerosl, Pol.
Przytyk, Pol.
Pulawy, Pol.
Pultusk, Pol.
Punsk, Pol.
Raalte, Neth.
Rabka, Pol.
Rachtig, Ger.
Raciaz, Pol.
Raczki, Pol.
Radekhov, Ukr.
Radom, Pol.
Radomsko, Pol.
Radomysl Wielki, Pol.
Radoshkovichi, Bel.
Radzanow, Pol.
Radzymin, Pol.
Radzyn Podlaski, Pol.
Raesfeld, Ger.
Rakhov, Ukr.
Rakospalota, Hun.
Rakow, Pol.
Randegg, Ger.
Rastice, Cz.
Ratno, Ukr.
Raum Bremerhaven,
 Ger.
Rava Russkaya, Ukr.

Rawicz, Pol.
Recklinghausen, Ger.
Regensburg, Ger.
Rembertow, Pol.
Reteag, Rom.
Rhein, Ger.
Rheine, Ger.
Rheurdt, Ger.
Rietavas, Lith.
Riga, Lat.
Rijeka, It.
Rimbach, Ger.
Rimse, Lith.
Rinteln, Ger.
Rogatin, Ukr.
Rokiskis, Lith.
Rokitnoye, Ukr.
Romanovo, Ukr.
Rossdorf, Ger.
Rostock, Ger.
Rotterdam, Neth.
Rovno, Ukr.
Rozan, Pol.
Rozhanka, Bel.
Rozhishche, Ukr.
Rozhnyatov, Ukr.
Rozprza, Pol.
Rozwadow, Pol.
Rubezhevichi, Bel.
Rudki, Ukr.
Ruscova, Rom.
Ruzhany, Bel.
Ryki, Pol.
Rymanow, Pol.
Rypin, Pol.
Rytwiany, Pol.
Rzeszow, Pol.
Safarikovo, Slov.
Sahy, Slov.
Saluzzo, It.
Salzburg, Ger.
Sambor, Ukr.
Samorin, Slov.
Sandomierz, Pol.
Sankt Ingbert, Ger.
Sanok, Pol.

Sarata, Ukr.
Sarnaki, Pol.
Sarny, Ukr.
Satoraljaujhely, Hun.
Schenklengsfeld, Ger.
Schifferstadt, Ger.
Schmalkalden, Ger.
Schmallenberg, Ger.
Schopfheim, Ger.
Schwelm, Ger.
Schwerte, Ger.
Schwetzingen, Ger.
Secovce, Slov.
Sedziszow (near
    Jedrzejow), Pol.
Sedziszow, Pol.
Seeheim, Ger.
Seesen, Ger.
Selets, Bel.
Seligenstadt, Ger.
Senica, Slov.
Senkuv, Ukr.
Serock, Pol.
Shabo, Ukr.
Sharkovshchina, Bel.
Shchedrin, Bel.
Shchurovichi, Ukr.
Shereshevo, Bel.
Shpola, Ukr.
Shumskoye, Ukr.
Siedlce, Pol.
Siedliszcze, Pol.
Siemiatycze, Pol.
Sierpc, Pol.
Sighet, Rom.
Sinyavka, Bel.
Skala Podolskaya, Ukr.
Skalat, Ukr.
Skarzysko Kamienna,
    Pol.
Skelivka, Ukr.
Skhodnitsa, Ukr.
Skierniewice, Pol.
Sknilov, Ukr.
Skole, Ukr.
Skuodas, Lith.

Slonim, Bel.
Slupia Nowa, Pol.
Slupsk, Ger.
Slupsk, Pol.
Slutsk, Bel.
Sluzewo, Pol.
Smorgon, Bel.
Smotrich, Ukr.
Sobibor, Pol.
Sobolew, Pol.
Sobota, Pol.
Sochaczew, Pol.
Sokal, Ukr.
Sokiryany, Ukr.
Sokolka, Pol.
Sokolovka, Ukr.
Sokolow, Pol.
Sokoly, Pol.
Solingen, Ger.
Sombor, Serbia
Sopotskin, Bel.
Sosnovoye, Ukr.
Sosnowiec, Pol.
Speyer, Ger.
Sprendlingen, Ger.
Stanislavchik, Ukr.
Starobin, Bel.
Staryy Sambor, Ukr.
Staryye Dorogi, Bel.
Staszow, Pol.
Stavishche, Ukr.
Stawiski, Pol.
Steinfurth, Ger.
Steinheim, Ger.
Stepan, Ukr.
Stoczek Wegrowski,
    Pol.
Stojaciszki, Pol.
Stok, Pol.
Stolbtsy, Bel.
Stolin, Bel.
Stommeln, Ger.
Stoyanov, Ukr.
Stropkov, Slov.
Strusov, Ukr.
Stryy, Ukr.

Strzegowo, Pol.
Strzemilcze, Ukr.
Strzyzow, Pol.
Stuttgart, Ger.
Sucha, Pol.
Suchocin, Pol.
Suchowola, Pol.
Sudlohn, Ger.
Sulzburg, Ger.
Suwalki, Pol.
Svarichov, Ukr.
Svencioneliai, Lith.
Svencionys, Lith.
Svir, Bel.
Svisloch, Bel.
Szczawnica Nizna, Pol.
Szczawnica, Pol.
Szczebrzeszyn, Pol.
Szczecin, Pol.
Szczekociny, Pol.
Szczuczyn (Bialystok
   area), Pol.
Szczuczyn (Novogrudok
   area), Bel.
Szikszo, Hun.
Szirak, Hun.
Szrensk, Pol.
Szydlow, Pol.
Szydlowiec, Pol.
Talheim, Ger.
Tarnobrzeg, Pol.
Tarnogrod, Pol.
Tarnow, Pol.
Tartakov, Ukr.
Tarutino, Ukr.
Tasnad, Rom.
Teglas, Hun.
Telekhany, Bel.
Telgte, Ger.
Telsiai, Lith.
Teplik, Ukr.
Terebovlya, Ukr.
Ternopol, Ukr.
Ternovka, Ukr.
Tesmak, Hun.
Thessaloniki, Greece

Tiengen, Ger.
Timkovichi, Bel.
Tirgu Lapus, Rom.
Tirgu Mures, Rom.
Tlumach, Ukr.
Tluszcz, Pol.
Tolstoye, Ukr.
Tomaszow Lubelski, Pol.
Tomaszow Mazowiecki,
   Pol.
Topolcany, Slov.
Toporov, Ukr.
Torchin, Ukr.
Torgovitsa, Ukr.
Trakai, Lith.
Trier, Ger.
Trzebinia, Pol.
Tubingen, Ger.
Tuchin, Ukr.
Tulln, Aus.
Turek, Pol.
Turets, Bel.
Turiysk, Ukr.
Turka (Lwow), Ukr.
Turna nad Bodvou,
   Slov.
Turobin, Pol.
Twello, Neth.
Twistringen, Ger.
Tykocin, Pol.
Tysmenitsa, Ukr.
Tyszowce, Pol.
Ubinie, Ukr.
Ugnev, Ukr.
Ujpest, Hun.
Ulm, Ger.
Urechye, Bel.
Ustilug, Ukr.
Ustrzyki Dolne, Pol.
Utena, Lith.
Uzhgorod, Ukr.
Uzlovoye, Ukr.
Valkininkas, Lith.
Vamosmikola, Hun.
Vamospercs, Hun.
Vas, Croatia

Vasilishki, Bel.
Velikiye Mosty, Ukr.
Velp, Neth.
Venice, It.
Vidzy, Bel.
Viersen, Ger.
Vileyka, Bel.
Vilnius, Lith.
Vilyampolskaya Slobo,
   Bel.
Vinnitsa, Ukr.
Vinogradov, Ukr.
Vishnevets, Ukr.
Vishnevo, Bel.
Vitebsk, Bel.
Vladimir Volynskiy,
   Ukr.
Vladimirets, Ukr.
Vlotho, Ger.
Volkovysk, Bel.
Volma, Bel.
Volontirovka, Mold.
Volozhin, Bel.
Volpa, Bel.
Voronovo, Bel.
Vranov nad Toplou,
   Slov.
Vrbove, Slov.
Vselyub, Bel.
Vyshgorodok, Ukr.
Vysotsk, Ukr.
Wadowice, Pol.
Wandsbek, Ger.
Warburg, Ger.
Warka, Pol.
Warszawa, Pol.
Warta, Pol.
Wasilkow, Pol.
Wasniow, Pol.
Weesp, Neth.
Wegrow, Pol.
Weingarten, Ger.
Weinheim, Ger.
Wenkheim, Ger.
Wesseling, Ger.
Wieliczka, Pol.

Wielun, Pol.
Wien, Aus.
Wieruszow, Pol.
Wierzbnik, Pol.
Wiesbaden, Ger.
Wildeshausen, Ger.
Windsheim, Ger.
Wiskitki, Pol.
Wislica, Pol.
Wisna, (Vizna)
Witten, Ger.
Wittlich, Ger.
Wizna, Pol.
Wloclawek, Pol.
Wlodawa, Pol.
Wodzislaw, Pol.
Wojslawice, Pol.
Wolborz, Pol.
Wolbrom, Pol.
Wolica Wygoda, Ukr.
Wolomin, Pol.
Worms, Ger.
Wunstorf, Ger.
Wurzburg, Ger.

Wysokie Mazowieckie,
    Pol.
Wyszkow, Pol.
Wyszogrod, Pol.
Yablonka, Pol.
Yampol (Wolyn), Ukr.
Yanovichi, Bel.
Yavorov, Ukr.
Yedintsy, Mold.
Yeremichi, Bel.
Zabludow, Pol.
Zabolotov, Ukr.
Zadneye, Ukr.
Zaglebie Dabrowskie,
    Pol.
Zakopane, Pol.
Zalaber, Hun.
Zambrow, Pol.
Zamekhov, Ukr.
Zamosc, Pol.
Zareby Koscielne, Pol.
Zarki, Pol.
Zarszyn, Pol.
Zassow, Pol.

Zastavye, Bel.
Zavidche, Ukr.
Zawiercie, Pol.
Zbarazh, Ukr.
Zborov, Ukr.
Zdunska Wola, Pol.
Zelechow, Pol.
Zelow, Pol.
Zeltingen, Ger.
Zelva, Lith.
Zgierz, Pol.
Zheludok, Bel.
Ziegenhain, Ger.
Zinkov, Ukr.
Zloczew, Pol.
Zoblas, Rom.
Zolochev, Ukr.
Zundorf, Ger.
Zuromin, Pol.
Zutphen, Neth.
Zwickau, Ger.
Zwolen, Pol.
Zychlin, Pol.
Zyrardow, Pol.

Oswiecim (Jewish community)	M–1/E–711/594; 761/623
	M–1/Q–1423/244; 1462/284; 1541/299; 1836/
	393; 2161/507
Deportations to Bedzin	M–1/E–1423/244; 1462/284; 1541/299
to Blechhammer, camp	M–1/Q–1541/299
to Buchenwald, camp	M–1/Q–1541/299
to Chrzanow	M–1/Q–1423/244; 2161/1507
to Sosnowiec	M–1/Q–1423/244; 1462/284; 1836/393; 2161/507
to Upper Silesia, forced labor camps in	M–1/Q–1423/224
Escape to Soviet Union	M–1/Q–2161/507
Forced labor	M–1/E–367/289; 2360/2407
at erection of camp Auschwitz	M–1/E–809/679
Camp, see: Auschwitz	
Oszmiana (Ašmena), see: Oshmyany	
Otnobroda, forced labor camp	
Aid by Red Cross	M–1/E–1162/1134
Ottmuth, Lower Silesia, forced labor camp	M–1/E–1835/1692
Deportees brought in	M–1/E–810/677; 2487/2584
Otwock, Warsaw area	M–1/E–854/700; 1781/1643
Collaborators, Jewish police	M–1/Q–2125/495
Cultural life	M–1/E–854/700
Deportations to Treblinka	M–1/E–2125/495
Escape	M–1/E–377/325; 881/755
Forced labor	M–1/E–854/700
Hiding	M–1/E–881/755
List of Jews	M–1/DN–28/2
Police, Jewish	M–1/E–854/700
War criminals	M–1/Q–2125/495
Ovruch, Zhitomir area, Soviet Union	
Forced labor	M–1/E–325/224
Ozarow, Kielce area	M–1/Q–1915/435
Aid by Soviets	M–1/E–1136/1104
Collaborators, Jewish	M–1/E–1136/1104
Deportations	M–1/E–1800/1659
to Skarzysko-Kamienna	M–1/E–1136/1104
to Treblinka	M–1/Q–1915/435
Escape	M–1/E–377/330; 2200/1992
Flight to	M–1/E–377/330; 2200/1992
Forced labor	M–1/E–1800/1659

Guide to Unpublished Materials of the Holocaust Period. An index to the record groups of the archives at Yad Vashem was published in a series of volumes. Few of the documents have information about individuals, but note under Otwock, there is mention of a "List of Jews."

APPENDIX B
TOWNS REFERENCED IN THE
GUIDE TO UNPUBLISHED MATERIALS OF
THE HOLOCAUST PERIOD

The archives at Yad Vashem in Jerusalem has documentation for more than 4,000 towns in Europe. (See the chapter on "Yad Vashem" for more detailed information.) The volumes of *Guide to Unpublished Materials of the Holocaust Period* also include numerous entries for camps and refugee centers during and after World War II throughout the world. Few, if any, such facilities are identified below. If you know that an individual went to a specific labor camp or refugee center, it would be worthwhile to look in the volumes of the Guide to see if they include information of interest. The names Czechoslovakia, USSR and Yugoslavia are used because the lists were compiled prior to the breakup of these countries.

List of Country Abbreviations

Alb.	Albania	Fr.	France	Pol.	Poland
Aus.	Austria	Ger.	Germany	Rom.	Romania
Bel.	Belarus	Hun.	Hungary	Serb.	Serbia
Belg.	Belgium	It.	Italy	Slov.	Slovakia
Bulg.	Bulgaria	Lat.	Latvia	Swed.	Sweden
Croat.	Croatia	Lith.	Lithuania	Switz.	Switzerland
Cz.	Czechoslovakia	Maced.	Macedonia	Ukr.	Ukraine
Est.	Estonia	Mold.	Moldova	Yug.	Yugoslavia
Fin.	Finland	Neth.	Netherlands		

Aachen, Ger.	Adjudu Vechi, Rom.	Aiud, Rom.
Abaujszanto, Hun.	Admont, Aus.	Akhtyrka, Ukr.
Abbeville, Fr.	Adutiskis, Lith.	Akmene, Lith.
Abkashevko, USSR	Agrinion, Greece	Akovo, Yugo.
Abony, Hun.	Ahaus, Ger.	Alba Iulia, Rom.
Ada, Serb.	Ahlem, Ger.	Aleksandriya, Ukr.
Ada, Yugo.	Ahlen, Ger.	Aleksandrow Kujawski,
Adamow, Pol.	Ahmecetca, Rom.	Pol.
Adelebsen, Ger.	Ahrensdorf, Ger.	Aleksandrow Lodzki,
Adelsberg, Ger.	Aichach, Ger.	Pol.
Adelsdorf, Ger.	Aidhausen, Ger.	Aleksotas, Lith.

Alesheim, Ger.
Alexandria, Rom.
Alexandrovka, Ukr.
Allendorf an der Lumda,
   Ger.
Allersheim, Ger.
Almelo, Neth.
Alpen, Ger.
Alsedziai, Lith.
Altaussee, Aus.
Altenburg, Ger.
Altenmuhr, Ger.
Altenschonbach, Ger.
Altenstadt, Ger.
Altona, Ger.
Alushta, Ukr.
Alytus, Lith.
Alzenau in
   Unterfranken, Ger.
Alzey, Ger.
Amberg, Ger.
Amersfoort, Neth.
Ammendorf, Ger.
Ammersee, Ger.
Ampfing, Ger.
Amsterdam, Neth.
Amstetten, Aus.
Ananyev, Ukr.
Anderlecht, Belg.
Andrychow, Pol.
Andrzejewo, Pol.
Andrzejow (Lodz area),
   Pol.
Angleur, Belg.
Anholt, Ger.
Annaberg, Ger.
Annopol (Lublin), Pol.
Ans, Belg.
Ansbach, Ger.
Antoninek, ?
Antopol, Bel.
Antwerpen, Belg.
Anyksciai, Lith.
Apolda, Ger.
Apsilsa, Ukr.
Aquila, It.
Arad, Rom.

Archangel, USSR
Ariogala, Lith.
Arlon, Belg.
Armyansk, Ukr.
Arnheem, Neth.
Arnoldstein, Aus.
Arnsberg, Ger.
Arolsen, Ger.
Arta, Greece
Artemovsk, Ukr.
Asare, Lat.
Aschach, Aus.
Aschaffenburg, Ger.
Aschbach, Ger.
Aschersleben, Ger.
Ascona, Switz.
Asino, USSR
Asperg, Ger.
Aszod, Hun.
Ataki, Mold.
Athens, Greece
Athus, Belg.
Attnang, Aus.
Aub, Ger.
Aufsess, Ger.
Augsburg, Ger.
Augustow, Pol.
Aukstadvaris, Lith.
Aurelow, Pol.
Aurich, Ger.
Avignon, Fr.
Babadag, Rom.
Babenhausen, Ger.
Babi Yar, Ukr.
Babiak, Pol.
Babice, Pol.
Babtai, Lith.
Bacau, Rom.
Bacia, Rom.
Bacieczki, Pol.
Backa Palanka, Yugo.
Backnang, Ger.
Bacstopolya, Hun.
Bad Aibling, Ger.
Bad Deutsch Altenburg,
   Aus.
Bad Durkheim, Ger.

Bad Ems, Ger.
Bad Godesberg, Ger.
Bad Harzburg, Ger.
Bad Hersfeld, Ger.
Bad Homburg vor der
   Hohe, Ger.
Bad Ischl, Aus.
Bad Kissingen, Ger.
Bad Lauchstadt, Ger.
Bad Mergentheim, Ger.
Bad Nauheim, Ger.
Bad Neustadt an der
   Saale, Ger.
Bad Pyrmont, Ger.
Bad Rappenau, Ger.
Bad Reichenhall, Ger.
Bad Salzschlirf, Ger.
Bad Salzuflen, Ger.
Bad Soden am Taunus,
   Ger.
Bad Vilbel, Ger.
Baden, Aus.
Baden Baden, Ger.
Bagolyuk, Hun.
Baia Mare, Rom.
Baisingen, Ger.
Baja, Hun.
Bakhchisarai, USSR
Bakhchisaray, Ukr.
Bakshty, Bel.
Balanovca, Ukr.
Balatonalmadi, Hun.
Balatonboglar, Hun.
Balatonujhely, Hun.
Balbieriskis, Lith.
Baleliai Antrieji, Lith.
Balf, Hun.
Baligrod, Pol.
Balki, Ukr.
Balmazujvaros, Hun.
Balta, Ukr.
Baltoja Voke, Lith.
Baltoji Voke, Lith.
Baltow, Pol.
Baltowka, Pol.
Bamberg, Ger.
Banilov, Ukr.

Banja Luka, Yugo.
Banja, Yugo.
Banovce nad Bebravou,
   Cz.
Banska Bystrica, Cz.
Banska Stiavnica, Cz.
Bar, Ukr.
Baran, Bel.
Baranovichi, Bel.
Baranovka, Ukr.
Baranow, Pol.
Baranow Sandomierski,
   Pol.
Barcares, Fr.
Barciai, Lith.
Barcs, Hun.
Bardejov, Cz.
Bari, It.
Barkasovo, Hun.
Barnabas, Ukr.
Barntrup, Ger.
Barsbaracska, Cz.
Bartenstein, Ger.
Barth, Ger.
Bartodzieje Podlesne,
   Pol.
Bartoszewo, Pol.
Baruth, Ger.
Barycz, Pol.
Barysh, Ukr.
Bastheim, Ger.
Batovo, Cz.
Batumi, Georgia
Baturnin, Ukr.
Bautzen, Ger.
Bayreuth, Ger.
Bazavluchok, Ukr.
Beau Soleil, Fr.
Beaujolais, Fr.
Bebra, Ger.
Bechhofen, Ger.
Beckum, Ger.
Beclean, Rom.
Bedo, Hun.
Bedzin, Pol.
Begoml, Bel.
Bekasmegyer, Hun.

Bekecs, Hun.
Bekescsaba, Hun.
Bela Pod Bezdezem, Cz.
Belaya Krinitsa, Ukr.
Belaya Tserkov, Ukr.
Belchatow, Pol.
Beled, Hun.
Belgorod Dnestrovskiy,
   Ukr.
Belina, Cz.
Belitsa, Bel.
Belogorsk, Ukr.
Belokorovichi, Ukr.
Belopolye, Ukr.
Beltsy, Mold.
Belyy Kamen, Ukr.
Belz, Ukr.
Belzec, Pol.
Belzyce, Pol.
Bendery, Mold.
Bendorf, Ger.
Benesov, Cz.
Benghazi, Libya
Benyakoni, Bel.
Beograd, Yugo.
Berbesti, Rom.
Bercel, Hun.
Berchem-Sainte-Agathe,
   Belg.
Berchtesgaden, Ger.
Berdechow, Pol.
Berdichev, Ukr.
Berdyansk, Ukr.
Beregomet, Ukr.
Beregovo, Ukr.
Beremyany, Ukr.
Berestechko, Ukr.
Berettyoujfalu, Hun.
Bereza, Bel.
Berezhany, Ukr.
Berezhnitsa, Bel.
Berezino, Bel.
Berezna, Ukr.
Berezno, Ukr.
Berezovka, Ukr.
Berezovo, Ukr.
Berge, Ger.

Bergen Enkheim, Ger.
Berleburg, Ger.
Berlin, Ger.
Bernau, Ger.
Bernburg, Ger.
Berndorf, Aus.
Bernhausen, Ger.
Bernkastel Kues, Ger.
Bershad, Ukr.
Berwangen, Ger.
Besancon, Fr.
Bessarabka, Mold.
Beutzenburg, Ger.
Bezdan, Yugo.
Bezdonys, Lith.
Biala Podlaska, Pol.
Biala Rawska, Pol.
Bialaczow, Pol.
Bialka, Pol.
Bialobrzegi, Pol.
Bialogard, Pol.
Bialogon, Pol.
Bialowieza, Pol.
Bialoworce, Cz.
Bialystok, Pol.
Biecz, Pol.
Biel, Cz.
Bielawa Dolna, Pol.
Bielefeld, Ger.
Bielsk, Pol.
Bielsk Podlaski, Pol.
Bielsko Biala, Pol.
Bielszowice, Pol.
Biesiadka, Pol.
Bietigheim, Ger.
Biezanow, Pol.
Bilaevka, Rom.
Bilche Zolotoye, Ukr.
Bilgoraj, Pol.
Bilki, Ukr.
Billigheim (Rhineland
   Pfalz), Ger.
Bilthoven, Neth.
Bindermichl, Aus.
Bingen, Ger.
Bircza, Pol.
Birzai, Lith.

Biskupice, Pol.
Bissum, Neth.
Bistrita, Rom.
Bitola, Yugo.
Bitolj, Maced.
Bitterfeld, Ger.
Bivolari, Rom.
Blagovshchina, Bel.
Blaszki, Pol.
Blazki, Pol.
Blazowa, Pol.
Blizyn, Pol.
Blonie, Pol.
Blumenthal bei
    Hellenthall, Ger.
Bobigny, Fr.
Bobowa, Pol.
Bobr, Bel.
Bobrka, Ukr.
Bobruysk, Bel.
Bochnia, Pol.
Bocholt, Ger.
Bochum, Ger.
Boczki Swidrowo, Pol.
Bodrogkeresztur, Hun.
Bodzanow, Pol.
Bodzentyn, Pol.
Boehl, Ger.
Bogdan, Ukr.
Bogdanovka (Tarnopol),
    Ukr.
Bogdanuvka (Zboruv
    area), Ukr.
Bogoria, Pol.
Bogorodchany, Ukr.
Bohumin, Cz.
Boizenburg, Ger.
Bolekhov, Ukr.
Boleslawiec, Pol.
Bolganymajor, Hun.
Bolgrad, Ukr.
Bolkenhain, Pol.
Bolshaya Verbcha, Ukr.
Bolshiye Luki, Bel.
Bolshovtsy, Ukr.
Bonn, Ger.
Bonyhad, Hun.

Boppard, Ger.
Bor (Yugoslavia), Yug.
Bordeaux, Fr.
Borek Falecki, Pol.
Borislav, Ukr.
Borisov, Bel.
Borken (near Essen),
    Ger.
Borki (Lublin area),
    Pol.
Borki (Lvov area), Ukr.
Borodina, Ukr.
Borsa Maramures, Rom.
Borshchev, Ukr.
Borshchevka, Ukr.
Borysuvka, Bel.
Bosen, Ger.
Botosani, Rom.
Bourges, Fr.
Boyany, Ukr.
Brabant, Belg.
Brad, Rom.
Braila, Rom.
Brandenburg, Ger.
Brandys nad Labem,
    Cz.
Bransk, Pol.
Braslav, Bel.
Brasov, Rom.
Bratislava, Cz.
Brauneberg, Ger.
Braunlage, Ger.
Braunsbach, Ger.
Braunschweig, Ger.
Brcko, Yugo.
Breclav, Cz.
Breendonk, Belg.
Breitenau, Ger.
Breitenberg, Ger.
Bremen, Ger.
Bremerhaven, Ger.
Bressoux, Belg.
Brest, Bel.
Brezno nad Hronom,
    Cz.
Brezova Pod Bradlom,
    Cz.

Brichany, Mold.
Brilon, Ger.
Briukhovo, Bel.
Brnenec, Cz.
Brno, Cz.
Brodnica, Pol.
Brody, Ukr.
Brok (Warszawa area),
    Pol.
Brok, Pol.
Bronislawowka, Ukr.
Broshnev Osada, Ukr.
Broumov, Cz.
Bruckenau, Ger.
Bruges, Belg.
Bruhl, Ger.
Brusnik, Pol.
Bruxelles, Belg.
Brwinow, Pol.
Brzeg, Pol.
Brzeg Dolny, Pol.
Brzesko Nowe, Pol.
Brzesko, Pol.
Brzezinki, Pol.
Brzeziny, Pol.
Brzeznica, Pol.
Brzozow, Pol.
Bucecea, Rom.
Buchach, Ukr.
Buchau, Ger.
Buchberg, Ger.
Buchel, Ger.
Buchloe, Ger.
Buckeburg, Ger.
Bucki, Pol.
Bucovice, Cz.
Bucuresti, Rom.
Buda Koshelevo, Bel.
Budafok, Hun.
Budakalasz, Hun.
Budanov, Ukr.
Budapest, Hun.
Budesti Maramures,
    Rom.
Budy, Ukr.
Budzyn (Lublin area),
    Pol.

Bugaj, Pol.
Buhl, Ger.
Buhusi, Rom.
Bujakow, Pol.
Bukachevtsy, Ukr.
Bukovinka, Ukr.
Bukowsko, Pol.
Bunde, Ger.
Burdujeni, Rom.
Buren, Ger.
Burg, Ger.
Burgas, Bulg.
Burgau, Ger.
Burghaslach, Ger.
Burgkunstadt, Ger.
Burgpreppach, Ger.
Burgsinn, Ger.
Burgsteinfurt, Ger.
Burshtyn, Ukr.
Busk, Ukr.
Busko Zdroj, Pol.
Buskovice, Cz.
Butrimoniai, Lith.
Butthart, Ger.
Buxtehude, Ger.
Buzau, Rom.
Byala (near Chortkov),
   Ukr.
Bychawa, Pol.
Bydgoszcz, Pol.
Bykhov, Bel.
Byki, Bel.
Bysen, Cz.
Bystra, Pol.
Bystrzyca, Pol.
Byten (Kovel area),
   Ukr.
Byten, Bel.
Bytom, Pol.
Bzesko Nowe, Pol.
Cadca, Cz.
Cakovec, Yugo.
Calbe, Ger.
Calle, Ger.
Calw, Ger.
Caputh, Ger.
Caracal, Rom.

Caransebes, Rom.
Cechowka, Pol.
Cecylowka, Pol.
Cegled, Hun.
Ceglow, Pol.
Celldomolk, Hun.
Celle, Ger.
Ceranow, Pol.
Ceske Budejovice, Cz.
Chabowka, Pol.
Cham, Ger.
Chamonix, Fr.
Charleroi, Belg.
Charsznica, Pol.
Chatelineau, Belg.
Chechelnik, Ukr.
Checiny, Pol.
Chelm, Pol.
Chelmek, Pol.
Chelmno, Pol.
Chelmza, Pol.
Chene, Belg.
Cherkassy, Ukr.
Chernelitsa, Ukr.
Chernigov, Ukr.
Chernovtsy, Ukr.
Chernyakhov, Ukr.
Cherven, Bel.
Chervonoarmeisk, Ukr.
Chervonograd, Ukr.
Chetvertinovka, Ukr.
Chimay, Belg.
Chmieliska, Ukr.
Chmielnik, Pol.
Chmielnik Potoki, Pol.
Chobedza, Pol.
Chocianowice, Pol.
Chocim (Lodz area),
   Pol.
Chocz, Pol.
Chodel, Pol.
Chodkow Nowy, Pol.
Choroszcz, Pol.
Chortkov, Ukr.
Chorzele, Pol.
Chorzow, Pol.
Choszczno, Pol.

Chrzanow, Pol.
Chuguyev, Ukr.
Chyzyny, Pol.
Ciechanow, Pol.
Ciechanowiec, Pol.
Ciechocinek, Pol.
Ciepielow, Pol.
Cieszanow, Pol.
Cieszyn, Pol.
Cieszyny, Pol.
Ciezkowice, Pol.
Cimpinita, Rom.
Cimpulung Moldovenesc,
   Rom.
Ciudin, Ukr.
Clermont, Fr.
Cluj, Rom.
Cmielow, Pol.
Coburg, Ger.
Cochem, Ger.
Codaesti, Rom.
Compiegne, Fr.
Constanta, Rom.
Constanza, Rom.
Convatin, Rom.
Corabia, Rom.
Corinth, Greece
Cottbus, Ger.
Cotu Lung, Rom.
Craiova, Rom.
Crasna, Rom.
Creglingen, Ger.
Creussen, Ger.
Cristesti, Rom.
Crna Gora, Yugo.
Cronheim, Ger.
Csenger, Hun.
Csepel, Hun.
Csillaghegy, Hun.
Csurgo, Hun.
Cuhea, Rom.
Cycow, Pol.
Czajkin, Lith.
Czarkow, Pol.
Czarna (near Pilzno),
   Pol.
Czarne, Pol.

Czarny Dunajec, Pol.
Czchow, Pol.
Czeladz, Pol.
Czemierniki, Pol.
Czeremcha, Pol.
Czerniejewo, Pol.
Czerniejow, Pol.
Czerniewicze, Bel.
Czerwin, Pol.
Czerwony Bor, Pol.
Czestochowa, Pol.
Czestoniew, Pol.
Czudec, Pol.
Czystylow, Ukr.
Czyzew, Pol.
Czyzykow, Ukr.
Czyzyny, Pol.
Dabie, Pol.
Dabrowa, Pol.
Dabrowa (near Kielce),
  Pol.
Dabrowa Gornicza, Pol.
Dabrowa Tarnowska,
  Pol.
Dabrowice, Pol.
Dachau, Ger.
Daleszyce, Pol.
Damborice, Cz.
Dandowka, Pol.
Danilowicze, Bel.
Darabani, Rom.
Darda, Yugo.
Darevnaya, Bel.
Darmstadt, Ger.
Darnitsa, Ukr.
Daruvar, Yugo.
Dashkevichi, Bel.
Datyn, Ukr.
Daugailiai, Lith.
Daugavpils, Lat.
Dautmergen, Ger.
David Gorodok, Bel.
Davideshte, Ukr.
Davidka, ?
Davidovka, Ukr.
Debica, Pol.
Deblin, Pol.

Debnik, Pol.
Debrecen, Hun.
Deggendorf, Ger.
Dej, Rom.
Deksznie, Lith.
Delft, Neth.
Delmenhorst, Ger.
Delyatichi, Bel.
Delyatin, Ukr.
Demidov, USSR
Demmelsdorf, Ger.
Demotika, Greece
Demyansk, USSR
Denkow, Pol.
Dennenlohe, Ger.
Derazhno, Ukr.
Derechin, Bel.
Derecske, Hun.
Derevok, Ukr.
Dermanka, Ukr.
Dernau, Ger.
Dettelbach, Ger.
Deurne, Belg.
Deutschkreutz, Aus.
Devavanya, Hun.
Devecser, Hun.
Didymotihou, Greece
Dieburg, Ger.
Diepholz, Ger.
Dierdorf, Ger.
Diespeck, Ger.
Dietenheim, Ger.
Dieveniskes, Lith.
Digne, Fr.
Diguri Putna, Rom.
Dillingen, Ger.
Dimidovca, Ukr.
Dinkelsbuhl, Ger.
Diosgyor, Hun.
Dirmstein, Ger.
Disna, Bel.
Dittlofsroda, Ger.
Divin, Bel.
Dlugosiodlo, Pol.
Dnepropetrovsk, Ukr.
Doaga, Rom.
Dobczyce, Pol.

Dobele, Lat.
Dobiegniew, Pol.
Dobra, Pol.
Dobra (near Limanowa),
  Pol.
Dobranowka, Ukr.
Dobreni, Rom.
Dobromil, Ukr.
Dobromysl, Bel.
Dobrzechow, Pol.
Dobrzyn nad Wisla, Pol.
Dobsina, Cz.
Doetinchem, Fr.
Dokshitsy, Bel.
Dolesheim, Aus.
Dolginovo, Bel.
Dolgorukovo, USSR
Dolhobyczow, Pol.
Dolina, Ukr.
Dolna Ludova, Cz.
Dolny Kubin, Cz.
Dolzhki, Ukr.
Domachevo, Bel.
Domanevka, Ukr.
Domaszowce Nowe,
  Ukr.
Dombovar, Hun.
Domene, Fr.
Domsod, Hun.
Donauworth, Ger.
Donets Basin, USSR
Donetsk, Ukr.
Dora, Ukr.
Dorfe Haaren, Ger.
Dornheim, Ger.
Dorohoi, Rom.
Dorohucza, Pol.
Doroshitse, Ukr.
Dorsten, Ger.
Dortmund, Ger.
Dragomiresti, Rom.
Drahisevo, Cz.
Drahovec, Ukr.
Drama, Greece
Drancy, Fr.
Drawsko, Pol.
Drensteinfurt, Ger.

Dresden, Ger.
Drnis, Yugo.
Drobin, Pol.
Drogichin, Bel.
Drogobych, Ukr.
Drohiczyn, Pol.
Dromersheim, Ger.
Drozdy, Bel.
Druskininkai, Lith.
Druya, Bel.
Druysk, Bel.
Drzewica, Pol.
Dubeczno, Pol.
Dubetsko, Pol.
Dubienka, Pol.
Dubinovo, Bel.
Dubno, Ukr.
Dubossary, Mold.
Dubovoye, Ukr.
Dubrovitsa, Ukr.
Dubrovka, ?
Dubrovnik, Yugo.
Dudelsheim, Ger.
Duderstadt, Ger.
Duisburg, Ger.
Dukla, Pol.
Dukstas, Lith.
Dukstos, Lith.
Dulmen, Ger.
Dumbraveny, Mold.
Dunaharaszti, Hun.
Dunajska Streda, Cz.
Dunarea, Rom.
Dunayev, Ukr.
Dunayevtsy, Ukr.
Dundaga, Lat.
Dunilovichi, Bel.
Durazzo, Alb.
Dusseldorf, Ger.
Dvorets, Bel.
Dworzysk, Pol.
Dyatlovo, Bel.
Dynow, Pol.
Dzerzhinsk, Bel.
Dzhankoy, Ukr.
Dzhurin, Ukr.
Dzialdowo, Pol.

Dzialki Morozowalskie,
   Pol.
Dzialoszyce, Pol.
Dziczki, Ukr.
Dzieczyna, Pol.
Dzierzbotki, Pol.
Dzierzoniow, Cz.
Dzikow Stary, Pol.
Dziwnowek, Pol.
Dzvinogrud, Ukr.
Ebelsbach, Ger.
Eberau, Aus.
Eberbach, Ger.
Ebersheim, Ger.
Eberswalde, Ger.
Echtenerburg, Neth.
Echzell, Ger.
Edeleny, Hun.
Eerbeek, Neth.
Egenhausen, Ger.
Eger, Hun.
Eggenfelden, Ger.
Eichenhausen, Ger.
Eichstatt, Ger.
Eisenbach, Ger.
Eisenberg, Ger.
Eisenerz, Aus.
Eisiskes, Lith.
Elasson, Greece
Elblag, Pol.
Ellar, Ger.
Ellingen, Ger.
Ellrich, Ger.
Elmshorn, Ger.
Eltmann, Ger.
Eltville, Ger.
Emden, Ger.
Emmetzheim, Ger.
Enschede, Neth.
Enskirchen, Ger.
Epe, Neth.
Eppingen, Ger.
Ercsi, Hun.
Erdmannsdorf, Ger.
Erfurt, Ger.
Erkelenz, Ger.
Erkner, Ger.

Erkrath, Ger.
Erlangen, Ger.
Ermershausen, Ger.
Ermetzhofen, Ger.
Ersekcsanad, Hun.
Erzvilkas, Lith.
Eschau, Ger.
Eschershausen, Ger.
Eschwege, Ger.
Essen, Ger.
Esslingen, Ger.
Estenfeld, Ger.
Esterwegen, Ger.
Etingen, Ger.
Etterbeek, Belg.
Ettlingen, Ger.
Evere, Belg.
Fajslawice, Pol.
Falenica, Pol.
Falenty, Pol.
Faleshty, Mold.
Falkenberg, Ger.
Falkensee, Ger.
Falkenstein, Ger.
Falstad, Norway
Falticeni, Rom.
Fatezh, USSR
Fechenbach, Ger.
Fehergyarmat, Hun.
Fehrbellin, Ger.
Fehring, Aus.
Fekete Ardo, Hun.
Felczyn, Pol.
Feldafing, Ger.
Feldbach, Aus.
Feldesz, Hun.
Feldmoching, Ger.
Fellheim, Ger.
Felsberg, Ger.
Felsogod, Hun.
Feodosiya, Ukr.
Ferramonti, It.
Feuchtwangen, Ger.
Filesti, Rom.
Finthen, Ger.
Firlej, Pol.
Flanders, Belg.

Flensburg, Ger.
Florence, It.
Floreshty, Mold.
Floridsdorf, Aus.
Florsheim, Ger.
Flossenburg, Ger.
Focsani, Rom.
Foltesti, Rom.
Forbach, Ger.
Forchheim, Ger.
Fossoli, It.
Framersheim, Ger.
Frampol, Pol.
Frankenberg, Ger.
Frankenthal, Ger.
Frankenwinheim, Ger.
Frankfurt am Main, Ger.
Frankfurt an der Oder,
    Ger.
Freiburg Im Breisgau,
    Ger.
Freilassing, Ger.
Freudenburg, Ger.
Freudenthal, Ger.
Friedberg, Ger.
Friesland, Neth.
Frondenberg, Ger.
Frumushika, Mold.
Frysztak, Pol.
Fulda, Ger.
Furstenberg, Ger.
Furstenfeldbruck, Ger.
Furstenzell, Ger.
Furth, Ger.
Gabin, Pol.
Gabrovo, Bulg.
Gadyach, Ukr.
Gaesti, Rom.
Gailingen, Ger.
Galanta, Cz.
Galati, Rom.
Galben, Rom.
Gambach, Ger.
Ganachevka, Ukr.
Ganacker, Ger.
Ganichi, Ukr.
Ganshoren, Belg.

Gantsevichi, Bel.
Garany, Cz.
Garbatka, Pol.
Gardelegen, Ger.
Gargzdai, Lith.
Garliava, Lith.
Garmisch Partenkirchen,
    Ger.
Garwolin, Pol.
Gasocin, Pol.
Gatchina, USSR
Gauersheim, Ger.
Gaukonigshofen, Ger.
Gauting, Ger.
Gava, Hun.
Gaysin, Ukr.
Gdansk, Pol.
Gdow, Pol.
Gdynia, Pol.
Geilenkirchen, Ger.
Geiselhoring, Ger.
Geisenheim, Ger.
Geislingen am Steige,
    Ger.
Geldern, Ger.
Geldersheim, Ger.
Gelsenkirchen, Ger.
Gemen, Ger.
Gemmingen, Ger.
Gemund, Ger.
Gemunden (Bavaria),
    Ger.
Genthin, Ger.
Georgensgmund, Ger.
Gera, Ger.
Germanovichi, Bel.
Germanuv, Ukr.
Gernrode, Ger.
Gernsbach, Ger.
Geroda, Ger.
Geroldshausen, Ger.
Gerolzhofen, Ger.
Gers, Fr.
Gerse, Hun.
Gersfeld, Ger.
Gertsa, Ukr.
Gesia Wolka, Pol.

Ghent, Belg.
Ghimes, Rom.
Ghirasa Ghira, Rom.
Gidigich, Mold.
Gidle, Pol.
Giebelstadt, Ger.
Giedraiciai, Lith.
Gielniow, Pol.
Giessen, Ger.
Giraltovce, Cz.
Giruliai, Lith.
Giulesti, Rom.
Gladenbach, Ger.
Glebokie, Bel.
Glebowice, Pol.
Gleina, Ger.
Glinice, Pol.
Glinojeck, Pol.
Glinyany, Ukr.
Gliwice, Pol.
Globino, Ukr.
Glod Maramures, Rom.
Glodowo, Pol.
Glogow, Pol.
Glowno, Pol.
Glubochek, Ukr.
Glusk, Pol.
Gnadenberg, Ger.
Gniewkowo, Pol.
Gniewoszow, Pol.
Gniezno, Pol.
Goch, Ger.
Gochsheim, Ger.
Godollo, Hun.
Gogolin, Pol.
Golab, Pol.
Goldbach, Ger.
Goldkops, Ger.
Golejow, Pol.
Goleszow, Pol.
Golina, Pol.
Gologory, Ukr.
Golovchyntse, Ukr.
Golshany, Bel.
Golta, Ukr.
Golubie, Pol.
Gomel, Bel.

Gomunice, Pol.
Goniadz, Pol.
Goppingen, Ger.
Gora Kalwaria, Pol.
Goraj Lubelski, Pol.
Gorecko, Pol.
Gorlice, Pol.
Gorlitz, Ger.
Gornostayevka, Ukr.
Gorodenka, Ukr.
Gorodishche
    (Dnepropetrovsk area),
    Ukr.
Gorodishche
    (Nowogrodek), Bel.
Gorodnitsa, Ukr.
Gorodnya, Ukr.
Gorodok (near Vitebsk),
    Bel.
Gorodok (near
    Molodechno), Bel.
Gorokhov, Ukr.
Goryngrad, Ukr.
Gorzkow (Kielce area),
    Pol.
Gorzkow, Pol.
Gorzkowice, Pol.
Goscieradow, Pol.
Goshcha, Ukr.
Goshchevo, Bel.
Goslar, Ger.
Gospic, Yugo.
Gosselies, Belg.
Gossmannsdorf am
    Main, Ger.
Gostynin, Pol.
Goteborg, Swed.
Gotha, Ger.
Gotse Delchev, Bulg.
Gottingen, Ger.
Gottwaldov, Cz.
Gowarczow, Pol.
Goworowo, Pol.
Grabce Wreckie, Pol.
Graben, Ger.
Grabkow, Pol.
Grabow (Bialystok

area), Pol.
Grabow, Pol.
Grabowa, Pol.
Grabowiec, Pol.
Grabowka (near
    Bialystok), Pol.
Gradistea, Rom.
Grafelfing, Ger.
Grajewo, Pol.
Gralewo, Pol.
Graz, Aus.
Grebenki, Ukr.
Grebenstein, Ger.
Greboszow, Pol.
Grebow, Pol.
Gregorov, Ukr.
Greifswald, Ger.
Greiz, Ger.
Gremyach, Ukr.
Greussenheim, Ger.
Grimaylov, Ukr.
Grinkiskis, Lith.
Grochow, Pol.
Grodek, Pol.
Grodkowice, Pol.
Grodno, Bel.
Grodziec (near Konin),
    Pol.
Grodzisk Mazowiecki,
    Pol.
Grodzisko Dolne, Pol.
Grojec, Pol.
Gromnik, Pol.
Gronau, Ger.
Grosolovo, Ukr.
Gross Rohrheim, Ger.
Gross Breesen, Ger.
Grossau, Aus.
Grossen Buseck, Ger.
Grossenlinden, Ger.
Grosskarben, Ger.
Grosskarlbach, Ger.
Grossostheim, Ger.
Grudziadz, Pol.
Grugliasco, It.
Grun, Ukr.
Grunow Spiegelberg,

Ger.
Grybow, Pol.
Grygorowicze, Ukr.
Gualdo Tadino, It.
Guardiagrele, It.
Gudigai, Lith.
Gulbene, Lat.
Gumniska, Pol.
Guntersblum, Ger.
Gunzenhausen, Ger.
Gura Humorului, Rom.
Gusyatin, Ukr.
Gutersloh, Ger.
Guzar, Uzbekistan
Gwozdziec, Pol.
Gyoma, Hun.
Gyor, Hun.
Hadmersleben, Ger.
Hagen, Ger.
Hagenbach, Ger.
Hague, The, Neth.
Haigerloch, Ger.
Hainsfarth, Ger.
Hajdabesernin, Hun.
Hajdubagos, Hun.
Hajduboszormeny, Hun.
Hajdudorog, Hun.
Hajduhadhaz, Hun.
Hajdunanas, Hun.
Hajnowka, Pol.
Halberstadt, Ger.
Halic, Cz.
Hallenberg, Ger.
Hamborn, Ger.
Hamburg, Ger.
Hamm, Ger.
Hammelburg, Ger.
Han Pijesak, Yugo.
Hanau am Main, Ger.
Handlova, Cz.
Hango, Fin.
Hannover, Ger.
Hansk, Pol.
Hantesti, Rom.
Hanusovce nad Toplou,
    Cz.
Hanusovice, Cz.

Harburg, Ger.
Haren, Ger.
Harlingen, Neth.
Hasenhecke Siedlung,
    Ger.
Haslach, Ger.
Hasselt, Belg.
Hassfurt, Ger.
Hassloch, Ger.
Hatvan, Hun.
Hausberge an der Porta,
    Ger.
Hauzenberg, Ger.
Hechingen, Ger.
Heci, Rom.
Hegyeshalom, Hun.
Heidelberg, Ger.
Heidenheim, Ger.
Heilbronn, Ger.
Heiligenstadt (Bavaria),
    Ger.
Heinichen, Ger.
Heinsberg, Ger.
Hejobaba, Hun.
Hejocsaba, Hun.
Hel, Pol.
Heldenbergen, Ger.
Helenow, Pol.
Helmond, Neth.
Helmstedt, Ger.
Hemer, Ger.
Hengelo, Neth.
Heppenheim an der
    Bergstrasse, Ger.
Herault, Fr.
Hernadcsany, Cz.
Herne, Ger.
Herrlingen, Ger.
Hersbruck, Ger.
Herstal, Belg.
Hertogenbosch, Neth.
Herxheim, Ger.
Herzfeld, Ger.
Hessdorf, Ger.
Hessental, Ger.
Hessisch Lichtenau, Ger.
Heuberg, Ger.

Heusden, Belg.
Hildesheim, Ger.
Hilversum, Neth.
Himbach, Ger.
Hindesdorf, Aus.
Hinzert, Ger.
Hirlau, Rom.
Hirschaid, Ger.
Hlohovec, Cz.
Hluboczek Wielki, Ukr.
Hnidawa, Ukr.
Hochberg, Ger.
Hochheim am Main, Ger.
Hochst Im Odenwald,
    Ger.
Hockenheim, Ger.
Hodmezovasarhely, Hun.
Hodonin, Cz.
Hof, Ger.
Hoffenheim, Ger.
Hofgeismar, Ger.
Hofheim am Taunus,
    Ger.
Hohenlimburg, Ger.
Holberg, Ger.
Hollenberg, Ger.
Holobutow, Ukr.
Homberg, Ger.
Homburg am Main, Ger.
Homokterenye, Hun.
Honningen, Ger.
Horb, Ger.
Horde, Ger.
Horincevo, Cz.
Horni Hyncina, Cz.
Horodyszcze, Pol.
Horstein, Ger.
Horstmar, Ger.
Hoxter, Ger.
Hrubieszow, Pol.
Huciska, Pol.
Huckelhoven, Ger.
Huffenhardt, Ger.
Huls, Ger.
Humenne, Cz.
Huncovce, Cz.
Hundsfeld, Ger.

Hunfeld, Ger.
Hungen, Ger.
Hurby, Ukr.
Huta (near Kielce), Pol.
Huta (Lwow), Pol.
Huta (Wolyn), Ukr.
Huta Komorowska, Pol.
Huttendorf, Ger.
Huttenheim, Ger.
Iacobeni, Rom.
Iasi, Rom.
Ibrany, Hun.
Ichenhausen, Ger.
Idar Oberstein, Ger.
Igling, Ger.
Iglita, Rom.
Ignalina, Lith.
Ignatovka, Ukr.
Iklad, Hun.
Ilanets, Ukr.
Ilava, Cz.
Ilawa, Pol.
Ileanda, Rom.
Ilintsy, Ukr.
Ilvesheim, Ger.
Ilvov, Rom.
Ilya, Bel.
Ilza, Pol.
Indura, Pol.
Ingelheim, Ger.
Inheiden, Ger.
Innsbruck, Aus.
Inowlodz, Pol.
Inowroclaw, Pol.
Invancice, Cz.
Ioannina, Greece
Iody, Bel.
Irshava, Ukr.
Isaccea, Rom.
Itcani, Rom.
Ivanichi, Ukr.
Ivanka Pri Dunaji, Cz.
Ivano Frankovsk, Ukr.
Ivano Frankovo, Ukr.
Ivanovka (near
    Zhitomir), Ukr.
Ivanovo, Bel.

Ivatsevichi, Bel.
Ivenets, Bel.
Ivye, Bel.
Iwaniska, Pol.
Iwonicz Zdroj, ?
Iza, Ukr.
Izabelin, Bel.
Izbica (Lubelska), Pol.
Izbica Kujawska, Pol.
Izbica, Pol.
Izdebnik, Pol.
Izluchistoye, Ukr.
Izyaslav, Ukr.
Jablon, Pol.
Jablonna, Pol.
Jablonna Legionowo,
   Pol.
Jablunkov, Cz.
Jadow, Pol.
Jajinci, Yugo.
Jaksice, Pol.
Jalowka, Pol.
Jambes, Belg.
Janoshaza, Hun.
Janow Lubelski, Pol.
Janow Sokolski, Pol.
Janowice, Pol.
Janowo, Pol.
Jarczew, Pol.
Jarocin (near
   Tarnobrzeg), Pol.
Jaroslaw, Pol.
Jaroszyn, Pol.
Jarzt, Ger.
Jasenovac, Yugo.
Jasienica (Bialystok
   area), Pol.
Jasienica (Kielce area),
   Pol.
Jasionowka, Pol.
Jasiunai, Lith.
Jasliska, Pol.
Jaslo, Pol.
Jastkow, Pol.
Jaszbereny, Hun.
Jawiszowice, Pol.
Jawornik Polski, Pol.

Jaworzno, Pol.
Jaworzyna Slaska, Pol.
Jedlicze, Pol.
Jedlnia, Pol.
Jedrzejow, Pol.
Jedwabne, Pol.
Jelenia Gora, Pol.
Jelgava, Lat.
Jelnia, Pol.
Jelsava, Cz.
Jennersdorf, Aus.
Jesberg, Ger.
Jesenik, Cz.
Jette, Belg.
Jever, Ger.
Jeziorna Krolewska,
   Pol.
Jiblea, Rom.
Jibou, Rom.
Jieznas, Lith.
Jilava, Rom.
Jodlowa, Pol.
Jodlownik, Pol.
Jonava, Lith.
Joniskis, Lith.
Jordanow, Pol.
Jozefka, Ukr.
Jozefow (Nad Wisla),
   Pol.
Jozefow Stary (Kielce),
   Pol.
Judenburg, Aus.
Jugenheim, Ger.
Jumet, Belg.
Jumpravmuiza, Lat.
Jurbarkas, Lith.
Jurcauti, Ukr.
Jutas, Hun.
Juterbog, Ger.
Kadarkut, Hun.
Kadobovtsy, Ukr.
Kadzielnia, Pol.
Kaerpen bei Bergheim,
   Ger.
Kaiserslautern, Ger.
Kaisiadorys, Lith.
Kakhovka, Ukr.

Kalami, Greece
Kalarash, Mold.
Kaldenkirchen, Ger.
Kaliningrad, USSR
Kalisz, Pol.
Kalkar, Ger.
Kallo, Hun.
Kallosemjen, Hun.
Kalnik, Ukr.
Kalocsa, Hun.
Kaltinenai, Lith.
Kalush, Ukr.
Kaluszyn, Pol.
Kalvarija, Lith.
Kalwaria Zebrzydowska,
   Pol.
Kamecze, Hun.
Kamen, Bel.
Kamen Kashirskiy, Ukr.
Kamenets, Bel.
Kamenets Podolskiy,
   Ukr.
Kamenka Bugskaya,
   Ukr.
Kamenka Dneprovskaja,
   Ukr.
Kamenki, Ukr.
Kamennoye, Ukr.
Kamiensk, Pol.
Kamilonisi, Greece
Kamionka (Bialystok),
   Pol.
Kamionka Wielka (near
   Nowy Sacz), Pol.
Kampinos, Pol.
Kanczuga, Pol.
Kanie, Pol.
Kaniowka, Pol.
Kaposvar, Hun.
Kapustyany, Ukr.
Karait, Ukr.
Karanac, Yugo.
Karbach, Ger.
Karcag, Hun.
Karczew, Pol.
Karlmarxstadt, Ger.
Karlovka, Ukr.

Karlovy Vary, Cz.
Karlsruhe, Ger.
Karlstadt, Ger.
Karmacs, Hun.
Karnich, Bel.
Karniewo, Pol.
Karolinka, Bel.
Karolyuvka, Ukr.
Karsfeld Allach, Ger.
Karsy, Pol.
Kartuzy, Pol.
Kassel, Ger.
Kastellaun, Ger.
Kastoria, Greece
Kasubassa, Ukr.
Katowice, Pol.
Kaufbeuren, Ger.
Kaufering, Ger.
Kaunas, Lith.
Kaushany, Mold.
Kavaja, Alb.
Kavalla, Greece
Kazakhstan
Kazan, USSR
Kazanow, Pol.
Kazimierowka, Pol.
Kazimierz Dolny, Pol.
Kazimierza Wielka, Pol.
Kazimirka, Ukr.
Kazlu Ruda, Lith.
Kecskemet, Hun.
Kedainiai, Lith.
Kehl, Ger.
Kelme, Lith.
Kemecse, Hun.
Kempten, Ger.
Kepa Tarchominska,
Kepno, Pol.
Kerch, Ukr.
Kerkira, Greece
Kessel, Neth.
Keszthely, Hun.
Ketrzyn, Pol.
Keturiasdesimt Totoriu,
  Lith.
Kezmarok, Cz.
Khalkis, Greece

Kharkov, Ukr.
Kherson, Ukr.
Khislavichi, USSR
Khmelnitskiy, Ukr.
Khmelno, Ukr.
Khodorov, Ukr.
Kholmy, Ukr.
Khomsk, Bel.
Khorokhorin, Ukr.
Khorol, Ukr.
Khoroshovtsy, Ukr.
Khorostkov, Ukr.
Khoslavichi, Bel
Khotimsk, Bel.
Khotin, Ukr.
Khoyniki, Bel.
Khust, Ukr.
Khutor Tarasivka, Ukr.
Kiel, Ger.
Kielbasy, Pol.
Kielce, Pol.
Kine, Lith.
Kirchberg, Ger.
Kirchhain, Ger.
Kirchheim
  (Unterfranken), Ger.
Kirn, Ger.
Kirovograd, Ukr.
Kirschberg, Ger.
Kiselin, Ukr.
Kishinev, Mold.
Kiskoros, Hun.
Kiskunhalas, Hun.
Kislovodsk, USSR
Kispest, Hun.
Kistarcsa, Hun.
Kisterenye, Hun.
Kisvarda, Hun.
Kitzingen, Ger.
Kivertsy, Ukr.
Kiyev, Ukr.
Kladno, Cz.
Klagenfurt, Aus.
Klaipeda, Lith.
Klatovy, Cz.
Kleczew, Pol.
Kleinbardorf, Ger.

Kleindexen, Ger.
Kleineibstadt, Ger.
Kleinheubach, Ger.
Kleinlangheim, Ger.
Kleinsteinach, Ger.
Kleinwallstadt, Ger.
Klemensow, Pol.
Klesov, Ukr.
Kleszczele, Pol.
Kletnya, USSR
Kletsk, Bel.
Klevan, Ukr.
Kleve, Ger.
Klimontow, Pol.
Klimonty, Pol.
Klimovo, USSR
Klin, USSR
Klingenberg am Main,
  Ger.
Klintsy, USSR
Klobuck, Pol.
Kloczew, Pol.
Klokotyna, Bel.
Klooga, Est.
Knyszyn, Pol.
Kobaj, Ukr.
Kobaki, Ukr.
Kobelyaki, Ukr.
Kobern, Ger.
Kobiljak, Ukr.
Koblenz, Ger.
Kobrin, Bel.
Kobylany, Pol.
Kobylczyna, Pol.
Kobyle Pole, Pol.
Kobylin, Pol.
Kobylnik, Bel.
Kochendorf, Ger.
Kock, Pol.
Kocmyrzow, Pol.
Koczanow, Pol.
Koden, Pol.
Kodyma, Ukr.
Koekelberg, Belg.
Koflach, Aus.
Kolacze, Pol.
Kolbiel, Pol.

Kolbuszowa, Pol.
Koldychevo, Bel.
Kolendzyany, Ukr.
Kolki, Ukr.
Kolleda, Ger.
Koln, Ger.
Kolno, Pol.
Kolo, Pol.
Kolobrzeg, Pol.
Kolodishchi, Bel.
Kolomyya, Ukr.
Kolonie Zoludzk, Ukr.
Kolpino, USSR
Koluszki, Pol.
Komarniki, Ukr.
Komarno (near Lvov),
    Ukr.
Komarno, Cz.
Komarom, Hun.
Komarow, Pol.
Komarowka, Pol.
Kommunarsk, Ukr.
Konary, Pol.
Kondraciszki, Bel.
Koniecpol, Pol.
Konigsberg (Bavaria),
    Ger.
Konigsfeld, Ger.
Konigshofen, Ger.
Konin, Pol.
Konopki, Pol.
Konskie, Pol.
Konskowola, Pol.
Konstantinovka, Ukr.
Konstantynovka, Ukr.
Konstantynow Lodzki,
    Pol.
Konstantynow, Pol.
Konstanz, Ger.
Konyushki (Tarnopol),
    Ukr.
Konz, Ger.
Kopachovka, Ukr.
Kopaliny, Pol.
Kopaygorod, Ukr.
Kopeisk, USSR
Kopetkowa, Pol.

Kopishche, Bel.
Koprzywnica, Pol.
Kopychintsy, Ukr.
Kopyl, Bel.
Kopys, Bel.
Korcula, Yugo.
Korczyn, Pol.
Korczyna, Pol.
Korelichi, Bel.
Korets, Ukr.
Korezule, Ukr.
Korfantow, Pol.
Kormend, Hun.
Kornwestheim, Ger.
Korobcheny, Mold.
Korolevo, Ukr.
Korond, Ukr.
Koronowo, Pol.
Koropets, Ukr.
Korost, Ukr.
Korosten, Ukr.
Korostyshev, Ukr.
Korycin, Pol.
Korynkovka, Ukr.
Korzeniec, Pol.
Korzenna, Pol.
Kos, Greece
Koshelevo, Ukr.
Kosice, Cz.
Kosiny, Ukr.
Kosov, Ukr.
Kosow Lacki, Pol.
Kossovo, Bel.
Kostolna, Cz.
Kostopol, Ukr.
Koszeg, Hun.
Koszow, Ukr.
Koszyce, Pol.
Kotaj, Hun.
Kotzting, Ger.
Kovarberence, Rom.
Kovel, Ukr.
Kowale Panskie, Pol.
Kozaki, Ukr.
Kozia Gora, Ukr.
Kozienice, Pol.
Kozin, Ukr.

Koziny, Pol.
Kozlovshchina, Bel.
Kozlow (near Miechow),
    Pol.
Kozlow, Ukr.
Kozminek, Pol.
Kozova, Ukr.
Kozyany, Bel.
Krajow Nowy, Ukr.
Krajowice, Pol.
Krakow, Pol.
Kraljevica, Yugo.
Kralovsky Chlmec, Cz.
Kramsk, Pol.
Kranjska Gora, Yugo.
Krapkowice, Pol.
Kraskow, Pol.
Krasne (Wolyn), Ukr.
Krasne (near
    Molodechno), Bel.
Krasne (near Vilnius),
    Lith.
Krasniczyn, Pol.
Krasnik, Pol.
Krasnobrod, Pol.
Krasnodar, USSR
Krasnograd, Ukr.
Krasnopolye, Ukr.
Krasnosielc, Pol.
Krasnystaw, Pol.
Kraziai, Lith.
Krefeld, Ger.
Krekenava, Lith.
Krekhovichi, Ukr.
Kremenchug, Ukr.
Kremenets, Ukr.
Kremintsy, Ukr.
Kremnica, Cz.
Kretinga, Lith.
Kretowce, ?
Krevo, Bel.
Krichevo, Ukr.
Kripuli, Bel.
Kriukai, Lith.
Krivichi, Bel.
Krivitsa, Bel.
Krivoklat, Cz.

Krivoy Rog, Ukr.
Krivoye Ozero, Ukr.
Krnov, Cz.
Krole Duze, Pol.
Krolikow, Pol.
Kropevnik, Ukr.
Kroscienko (near Nowy Targ), Pol.
Krosenko, Ukr.
Krosniewice, Pol.
Krosno, Pol.
Krotzenburg, Ger.
Krugloye, Bel.
Krumbach, Ger.
Krupki, Bel.
Krusznik, Pol.
Kruszyna, Pol.
Krychow, ?
Krylow, Pol.
Krynica Wies, Pol.
Krynki, Pol.
Kryzhopol, Ukr.
Krzemienica (near Mielec), Pol.
Krzepice, Pol.
Krzeszow, Pol.
Krzeszowiec, Pol.
Krzeszowka, Pol.
Krzystkowice, Pol.
Krzywiczki, Pol.
Ksiaz Wielki, Pol.
Kuban, Mold.
Kubarty, Lith.
Kubayuvka, Ukr.
Kublichi, Bel.
Kudirkos Naumiestis, Lith.
Kukucze, Lith.
Kulesze Koscielne, Pol.
Kulikov, Ukr.
Kumow Majoracki, Pol.
Kunmadaras, Hun.
Kunow, Pol.
Kupel, Ukr.
Kuppenheim, Ger.
Kurdwanowka, Ukr.
Kurdyban, Ukr.

Kurenets, Bel.
Kurovichi, Ukr.
Kurow, Pol.
Kursenai, Lith.
Kursk, USSR
Kurtuvenai, Lith.
Kurzyna, Pol.
Kutno, Pol.
Kuty, Ukr.
Kuziai, Lith.
Kuzmintsy, Ukr.
Kuznica, Pol.
Kybartai, Lith.
Laasphe, Ger.
Labunki, Pol.
Lackie Wielkie, Ukr.
Lacko, Pol.
Lad, Pol.
Ladce, Cz.
Ladenburg, Ger.
Ladosno, Bel.
Ladyzhin, Ukr.
Lagedi, Est.
Lager Lechfeld, Ger.
Lagisza, Pol.
Lagow, Pol.
Lakhva, Bel.
Lampertheim, Ger.
Lanchin, Ukr.
Lancut, Pol.
Landau an der Isar, Ger.
Landeck (Austria), Aus.
Landsberg am Lech, Ger.
Landshut, Ger.
Landstuhl, Ger.
Langen, Ger.
Langenaltheim, Ger.
Langendiebach, Ger.
Langenfeld (Rhineland), Ger.
Langenselbold, Ger.
Lanovtsy, Ukr.
Lanowice, Ukr.
Lapanow, Pol.
Lapy, Pol.
Laren, Neth.

Larissa, Greece
Lask, Pol.
Laskarzew, Pol.
Laskowice Olawskie, Pol.
Lasocin, Pol.
Lastovo, Yugo.
Laszczow, Pol.
Lathen, Ger.
Latowicz, Pol.
Laubach, Ger.
Laudenbach, Ger.
Laufenselden, Ger.
Laukuva, Lith.
Lautrec, Fr.
Lavochne, Ukr.
Lavrov, Ukr.
Lebedevo, Bel.
Lebedin, Ukr.
Lebork, Pol.
Lechow, Pol.
Lechowek, Pol.
Lecsmer, Hun.
Leczna, Pol.
Leczyca, Pol.
Leeuharden, Neth.
Legden, Ger.
Legionowo, Pol.
Legnica, Pol.
Leh, Hun.
Leiha, Ger.
Leihgestern, Ger.
Leimersheim, Ger.
Leipheim, Ger.
Leipzig, Ger.
Leiwen, Ger.
Leki (Krakow area), Pol.
Leki (Lwow), Pol.
Lelow, Pol.
Lemforde, Ger.
Lemgo, Ger.
Lendershausen, Ger.
Lengerich, Ger.
Lenin, Bel.
Leningrad, USSR
Leordina, Rom.

Lepel, Bel.
Lerche, Ger.
Leros, Greece
Lesienice, Ukr.
Lesko, Pol.
Lesno Brdo, Yug.
Lesnowo, Pol.
Lesnoy Khlebichin, Ukr.
Lespezi, Rom.
Letichev, Ukr.
Leubsdorf, Ger.
Leutershausen, Ger.
Leverkusen, Ger.
Levice, Cz.
Levoca, Cz.
Lezajsk, Pol.
Lezhanovka, Ukr.
Liberec, Cz.
Libna, Cz.
Librantowa, Pol.
Lich, Ger.
Lichtenau (Westphalia), Ger.
Lichtenberg (Brandenburg area), Ger.
Lichtenfels, Ger.
Lichterfelde, Ger.
Lida, Bel.
Lidice, Cz.
Liebarska Lucka, Cz.
Liebenau, Aus.
Lieberose, Ger.
Liege, Belg.
Liepaja, Lat.
Liezen, Aus.
Lika, Yug.
Likavitos, Greece
Limanowa, Pol.
Limburg an der Lahn, Ger.
Limburg, Belg.
Limoges, Fr.
Lindau, Ger.
Lindheim, Ger.
Lingen, Ger.
Linkmenys, Lith.

Linkuva, Lith.
Linz, Aus.
Liozno, Bel.
Lipiczany, Bel.
Lipkany, Mold.
Lipnishki, Bel.
Lipno, Pol.
Lipova, Cz.
Lipowa, ?
Lippstadt, Ger.
Lipsko, Pol.
Lipsko (near Zamosc), Pol.
Liptovsky Hradok, Cz.
Liptovsky Svaty Mikulas, Cz.
Lisnyaki, Ukr.
Lisowce, Ukr.
Liszno, Pol.
Litomerice, Cz.
Ljubljana, Yugo.
Lochow, Pol.
Lodz, Pol.
Logosk, Bel.
Logoysk, Bel.
Lohr, Ger.
Lokhvitsa, Ukr.
Lom, Bulg.
Lomazy, Pol.
Lomianki, Pol.
Lomza, Pol.
Loosdrechtsche, Neth.
Lopatin, Ukr.
Lopuszno, Pol.
Loretto, Aus.
Losice, Pol.
Lososno, Bel.
Louvain, Pol.
Louviere, La, Belg.
Lovosice, Cz.
Lowcza, Pol.
Lowicz, Pol.
Loyev, Bel.
Lozno Aleksandrovka, Ukr.
Lubaczow, Pol.
Lubartow, Pol.

Lubavichi, USSR
Lubeck, Ger.
Lublin, Pol.
Lubny, Ukr.
Lucenec, Cz.
Luchinets, Ukr.
Luchkovtsy, Ukr.
Luckenwalde, Ger.
Lucmierz, Pol.
Luczyce, Pol.
Ludcrinetz, Ukr.
Ludenscheid, Ger.
Ludinghausen, Ger.
Ludus, Rom.
Ludwigsburg, Ger.
Ludwigshafen, Ger.
Ludwigslust, Ger.
Ludwikowo, Pol.
Ludwisin, ?
Luginy, Ukr.
Luka (Stanislawow), Ukr.
Lukovitsa, Ukr.
Lukow, Pol.
Lukowo, Pol.
Lulsfeld, Ger.
Luneburg, Ger.
Luneburger Heide, Ger.
Lunen, Ger.
Luninets, Bel.
Luoke, Lith.
Luta, Pol.
Lutherstadt Wittenberg, Ger.
Lutomiersk, Pol.
Lutsk, Ukr.
Lututow, Pol.
Luzhany, Ukr.
Lvov, Ukr.
Lyakhovichi, Bel.
Lygumai, Lith.
Lyntupy, Bel.
Lyon, Fr.
Lyskovo, Bel.
Lysobyki, Pol.
Lyuban (near Volozhin), Bel.

Lyubashevo, Bel.
Lyubcha, Bel.
Lyubeshov, Ukr.
Lyuboml, Ukr.
Lyubyaz, Ukr.
Maastricht, Neth.
Macedonia
Maciejowa, Pol.
Maciejowice, Pol.
Macin, Rom.
Mad, Hun.
Magdeburg, Ger.
Magnuszew, Pol.
Magyarfalva, Hun.
Magyarszek, Hun.
Maikop, ?
Mainbernheim, Ger.
Mainstockheim, Ger.
Mainz, Ger.
Mainz Weisenau, Ger.
Maisiagala, Lith.
Majdan Krolewski, Pol.
Majdanek, Pol.
Majowka, Pol.
Mako, Hun.
Makoszyn, Pol.
Makow Mazowiecki,
 Pol.
Makow Podhalanski,
 Pol.
Maksimets, Ukr.
Mala, Pol.
Malacky, Cz.
Malaya Glusha, Ukr.
Malchow, Ger.
Male Sedlishche, Ukr.
Malin, Ukr.
Malines, Belg.
Malki, Pol.
Malkinia Gorna, Pol.
Malmo, Swed.
Malogoszcz, Pol.
Maloyaroslavets, USSR
Malsch, Ger.
Malynsk, Ukr.
Malyy Trostenets, Bel.
Manevichi, Ukr.

Mankovka, Ukr.
Mannheim, Ger.
Marburg an der Lahn,
 Ger.
Marcali, Hun.
Marcinelle, Belg.
Marcinkonys, Lith.
Marianske Lazne, Cz.
Marijampole, Lith.
Marina Gorka, Bel.
Markauciskes, Lith.
Marki, Pol.
Markkleeberg, Ger.
Markowa, Pol.
Markt Berolzheim, Ger.
Markt Erlbach, Ger.
Marktheidenfeld, Ger.
Marktredwitz, Ger.
Marktsteft, Ger.
Markuleshty, Mold.
Markuszow, Pol.
Maroldsweisach, Ger.
Marseilles, Fr.
Martynovka, Ukr.
Massbach, Ger.
Mateszalka, Hun.
Matsiov, Ukr.
Mauthausen, Aus.
Maxdorf, Ger.
Mazeikiai, Lith.
Mazury, Pol.
Mechernich, Ger.
Mechetinskaya, USSR
Mecklenburg, Ger.
Medebach, Ger.
Medias, Rom.
Medin, Ukr.
Medzilaborce, Cz.
Meiningen, Ger.
Melitopol, Ukr.
Mellrichstadt, Ger.
Melnitsa Podolskaya,
 Ukr.
Melsele, Belg.
Memmelsdorf, Ger.
Memmingen, Ger.
Menden, Ger.

Menschede, Ger.
Meppen, Ger.
Merkine, Lith.
Merzig, Ger.
Meudt, Ger.
Meuselwitz, Ger.
Mezaparks, Lat.
Mezhgorye, Ukr.
Mezhirichi, Ukr.
Mezocsat, Hun.
Mezokeresztes, Hun.
Mezokovesd, Hun.
Mezoladany, Hun.
Mezotur, Hun.
Miadziol, Lith.
Miadziol Nowy, Bel.
Miadziol Stary, Bel.
Miaskowo, Pol.
Michalovce, Cz.
Michalowo, Pol.
Michelbach (Bavaria),
 Ger.
Michelstadt, Ger.
Michow Lubartowski,
 Pol.
Miechow, Pol.
Miedzeszyn, Pol.
Miedzianka, Pol.
Miedzno, Pol.
Miedzychod, Pol.
Miedzyrzec Podlaski,
 Pol.
Mielec, Pol.
Mienia, Pol.
Miercurea Ciuc, Rom.
Migovoye, Ukr.
Mihaifalau, ?
Mihaileni, Rom.
Mikashevichi, Bel.
Mikepercs, Hun.
Mikhalishki, Bel.
Mikhaylovka, Ukr.
Mikolow, Pol.
Mikulichin, Ukr.
Mikulintsy, Ukr.
Mikulov, Cz.
Milano, It.

Milanow, Pol.
Milanowek, Pol.
Milcha, Bel.
Milejow, Pol.
Milosna, Pol.
Miltenberg, Ger.
Mindelheim, Ger.
Minden, Ger.
Minkovtsy, Ukr.
Minsk, Bel.
Minsk Mazowiecki, Pol.
Miory, Bel.
Mir, Bel.
Mirashasa, Hun.
Mircze, Pol.
Mirgorod, Ukr.
Mirocice, Pol.
Miroslav, Cz.
Miroslavas, Lith.
Miske, Hun.
Miskolc, Hun.
Miszewo, Pol.
Mitocu Balan, Rom.
Mitrovica, Yug.
Mittelsinn, Ger.
Mittenwald, Ger.
Mitulin, Ukr.
Mizoch, Ukr.
Mlawa, Pol.
Mlinov, Ukr.
Mlyny, Pol.
Modliborzyce, Pol.
Modlin, Pol.
Modrice, Cz.
Modrzejow, Pol.
Mogielnica, Pol.
Mogila, Pol.
Mogilev, Bel.
Mogilev Podolskiy, Ukr.
Mogilno (near Poznan),
   Pol.
Mogneszty, Rom.
Mohacs, Hun.
Moinesti, Rom.
Moiseiu, Rom.
Mokobody, Pol.
Mokrovo, Bel.

Molchad, Bel.
Molodechno, Bel.
Molodziatycze, Pol.
Mologhia, Ukr.
Monastyriska, Ukr.
Monchen Gladbach,
   Ger.
Monchsroth, Ger.
Monor, Hun.
Montagne Noire, Fr.
Montegnee, Belg.
Montpellier, Fr.
Montreuil-sur-Mer, Fr.
Moosburg, Ger.
Moravska Trebova, Cz.
Mordy, Pol.
Moreni, Rom.
Moringen, Ger.
Morshin, Ukr.
Mortsel, Belg.
Moscice, Pol.
Mosonmagyarovar,
   Hun.
Mostar, Yugo.
Mostiska, Ukr.
Mostovoye, Ukr.
Moszczenica (Lodz area),
   Pol.
Mrozy, Pol.
Mstow, Pol.
Mszana Dolna, Pol.
Mszczonow, Pol.
Much, Ger.
Muchea, Rom.
Muhldorf, Ger.
Muhlhausen (Bavaria),
   Ger.
Muhlhausen, Ger.
Muhringen, Ger.
Mukachevo, Ukr.
Mulheim (near Koblenz),
   Ger.
Mulheim an der Ruhr,
   Ger.
Munchberg, Ger.
Munchen, Ger.
Munster, Ger.

Muntenia, Rom.
Murafa, Ukr.
Murau, Aus.
Murava, Ukr.
Murnau, Ger.
Muryjovo, Ukr.
Musninkai, Lith.
Muszaly, Hun.
Muszyna, Pol.
Mutterstadt, Ger.
Myjava, Cz.
Myshkovtse, Ukr.
Myslenice, Pol.
Myslow, Pol.
Myslowice, Pol.
Myszkow, Pol.
Nacha, Bel.
Nacina Ves, Cz.
Nadvornaya, Ukr.
Nagyborzsova, Cz.
Nagyecsed, Hun.
Nagykallo, Hun.
Nagykanizsa, Hun.
Nagykata, Hun.
Nagyoroszi, Hun.
Nagyvarsany, Hun.
Naleczow, Pol.
Naliboki, Bel.
Namur, Belg.
Narayev, Ukr.
Narayevka, Ukr.
Narew, Pol.
Narocz, Bel.
Narol, Pol.
Narva, Est.
Nasielsk, Pol.
Nassau, Ger.
Naujasis Daugeliskis,
   Lith.
Naujoji Vilna, Lith.
Naumburg, Ger.
Nebylov, Ukr.
Neckarbischofsheim, Ger.
Negresti, Rom.
Nehoiu, Rom.
Neidenstein, Ger.
Nekhvoroshcha, Ukr.

Nellingen, Ger.
Nemaksciai, Lith.
Nemencine, Lith.
Nemesvid, Hun.
Nemirov (near Lvov), Ukr.
Nemirov, Ukr.
Nenzenheim, Ger.
Nepolokovtsy, Ukr.
Nerezice, Ukr.
Nesterov, Ukr.
Nesvizh, Bel.
Neu Isenburg, Ger.
Neu Ulm, Ger.
Neubrandenburg, Ger.
Neuendorf Uber Furstenwald, Ger.
Neuengamme, Ger.
Neuhammer, Ger.
Neuhaus, Ger.
Neuhof, Ger.
Neuilly, Fr.
Neumagen, Ger.
Neumark, ?
Neumarkt in der Oberpfalz, Ger.
Neunkirchen (Germany), Ger.
Neustadt, Ger.
Neustadt an der Aisch, Ger.
Neustadt an der Weinstrasse, Ger.
Neustadt bei Coburg, Ger.
Neuwied, Ger.
Nevel, USSR
Nezhin, Ukr.
Nezviska, Ukr.
Nice, Fr.
Nidzica, Pol.
Niebylec, Pol.
Nieder Mockstadt, Ger.
Nieder Olm, Ger.
Nieder Selters, Ger.
Niederbieber, Ger.
Niederbuhl, Ger.

Niederlahnstein, Ger.
Niedermarsberg, Ger.
Niedermemmel, Ger.
Niederwerrn, Ger.
Niemen, Bel.
Niemirki, Pol.
Niemojki, Pol.
Nienburg, Ger.
Niepolomice, Pol.
Nieprzesnia, Pol.
Nierendorf, Ger.
Nietkow, Pol.
Nieuport, Belg.
Niewierz, Ukr.
Niewirkow, Pol.
Nikolayev, Ukr.
Nikopol, Ukr.
Niksdorf, Ger.
Nis, Yugo.
Nisko, Pol.
Nitra, Cz.
Niwka, Pol.
Nizhnev, Ukr.
Nizhneye Selishche, Ukr.
Nizhniye Veretski, Ukr.
Norden, Ger.
Nordhausen, Ger.
Nordheim vor der Rhon, Ger.
Nordhorn, Ger.
Nordlingen, Ger.
Nosarzewo, Pol.
Nova Gradiska, Yugo.
Novaky, Cz.
Nove Mesto, ?
Nove Mesto nad Vahom, Cz.
Nove Zamky, Cz.
Novgorod, Ukr.
Novi Becej, Yugo.
Novi Sad, Yugo.
Novo Pashkovo, Bel.
Novo Ukrainka, Ukr.
Novograd Volynskiy, Ukr.
Novogrudok, Bel.

Novomoskovsk, Ukr.
Novoselovskoye, Ukr.
Novoseltsy, Ukr.
Novosyulki, Ukr.
Novoukrainka, Ukr.
Novoyelnya, Bel.
Novy Hrozenkov, Cz.
Novyy Sverzhen, Bel.
Novyy Vitkov, Ukr.
Novyy Yarychev, Ukr.
Novyye Selishty, Mold.
Nowa Sol, Pol.
Nowe Miasto, Pol.
Nowosiolki, ?
Nowy Dwor Mazowiecki, Pol.
Nowy Dwor, Pol.
Nowy Korczyn, Pol.
Nowy Sacz, Pol.
Nowy Swierzen, Bel.
Nowy Targ, Pol.
Nowy Tomysl, Pol.
Nur, Pol.
Nurnberg, Ger.
Nyirbator, Hun.
Nyiregyhaza, Hun.
Nyirmada, Hun.
Nysa, Pol.
Obbach, Ger.
Obeliai, Lith.
Oberaltertheim, Ger.
Oberelsbach, Ger.
Oberlahnstein, Ger.
Oberlauringen, Ger.
Oberlustadt, Ger.
Obernbreit, Ger.
Obernzell, Ger.
Oberriedenberg, Ger.
Oberthulba, Ger.
Obertin, Ukr.
Obodovka, Ukr.
Ochakov, Ukr.
Ochotnica Dolna, Pol.
Ochsenfurt, Ger.
Odenwaldstettin, Ger.
Odessa, Ukr.
Odobesti, Rom.

Odorhei, Rom.
Oelde, Ger.
Offenbach, Ger.
Offenburg, Ger.
Ogre, Lat.
Ohrdruf, Ger.
Okno, Ukr.
Okolitsa, Lith.
Okrzeja, Pol.
Oktyabrskiy, Bel.
Okuniew, Pol.
Olching, Ger.
Olchowczyk, Ukr.
Oldenburg, Ger.
Olecko, Pol.
Olesnica, Pol.
Olesznica, Pol.
Oleszyce, Pol.
Oleyevo Korolevka,
 Ukr.
Olgopol, Ukr.
Olizarka, Ukr.
Olkhovtsy, Bel.
Olkusz, Pol.
Olomouc, Cz.
Olpiny, Pol.
Olshany (near Vilnius),
 Bel.
Olsztyn (Kielce area),
 Pol.
Olsztyn, Pol.
Olsztynek, Pol.
Olyka, Ukr.
Ondava, Cz.
Onut, Ukr.
Opalin, Ukr.
Opatow, Pol.
Opatowek, Pol.
Opatowiec, Pol.
Opava, Cz.
Opladen, Ger.
Opoczno, Pol.
Opole, Pol.
Opole Lubelskie, Pol.
Opory, Ukr.
Oppenheim, Ger.
Opsa, Bel.

Oradea, Rom.
Oraseni, Rom.
Orastie, Rom.
Ordzhonikidze, Ukr.
Orgeyev, Mold.
Orla, Pol.
Orlya, Bel.
Ornontowice, Pol.
Orsava, Ukr.
Orsha, Bel.
Ortel Ksiazecy, Pol.
Orzeszkowka, Pol.
Orzysz, Pol.
Osada Lubicz, Pol.
Osann, Ger.
Oschatz, Ger.
Oschersleben, Ger.
Oshmyany, Bel.
Osiakow, Pol.
Osieciny, Pol.
Osiek, Pol.
Osijek, Yugo.
Osmolice, Pol.
Osnabruck, Ger.
Osowa Wysksa, Ukr.
Ossowa, Pol.
Ostapovo, Ukr.
Osterode am Harz, Ger.
Ostheim vor der Rhon,
 Ger.
Osthofen, Ger.
Ostra Mogila, Ukr.
Ostrava, Cz.
Ostrog, Ukr.
Ostroleka, Pol.
Ostropol, Ukr.
Ostrovets, Bel.
Ostrow Lubelski, Pol.
Ostrow Mazowiecka,
 Pol.
Ostrowek (near
 Wegrow), Pol.
Ostrowiec Swietokrzyski,
 Pol.
Ostrozhets, Ukr.
Ostruv (near Tarnopol),
 Ukr.

Ostryna, Bel.
Oswiecim, Pol.
Oszczow, Pol.
Otmet, Pol.
Otocac, Yugo.
Otoczna, Pol.
Ottensoos, Ger.
Otting, Ger.
Ottweiler, Ger.
Otwock, Pol.
Otynya, Ukr.
Ougree, Belg.
Ovruch, Ukr.
Ozarichi (Polesie), Bel.
Ozarow, Pol.
Ozd, Hun.
Ozernyany, Ukr.
Ozery, Bel.
Ozeryany (Stanislawow),
 Ukr.
Ozeryany, Ukr.
Ozorkow, Pol.
Ozyutichi, Ukr.
Pabianice, Pol.
Pabrade, Lith.
Pacanow, Pol.
Paderborn, Ger.
Padova, It.
Padubysys, Lith.
Pahres, Ger.
Pajeczno, Pol.
Pakosc, Pol.
Pakruojis, Lith.
Palade, Rom.
Palanga, Lith.
Palanka, Mold.
Pancevo, Yugo.
Panciu, Rom.
Panemune, Lith.
Panemunis, Lith.
Paneriai, Lith.
Panevezys, Lith.
Panne, La, Belg.
Papa, Hun.
Papenburg, Ger.
Papendorf, Ger.
Pappenheim, Ger.

Paradyz, Pol.
Parafyanovo, Bel.
Parczew, Pol.
Pardubice, Cz.
Parichi, Bel.
Paris, Fr.
Parkany, Hun.
Parma, It.
Partenheim, Ger.
Parysow, Pol.
Parzymiechy, Pol.
Pas-en-Artois, Fr.
Pascani, Rom.
Paskudy, Pol.
Pasrinca, Ukr.
Passau, Ger.
Pasvalys, Lith.
Patrauti, Rom.
Patroha, Hun.
Pau, Fr.
Pavlograd, Ukr.
Pavlov (Wolyn), ?
Pawlowka, Pol.
Pecel, Hun.
Pechenezhin, Ukr.
Pechora, Ukr.
Pecs, Hun.
Pecsvarad, Hun.
Peczurkes, Lith.
Pegnitz, Ger.
Pelkinie, Pol.
Peremyshlyany, Ukr.
Pereyaslav Khmelnitskiy,
    Ukr.
Perigeaux, Fr.
Perpigan, Fr.
Persenbeug, Aus.
Pervomaysk, Ukr.
Peschanoye, Ukr.
Pesterzsebet, Hun.
Pestimre, Hun.
Pestlorinc, Hun.
Peterswaldau, ?
Petlikowce Stare, Ukr.
Petrova Bisztra, Ukr.
Petrova Gora, USSR
Petrova, Rom.

Petrovaradin, Yugo.
Petrovka (near
    Kharkov), Ukr.
Petrvald, Cz.
Petrzalka, Cz.
Pezinok, Cz.
Pfarrkirchen, Ger.
Pforzheim, Ger.
Piaseczno, Pol.
Piaski Luterskie, Pol.
Piatek, Pol.
Piatlpwce, Ukr.
Piatra Neamt, Rom.
Piestany, Cz.
Pietkowo, Pol.
Pietrasze, Bel.
Pikeliai, Lith.
Pila, Pol.
Pilica, Pol.
Pilsach, Ger.
Pilviskiai, Lith.
Pilzno, Pol.
Pinczow, Pol.
Pinsk, Bel.
Pionki, Pol.
Piorkow, Pol.
Piotrkow Trybunalski,
    Pol.
Piotrkowice (near
    Poznan), Pol.
Piotrowice (near Lublin),
    Pol.
Piraeus, Greece
Pirmasens, Ger.
Pirna, Ger.
Pirot, Yugo.
Piryatin, Ukr.
Pistyn, Ukr.
Piszczac, Pol.
Piszczanica, Ukr.
Pitesti, Rom.
Piwniczna, Pol.
Plainesti, Rom.
Planegg, Ger.
Plaszow, Pol.
Plattling, Ger.
Platz, Ger.

Plawno, Pol.
Pleshchenitsy, Bel.
Plesna, Pol.
Pleszew, Pol.
Pleven, Bulg.
Pliskov, Ukr.
Plock, Pol.
Ploesti, Rom.
Plonsk, Pol.
Plopana Tirg, Rom.
Ploskie, Pol.
Plovdiv, Bulg.
Plugov, Ukr.
Plunge, Lith.
Plyussy, Bel.
Plzen, Cz.
Pnevno, Ukr.
Pochayev, Ukr.
Poddebice, Pol.
Podedworze, Pol.
Podgaychiki (Tarnopol),
    Ukr.
Podgaychiki, Ukr.
Podgaytsy, Ukr.
Podgorodishche, Ukr.
Podkamen, Ukr.
Podkamien
    (Stanislawow), Ukr.
Podmokly, Cz.
Podobovets, Ukr.
Podu Iloaie, Rom.
Podu Turcului, Rom.
Podvolochisk, Ukr.
Pogost, Bel.
Pohorelice, Cz.
Poitier, Fr.
Pokucie, Ukr.
Polaniec, Pol.
Polesskoye, Ukr.
Poligonowo, Lith.
Polochany, Bel.
Polonka, Bel.
Polonnoye, Ukr.
Polotsk, Bel.
Poltava, Ukr.
Polten, Ger.
Polyany, Ukr.

Pomaz, Hun.
Pombsen, Ger.
Pomiechowek, Pol.
Pomortsy, Ukr.
Pomoryany, Ukr.
Poniatow, Pol.
Poniatowa, Pol.
Ponikwa, Pol.
Ponizovye, Bel.
Popele, Ukr.
Popowo, Pol.
Poppenlauer, Ger.
Poprad, Cz.
Porechye, Bel.
Poronin, Pol.
Porozovo, Bel.
Postavy, Bel.
Postojna, Yugo.
Postoyno, Ukr.
Potok Senderski, Pol.
Potok Wielki (Lublin area), Pol.
Potsdam, Ger.
Pottenstein, Aus.
Pottmes, Ger.
Poulseur, Belg.
Povazska Bystrica, Cz.
Poznan, Pol.
Praga, Pol.
Praha, Cz.
Prahovo, Yugo.
Praszka, Pol.
Predeal, Rom.
Presov, Cz.
Presovtse, Ukr.
Prestice, Cz.
Pretzfeld, Ger.
Pribeta, Cz.
Pribor, Cz.
Prichsenstadt, Ger.
Prienai, Lith.
Prievidza, Cz.
Priluki, Ukr.
Pristina, Yugo.
Prizren, Yugo.
Probezhna, Ukr.
Prokocim, Pol.

Prostejov, Cz.
Proszowice, Pol.
Pruchnik, Pol.
Pruszkow, Pol.
Pruzhany, Bel.
Przasnysz, Pol.
Przeclaw, Pol.
Przedborz, Pol.
Przemysl, Pol.
Przeworsk, Pol.
Przyglow, Pol.
Przyrow, Pol.
Przysucha, Pol.
Przytyk, Pol.
Pskov, USSR
Pszon, ?
Puchaczow, Pol.
Puchiny, Bel.
Puck, Pol.
Puesti Sat, Rom.
Puiseaux, Fr.
Pulawy, Pol.
Pullach Im Isartal, Ger.
Pultusk, Pol.
Pushkin, USSR
Puspokladany, Hun.
Pustelnik, Pol.
Pustkow, Pol.
Putila, Ukr.
Putivl, Ukr.
Putnok, Hun.
Pyadyki, Ukr.
Pyasechna, Ukr.
Pyatigorsk, Bel.
Pyshno, Bel.
Pyszaca, Pol.
Pyszkowce, Ukr.
Pysznica, Pol.
Pyzdry, Pol.
Quakenbruck, Ger.
Rabenstein, Ger.
Rabka, Pol.
Raciaz, Pol.
Rackeve, Hun.
Radauti, Rom.
Radeberg, Ger.
Radekhov, Ukr.

Radiskis, Lith.
Radlow, Pol.
Radna, Rom.
Radogoszcz, Pol.
Radom, Pol.
Radomsko, Pol.
Radomysl Wielki, Pol.
Radoshkovichi, Bel.
Radoszyce, Pol.
Raducaneni, Rom.
Radun, Bel.
Radutiskiai, Lith.
Radviliskis, Lith.
Radymno, Pol.
Radzice, Pol.
Radziejowice, Pol.
Radzilow, Pol.
Radziszow, Pol.
Radzymin, Pol.
Radzyn Podlaski, Pol.
Rafalovka, Ukr.
Raguva, Lith.
Rainiai, Lith.
Rajgrod, Pol.
Rajsk, Pol.
Rajsko, Pol.
Rakhov, Ukr.
Rakita, Ukr.
Rakolupy, Pol.
Rakoskeresztur, Hun.
Rakospalota, Hun.
Rakosszentmihaly, Hun.
Rakow (near Volozhin), Bel.
Rakow, Pol.
Rakowice, Pol.
Ramien (near Radom), Pol.
Ramsbeck, Ger.
Ramsberg, Ger.
Ranizow, Pol.
Raseiniai, Lith.
Rastatt, Ger.
Rastoace, ?
Rathenow, Ger.
Ratno, Ukr.
Ratzeburg, Ger.

Raudondvaris, Lith.
Rava Russkaya, Ukr.
Ravensbruck, Ger.
Ravensburg, Ger.
Rawa Mazowiecka, Pol.
Rawicz, Pol.
Rechnitz, Aus.
Reckendorf, Ger.
Recklinghausen, Ger.
Reczno, Pol.
Regensburg, Ger.
Rehau, Ger.
Reichenau, Cz.
Reichenberg, Ger.
Rejowiec, Pol.
Rekoraj, Pol.
Remagen, Ger.
Rembertow, Pol.
Reppine, Cz.
Reshetilovka, Ukr.
Revfulop, Hun.
Rexingen, Ger.
Rezekne, Lat.
Rezina, Mold.
Rheinbischofsheim, Ger.
Rheinbrohl, Ger.
Rheine, Ger.
Rhodes, Greece
Rieneck, Ger.
Riese, Lith.
Rietavas, Lith.
Riga, Lat.
Rimnicu Sarat, Rom.
Rimpar, Ger.
Ripiceni, Rom.
Rodelsee, Ger.
Rodheim, Ger.
Rogachev, Bel.
Rogatin, Ukr.
Rogowo, Pol.
Rogoznica, Pol.
Rogozno (near Lublin),
   Pol.
Rokatschuw, Rom.
Rokiskis, Lith.
Rokitnoye, Ukr.
Rollbach, Ger.

Roman, Rom.
Romanuv, Ukr.
Rona de Jos, Rom.
Ropczyce, Pol.
Rosenheim, Ger.
Rosieres, Fr.
Rosilno, Ukr.
Rosiori de Vede, Rom.
Roslavl, USSR
Rosokhovatets, Ukr.
Ross, Bel.
Rosslau, Ger.
Rossosz, Pol.
Rostock, Ger.
Rostov, USSR
Rotenburg, Ger.
Roth bei Nurnberg,
   Ger.
Rothenburg Ob der
   Tauber, Ger.
Rotmistrovka, Ukr.
Rotthalmunster, Ger.
Rottweil, Ger.
Rovenshiny, Ukr.
Rovno, Ukr.
Roxheim, Ger.
Rozan, Pol.
Rozanowka, ?
Rozavlea, Rom.
Rozdol, Ukr.
Rozhanka, Bel.
Rozhishche, Ukr.
Rozhnov, Ukr.
Rozhnyatov, Ukr.
Roznava, Cz.
Rozprza, Pol.
Rozwadow, Pol.
Rubel, Bel.
Rubezhevichi, Bel.
Ruckersdorf, Ger.
Ruda Huta, Pol.
Ruda Pabianicka, Pol.
Ruda, Pol.
Ruda Yavorskaya, Bel.
Rudersberg, Ger.
Rudesheim, Ger.
Rudki, Ukr.

Rudnik, Pol.
Rudniki, Ukr.
Rudninkai, Lith.
Rudnitz, Ger.
Rudnya Bobrovska,
   Ukr.
Rudnya, Bel.
Rukainiai, Lith.
Rulzheim, Ger.
Rumburk, Cz.
Runkel, Ger.
Rusakovichi, Bel.
Ruse, Bulg.
Russenbach, Ger.
Ruthen, Ger.
Rutka, Cz.
Rutki, Pol.
Ruzhin, Ukr.
Ruzomberok, Cz.
Rybczewice, Pol.
Rybnitsa, Mold.
Rychwal, Pol.
Ryglice, Pol.
Ryki, Pol.
Rylsk, Ukr.
Rymanow, Pol.
Rypin, Pol.
Rytro, Pol.
Rzasnia, Pol.
Rzeczyca, Pol.
Rzepiennik Strzyzewski,
   Pol.
Rzepin, Pol.
Rzeszow, Pol.
Rzhev, USSR
Saarbrucken, Ger.
Saarburg, Ger.
Saarwellingen, Ger.
Saba, Ukr.
Sabac, Yugo.
Sabile, Lat.
Sabinov, Cz.
Sacel, Rom.
Sachsenburg, Ger.
Sachsenhausen, Ger.
Sadgura, Ukr.
Sadov, Ukr.

Sadowne, Pol.
Sadurki, Pol.
Safarikovo, Cz.
Saint Gilles, Belg.
Saint Nicolau Mare,
   Rom.
Saint-Etienne, Fr.
Saint-Gervais, Fr.
Saint-Mande, Fr.
Sajoszentpeter, Hun.
Sakiai, Lith.
Sakrau, Ger.
Salakas, Lith.
Salantai, Lith.
Salaspils, Lat.
Salgotarjan, Hun.
Salos, Lith.
Salzburg, Aus.
Salzwedel, Ger.
Samani, Lat.
Sambor, Ukr.
Samokleski Male, Pol.
Samsonow, Pol.
Sandomierz, Pol.
Sankt Martin Im
   Muhlkreise, Aus.
Sankt Polten, Aus.
Sankt Tonis, Ger.
Sannicolal Mare, Rom.
Sanniki, Pol.
Sanok, Pol.
Sapci, Yugo.
Sapinta, Rom.
Sarajevo, Yugo.
Saratov, USSR
Sarbogard, Hun.
Sarmas, Rom.
Sarnaki, Pol.
Sarny, Ukr.
Sarospatak, Hun.
Sarvar, Hun.
Sascut Sat, Rom.
Sasd, Hun.
Sashalom, ?
Sasov, Ukr.
Sataviace, Yug.
Satoraljaujhely, Hun.

Satu Mare, Rom.
Satulung, Rom.
Saukenai, Lith.
Saulgau, Ger.
Saveni, Rom.
Sawin, Pol.
Scazinet, Ukr.
Schandorf, Ger.
Schattendorf, Aus.
Scheinfeld, Ger.
Schifferstadt, Ger.
Schluchtern, Ger.
Schmiedeberg, Ger.
Schnaitsee, Ger.
Schnaittach, Ger.
Scholanowo, Lith.
Schollkrippen, Ger.
Schonberg (Bavaria),
   Ger.
Schondra, Ger.
Schonebeck, Ger.
Schonungen, Ger.
Schopfloch, Ger.
Schorndorf, Ger.
Schorzingen, Ger.
Schotten, Ger.
Schupbach, Ger.
Schwabach, Ger.
Schwabisch Gmund, Ger.
Schwabisch Hall, Ger.
Schwabmunchen, Ger.
Schwandorf in Bayern,
   Ger.
Schwanfeld, Ger.
Schwarzenborn, Ger.
Schwarzenfeld, Ger.
Schwarzheide, Ger.
Schweinfurt, Ger.
Schwenningen am
   Neckar, Ger.
Scutari, Alb.
Secereni, Rom.
Sedlishche, Ukr.
Sedziszow, Pol.
Seesen, Ger.
Seeshaupt, Ger.
Seirijai, Lith.

Sejny, Pol.
Sela, Lith.
Selb, Ger.
Selets (Carpathia), Ukr.
Selets (Nowogrodek),
   Bel.
Seliba, Bel.
Selyatin, Ukr.
Semeliskes, Lith.
Semenki, Ukr.
Senica, Cz.
Senta, Yugo.
Sepenberg, Ger.
Sepopol, Pol.
Seraing, Belg.
Sered, Cz.
Seredneye, Ukr.
Serniki Pervyye, Ukr.
Serock, Pol.
Serokomla, Pol.
Seta, Lith.
Sevastopol, Ukr.
Severskaya, USSR
Sevlussky Ardov, Ukr.
Shanghai, China
Shargorod, Ukr.
Sharkovshchina, Bel.
Shashkowka, Bel.
Shatsk, Ukr.
Shaumyana, USSR
Shcherbakov, USSR
Shcherets, Ukr.
Shchetinka, Bel.
Shepel, Ukr.
Shepetovka, Ukr.
Shereshevo, Bel.
Shidlovtsy, Ukr.
Shirokoye, Ukr.
Shishaki, Ukr.
Shklov, Bel.
Shtefaneshty, Mold.
Shtirotava, Lat.
Shumilovo, Ukr.
Shumskoye, Ukr.
Siauliai, Lith.
Siberia, USSR
Sidra, Pol.

Siedlce, Pol.
Siedliska (near
Jaworow), Pol.
Siedliszcze, Pol.
Siefersheim, Ger.
Siegen, Ger.
Siegritz, Ger.
Sielec, Pol.
Siemianowice Slaskie,
Pol.
Siemiatycze, Pol.
Siemien, Pol.
Sieniawa, Pol.
Siennica Nadolna, Pol.
Siennica Rozana, Pol.
Sienno, Pol.
Sieradz, Pol.
Sierpc, Pol.
Sighet, Rom.
Sihnea, Rom.
Silale, Lith.
Silute, Lith.
Simferopol, Ukr.
Simkaiciai, Lith.
Simleu Silvaniei, Rom.
Sinelnikovo, Ukr.
Sinevir, Ukr.
Sinkevichi, Bel.
Sinsheim, Ger.
Siret, Rom.
Sirvintos, Lith.
Sisky, Cz.
Sitkowka, Pol.
Skala Podolskaya, Ukr.
Skala, Pol.
Skalat, Ukr.
Skalbmierz, Pol.
Skaryszew, Pol.
Skarzysko Kamienna,
Pol.
Skaudvile, Lith.
Skawina, Pol.
Skidel, Bel.
Skierniewice, Pol.
Sknilov, Ukr.
Skole, Ukr.
Skopje, Yugo.

Skrzydlna, Pol.
Skrzyszow, Pol.
Skuczynki, Lith.
Skulsk, Pol.
Skulyany, Mold.
Skuodas, Lith.
Skvira, Ukr.
Skwierzyna, Pol.
Slatioara, Rom.
Slavonska Pozega,
Yugo.
Slavuta, Ukr.
Slavyansk, Ukr.
Slawa, Pol.
Slawatycze, Pol.
Slawkow, Pol.
Sledy, Ukr.
Sloka, Lat.
Slomniki, Pol.
Slonim, Bel.
Slotwina, Pol.
Slupca, Pol.
Slupia Nowa, Pol.
Slupsk, Pol.
Slutsk, Bel.
Smalininkai, Lith.
Smogorzow, Pol.
Smolensk, USSR
Smolevichi, Bel.
Smolnik, Cz.
Smolyany, Bel.
Smordva, Ukr.
Smorgon, Bel.
Sniadowo, Pol.
Snigirevka, Ukr.
Snov, Bel.
Snyatyn, Ukr.
Sob, Hun.
Sobibor, Pol.
Sobienie Jeziory, Pol.
Sobkow, Pol.
Sobolew (near Lublin),
Pol.
Sobrinowo, Bel.
Sochaczew, Pol.
Sofiya, Bulg.
Sogel, Ger.

Sokal, Ukr.
Sokirnitsa, Ukr.
Sokiryany, Ukr.
Sokolka, Pol.
Sokolniki (Lwow), Ukr.
Sokolniki, Pol.
Sokolov, Cz.
Sokolovka (Tarnopol),
Ukr.
Sokolow, Pol.
Sokolow (near Plock),
Pol.
Sokolow Podlaski, Pol.
Sokoly, Pol.
Solec nad Wisla, Pol.
Solec, Pol.
Solec Zdroj, Pol.
Solikamsk, USSR
Solingen, Ger.
Solipse, Pol.
Sollenau, Aus.
Solotvina, Ukr.
Sombor, Yugo.
Somlyocsehi, Rom.
Sommerau, Ger.
Sommerhausen, Ger.
Somogyvar, Hun.
Sompolno, Pol.
Sonsk, Pol.
Sopachiv, Ukr.
Sopot, Pol.
Sopotskin, Bel.
Sopron, Hun.
Soroki, Mold.
Soroksar, Hun.
Sosnki, Ukr.
Sosnovoye, Ukr.
Sosnowica, Pol.
Sosnowiec, Pol.
Sosnowiec Srodula, Pol.
Sosnowka, ?
Sovetsk, USSR
Sowin, Pol.
Spa, Belg.
Spaichingen, Ger.
Spandowerhagen, Ger.
Spassk, USSR

Spergau, Ger.
Speyer, Ger.
Spiegelau, Ger.
Spisska Nova Ves, Cz.
Spisske Podhradie, Cz.
Split, Yugo.
Sporkovshchizna, Bel.
Sprendlingen, Ger.
Sremska Mitrovica,
   Yugo.
Srock, Pol.
Sroda Wielkopolska,
   Pol.
Srodula, Pol.
Stadtlohn, Ger.
Stakliskes, Lith.
Stalinsk, Bel.
Stalowa Wola, Pol.
Staneleviche, Bel.
Staneshti de Sus, Ukr.
Stanislavchik, Ukr.
Staniszewskie, Pol.
Stanke Dimitrov, Bulg.
Staporkow, Pol.
Stara Lubovna, Cz.
Stara Paka, Cz.
Stara Zagora, Bulg.
Stargard Szczecinski,
   Pol.
Starkenburg, Ger.
Starnberg, Ger.
Starodub, USSR
Starogard, Pol.
Stary Oskol, USSR
Stary Sacz, Pol.
Starya Russa, Bel.
Staryy Sambor, Ukr.
Staryye Dorogi, Bel.
Stassfurt, Ger.
Staszow, Pol.
Stavishche, Ukr.
Stavochki, Ukr.
Stawiski, Pol.
Stawiszyn, Pol.
Steckelsdorf, Ger.
Steinach an der Saale,
   Ger.

Steinbruch, Ukr.
Stepan, Ukr.
Stepanki, Ukr.
Sterdyn, Pol.
Steyr, Aus.
Stockach, Ger.
Stockholm, Swed.
Stoczek (near Lochow),
   Pol.
Stoczek, Pol.
Stojaciszki, ?
Stok, Pol.
Stok Ruski, Pol.
Stolbtsy, Bel.
Stolin, Bel.
Stolovichi, Bel.
Stopnica, Pol.
Storozhinets, Ukr.
Stralo, Ukr.
Strassbourg, Fr.
Straubing, Ger.
Stredni Apsa, Rom.
Strimtura, Rom.
Strizhavka, Ukr.
Stropkov, Cz.
Strumpfelbrunn, Ger.
Strykow, Pol.
Stryy, Ukr.
Strzegom, Pol.
Strzegowo, Pol.
Strzelczyska, Ukr.
Strzelecin, Pol.
Strzelno, Pol.
Strzemieszyce Wielkie,
   Pol.
Strzyzow, Pol.
Stulln, Ger.
Stupki, ?
Stuttgart, Ger.
Subacius, Lith.
Subina, Pol.
Subotica, Yugo.
Suceava, Rom.
Sucha, Pol.
Suchedniow, Pol.
Suchodoly, Pol.
Suchowola (near

Parczew), Pol.
Sudlohn, Ger.
Sudovaya Vishnya, Ukr.
Sugenheim, Ger.
Sukhaya Balka Pervyy
   Uchastok, Ukr.
Sulejow, Pol.
Sulina, Rom.
Sumeg, Hun.
Suplingen, Ger.
Suprasl, Pol.
Susak, Yugo.
Suwalki, Pol.
Suzun, USSR
Svalavska Nelipa, Ukr.
Svalyava, Ukr.
Svaritsevichi, Ukr.
Svaty Jur, Cz.
Svaty Mikulas, Cz.
Sveksna, Lith.
Svencioneliai, Lith.
Svencionys, Lith.
Svidova, Ukr.
Svilengrad, Bulg.
Svinyukhi, Ukr.
Svir, Bel.
Svirzh, Ukr.
Svisloch, Bel.
Svitavy, Cz.
Svorotva, Bel.
Swider, Pol.
Swidnica, Pol.
Swiebodzin, Pol.
Swiecica, Pol.
Swierze, Pol.
Swietochlowice, Pol.
Swiety Krzyz, Pol.
Swilcza, Pol.
Swirydy, Pol.
Syanki, Ukr.
Syretsk, Ukr.
Szabolcs, Hun.
Szakmar, Hun.
Szalonna, Hun.
Szamosormezo, Rom.
Szarvas, Hun.
Szatmarcseke, Hun.

Szczakowa, Pol.
Szczawnica, Pol.
Szczebrzeszyn, Pol.
Szczecin, Pol.
Szczeglacin, Pol.
Szczekociny, Pol.
Szczucin, Pol.
Szczuczyn (Bialystok
  area), Pol.
Szczuczyn (Novogrudok
  area), Bel.
Szczurowa, Pol.
Szebnie, Pol.
Szeged, Hun.
Szekesfehervar, Hun.
Szeklencze, Ukr.
Szekszard, Hun.
Szentendre, Hun.
Szentes, Hun.
Szeremle, Hun.
Szob, Hun.
Szojva, Hun.
Szolnok, Hun.
Szombathely, Hun.
Szopienice, Pol.
Szrensk, Pol.
Sztrojna, Ukr.
Sztutowo, Pol.
Szubin, Pol.
Szydlow, Pol.
Szydlowiec, Pol.
Tab, Hun.
Tabarz, Ger.
Taganrog, USSR
Tailfingen, Ger.
Taksony, Hun.
Taktaharkany, Hun.
Talka, Bel.
Tallinn, Est.
Talnoye, Ukr.
Talsi, Lat.
Tann bei Fulda, Ger.
Tapiosuly, Hun.
Tarashcha, Ukr.
Tarcal, Hun.
Tarczyn, Pol.
Targul Bujor, Rom.

Tarlow, Pol.
Tarnava, Ukr.
Tarnobrzeg, Pol.
Tarnogrod, Pol.
Tarnorudka, Ukr.
Tarnow, Pol.
Tarnowice, Pol.
Tarpa, Hun.
Tartakov, Ukr.
Tartu, Est.
Tarutino, Ukr.
Tarvydai, Lith.
Tasnad, Rom.
Tata, Hun.
Tatarsk, USSR
Tauberbischofsheim, Ger.
Tauberrettersheim, Ger.
Taurage, Lith.
Tczew, Pol.
Teci, Ukr.
Tecuci, Rom.
Teitz, Cz.
Teius, Rom.
Telc, Cz.
Telekhany, Bel.
Telgte, Ger.
Telsiai, Lith.
Temerin, Yugo.
Templeuve, Belg.
Tenje, Yug.
Teplice, Cz.
Teplik, Ukr.
Terebovlya, Ukr.
Teremno, Ukr.
Tereszyn, Pol.
Terezin, Cz.
Ternopol, Ukr.
Ternova, Ukr.
Ternovka, Ukr.
Ternovo, Ukr.
Tetetlen, Hun.
Thalmassing, Ger.
Thebes, Greece
Theilheim, Ger.
Thessaloniki, Greece
Thessaly, Greece
Thungen, Ger.

Tibulovca, Ukr.
Tiengen, Ger.
Tilburg, Neth.
Tilff, Belg.
Tilleur, Belg.
Tilza, Lat.
Timisoara, Rom.
Tinets, Pol.
Tipolovka Veche, Ukr.
Tirana, Alb.
Tirashpol, Mold.
Tirgu Frumos, Rom.
Tirgu Jiu, Rom.
Tirgu Mures, Rom.
Tirgu Ocna, Rom.
Tirksliai, Lith.
Tirschenreuth, Ger.
Tiszafured, Hun.
Tiszalok, Hun.
Tiszalonka, Rom.
Tiszaszalka, Hun.
Titel, Yugo.
Tittmoning, Ger.
Tlumach, Ukr.
Tluszcz, Pol.
Tokaj, Hun.
Tokmak, Ukr.
Tokol, Hun.
Tolbukhin, Bulg.
Tole, Ukr.
Tolstoye, Ukr.
Tomaszow Lubelski,
  Pol.
Tomaszow Mazowiecki,
  Pol.
Tomaszowka, Pol.
Topola, Yugo.
Topolcany, Cz.
Toporov, Ukr.
Topusko, Yugo.
Torchin, Ukr.
Torgau, Ger.
Torokszentmiklos, Hun.
Toropets, USSR
Torun, Pol.
Totkomlos, Hun.
Toulouse, Fr.

Tovarnik, Yugo.
Trabelsdorf, Ger.
Trakai, Lith.
Trappstadt, Ger.
Traunstein, Ger.
Travnik, Yugo.
Trawniki, Pol.
Trebisov, Cz.
Treblinka, Pol.
Tremeloo, Belg.
Trencianske Teplice,
    Cz.
Trencin, Cz.
Treuchtlingen, Ger.
Treysa, Ger.
Trichaty, Ukr.
Trier, Ger.
Trieste
Trihati, Rom.
Trinec, Cz.
Trnava, Cz.
Trobitz, Ger.
Trofaiach, Aus.
Trondheim, Norway
Tropovo, Ukr.
Troscianka, Pol.
Trostberg, Ger.
Trostinets, Bel.
Trostyanets, Ukr.
Troyanovka, Ukr.
Truskavets, Ukr.
Trzcianne, Pol.
Trzebinia, Pol.
Trzydnik, Pol.
Tsuman, Ukr.
Tsyurupinsk, Ukr.
Tubingen, Ger.
Tuchin, Ukr.
Tuchola, Pol.
Tuchow, Pol.
Tukhovichi, Bel.
Tukums, Lat.
Tulcea, Rom.
Tulchin, Ukr.
Tulovo (Vitebsk area),
    Bel.
Tuluga, Rom.

Turc, ?
Turda, Rom.
Turek, Pol.
Turets, Bel.
Turgu Ocna, Rom.
Turiysk, Ukr.
Turka (Lwow), Ukr.
Turka (near Chelm),
    Pol.
Turka, Ukr.
Turnu Severin, Rom.
Turobin, Pol.
Turobowice, Pol.
Turovka, Ukr.
Turza, Pol.
Tustoglowy, ?
Tuszow, Pol.
Tuszyn, Pol.
Tvarozna, Cz.
Tverai, Lith.
Tverecius, Lith.
Twistringen, Ger.
Tyachev, Ukr.
Tyczyn, Pol.
Tykocin, Pol.
Tylicz, Pol.
Tyrawa Woloska, Pol.
Tyrnavos, Greece
Tyszowce, Pol.
Tytuvenai, Lith.
Uberlingen, Ger.
Uccle, Belg.
Uchanie, Pol.
Udingen, Ger.
Uffenheim, Ger.
Uglya, Ukr.
Ugnev, Ukr.
Uhersky Brod, Cz.
Uhlfeld, Ger.
Uhrusk, Pol.
Ujanowice, Pol.
Ujazd, Pol.
Ujfeherto, Hun.
Ujpest, Hun.
Ujvasar, ?
Ukmerge, Lith.
Ulan, Pol.

Ulanow, Pol.
Ulashkovtsy, Ukr.
Ulm, Ger.
Ulyaniki, Ukr.
Uman, Ukr.
Ungeny, Mold.
Unkel, Ger.
Unsleben, Ger.
Unteraltertheim, Ger.
Untererthal, Ger.
Untergrombach, Ger.
Unterriedenberg, Ger.
Unterriexingen, Ger.
Unterwalden (Tarnopol
    area), Ukr.
Urspringen, Ger.
Ursus, Pol.
Urzedow, Pol.
Ushachi, Bel.
Usichi, Ukr.
Ustchorna, Ukr.
Usti nad Labem, Cz.
Ustrzyki Dolne, Pol.
Ustse Zelene, Ukr.
Utena, Lith.
Utrecht, Neth.
Uvarovichi, Bel.
Uzda, Bel.
Uzhgorod, Ukr.
Uzlovoye, Ukr.
Uzventis, Lith.
Vabalninkas, Lith.
Vac, Hun.
Vacaresti, Rom.
Vad Maramures, Rom.
Vaiguva, Lith.
Vaihingen an der Enz,
    Ger.
Vainutas, Lith.
Vajszlo, Hun.
Valana, Cz.
Valcau de Jos, Rom.
Valea Rea, Rom.
Valki, Ukr.
Valkininkas, Lith.
Vama Turului, Rom.
Vamosmikola, Hun.

Vamosujfalu, Hun.
Vandziogala, Lith.
Vapnyarka, Ukr.
Varena, Lith.
Varkovichi, Ukr.
Varna (Bulgaria), Bulg.
Vasarhely, Cz.
Vasarosnameny, Hun.
Vashkovtsy, Ukr.
Vasilishki, Bel.
Vaslui, Rom.
Vatra Dornei, Rom.
Vechelde, Ger.
Vechorki, Ukr.
Vegeriai, Lith.
Veisiejai, Lith.
Veitshochheim, Ger.
Veivirzenai, Lith.
Veldes, Yug.
Velikaya Khodachka, Ukr.
Velikiy Bereznyy, Ukr.
Velikiye Borki, Ukr.
Velikiye Mosty, Ukr.
Velikiye Zagaytsy, Ukr.
Velka Bytca, Cz.
Velka Polana, Cz.
Velke Kopany, Ukr.
Velletri, It.
Ventspils, Lat.
Verhovca, Ukr.
Verice, Cz.
Verkhnedvinsk, Bel.
Verkhneye Sinevidnoye, Ukr.
Verkhneye Vodyanoye, Ukr.
Verkhovina, Ukr.
Verovice, Cz.
Verviers, Belg.
Vesenberg, Ukr.
Veszprem, Hun.
Vetis, Rom.
Vetka, Bel.
Vettweiss, Ger.
Vevinceni, Rom.
Vicovu de Sus, Rom.

Vidin, Bulg.
Vidukle, Lith.
Vidzy, Bel.
Viechtach, Ger.
Vieksniai, Lith.
Viesintos, Lith.
Vievis, Lith.
Vileyka, Bel.
Vilkaviskis, Lith.
Vilkija, Lith.
Villach, Aus.
Villmar, Ger.
Vilnius, Lith.
Vilok, Ukr.
Vilshofen, Ger.
Vilvoorde, Belg.
Vinniki, Ukr.
Vinnitsa, Ukr.
Vinogradov, Ukr.
Virbalis, Lith.
Virismort, Rom.
Viseu de Jos, Rom.
Viseu de Sus, Rom.
Vishnevets, Ukr.
Vishnevo, Bel.
Vitebsk, Bel.
Vivikoni, Est.
Vizhnitsa, Ukr.
Vladimir Volynskiy, Ukr.
Vladimirets, Ukr.
Vojka, Cz.
Volchovec, Ukr.
Volgograd, USSR
Volkersleier, Ger.
Volkolata, Bel.
Volkovysk, Bel.
Volodarsk Volynskiy, Ukr.
Volos, Greece
Volozhin, Bel.
Volpa, Bel.
Vorokhta, Ukr.
Voronovo, Bel.
Voroshilovgrad, Ukr.
Voynitsa, Ukr.
Voytovka, Ukr.

Voyutin, Ukr.
Vrable, Cz.
Vranov nad Toplou, Cz.
Vratsa, Bulg.
Vrbas, Yugo.
Vrbove, Cz.
Vreden, Ger.
Vrutky, Cz.
Vselyub, Bel.
Vukovar, Yugo.
Vulcan, Rom.
Vyazma, USSR
Vygoda (Transnistria), Ukr.
Vyshgorodok, Ukr.
Vyshkovo, Bel.
Vysoke Myto, Cz.
Vysotsk, Ukr.
Wachenhofen, Ger.
Wachock, Pol.
Wadowice, Pol.
Waging am See, Aus.
Waiblingen, Ger.
Walbrzych, Pol.
Waldbreitbach, Ger.
Waldheim, Ger.
Waldmunchen, Ger.
Waldorf, Ger.
Wallau, Ger.
Wallerstein, Ger.
Wallertheim, Ger.
Waltershausen, Ger.
Wangen, Ger.
Wannbach, Ger.
Wanrispertz, Hun.
Warburg, Ger.
Warka, Pol.
Warstein, Ger.
Warszawa, Pol.
Warta, Pol.
Wasilkow, Pol.
Wasniow, Pol.
Wasosz, Pol.
Wassenberg, Ger.
Wasseralfingen, Ger.
Wasserlos, Ger.
Wassertrudingen, Ger.

Waszkowica, Ukr.
Watermaal-Boitsfort, Belg.
Watzing, Ger.
Wawer, Pol.
Wawolnica, Pol.
Wegrow, Pol.
Wehen, Ger.
Weidach Durach, Ger.
Weiden, Ger.
Weidenberg, Ger.
Weigenheim, Ger.
Weilheim, Ger.
Weimar, Ger.
Weinheim, Ger.
Weissenbach, Ger.
Weissenberg, Ger.
Weissenburg in Bayern, Ger.
Weissenfels, Ger.
Weisweiler, Ger.
Wejherowo, Pol.
Welbhausen, Ger.
Wels, Aus.
Welzheim, Ger.
Wenings, Ger.
Werba, Ukr.
Wereszczyn, Pol.
Wereszyn, Pol.
Werlte, Ger.
Wernigerode, Ger.
Wertheim, Ger.
Westerburg, Ger.
Westeregeln, Ger.
Westheim, Ger.
Westheim bei Hammelburg, Ger.
Westheim bei Hassfurt, Ger.
Wetzlar, Ger.
Weyer, Ger.
Wezembeek, Belg.
Wieliczka, Pol.
Wielkie Oczy, Pol.
Wielopole Skrzynskie, Pol.
Wielun, Pol.
Wien, Aus.

Wiener Neustadt, Aus.
Wieruszow, Pol.
Wierzbica (near Pinczow), Pol.
Wierzbnik, Pol.
Wierzchownia, Pol.
Wiesbaden, Ger.
Wiesenbronn, Ger.
Wiesenfeld, Ger.
Wiesloch, Ger.
Wilanow, Pol.
Wilanowo, Pol.
Wilcze Nory, Bel.
Wilczyn, Pol.
Wilga, Pol.
Wilhelmpieckstadt Guben, Ger.
Wilhelmsburg, Aus.
Wilhelmshaven, Ger.
Wilhermsdorf, Ger.
Willmars, Ger.
Wilrijk, Belg.
Windsbach, Ger.
Windsheim, Ger.
Winterhausen, Ger.
Wiskitki, Pol.
Wislica, Pol.
Wislowiec, Pol.
Wisnicz Nowy, Pol.
Wisniowa Gora, Pol.
Wisznice, Pol.
Witkow, Pol.
Wittelshofen, Ger.
Witten, Ger.
Wittenberge, Ger.
Wittlich, Ger.
Wizna, Pol.
Wlochy, Pol.
Wloclawek, Pol.
Wlodawa, Pol.
Wlodzierzow, Pol.
Wlodzimierzow, Pol.
Wloszczowa, Pol.
Wodzislaw, Pol.
Wohra, Ger.
Wohyn, Pol.
Wojcieszkow, Pol.
Wojcza, Pol.

Wojnicz, Pol.
Wojslawice, Pol.
Wola Duchacka, Pol.
Wola Okrzejska, Pol.
Wola Przybyslawska, Pol.
Wola Ranizowska, Pol.
Wolanow, Pol.
Wolborz, Pol.
Wolbrom, Pol.
Wolfenbuttel, Ger.
Wolfratshausen, Ger.
Wolfsberg, Aus.
Wolfsegg, Ger.
Wolfskehlen, Ger.
Wolka Kanska, Pol.
Wolka Leszczanska, Pol.
Wolomin, Pol.
Wolow, Pol.
Wolozyce, Bel.
Wolsztyn, Pol.
Worms, Ger.
Worrstadt, Ger.
Worth an der Donau, Ger.
Wrexen, Ger.
Wroclaw, Pol.
Wronki, Pol.
Wrzesnia, Pol.
Wuppertal, Ger.
Wurzburg, Ger.
Wustensachsen, Ger.
Wysokie Mazowieckie, Pol.
Wysokie, Pol.
Wyszkow, Pol.
Wzdow, Pol.
Yablonitsa (near Kuty), Ukr.
Yablonka (Wolyn), Ukr.
Yablonov, Ukr.
Yagelnitsa, Ukr.
Yagotin, Ukr.
Yaktoruv, Ukr.
Yalta, Ukr.
Yambol, Bulg.
Yampol (Podolia), Ukr.
Yanovichi, Bel.

Yantarnyy, USSR
Yaremcha, Ukr.
Yasenov, Ukr.
Yasinuvka, Ukr.
Yasinya, Ukr.
Yavorov, Ukr.
Yedintsy, Mold.
Yefremov, USSR
Yelekhovichi, Ukr.
Yemilchino, Ukr.
Yevpatoriya, Ukr.
Zabava, Ukr.
Zabki, Pol.
Zablocie, Pol.
Zabludow, Pol.
Zabno, Pol.
Zabolotov, Ukr.
Zabrze, Pol.
Zabuze, Pol.
Zadvyzhe, ?
Zagan, Pol.
Zagare, Lith.
Zaglebie Dabrowskie, ?
Zagnansk, Pol.
Zagorow, Pol.
Zagorze (near Krakow), Pol.
Zagorze (Warszawa area), Pol.
Zagreb, Yugo.
Zaharesti, Rom.
Zakliczyn, Pol.
Zaklikow, Pol.
Zakopane, Pol.
Zakroczym, Pol.
Zakrzew, Pol.
Zakrzowek, Pol.
Zalaegerszeg, Hun.
Zaleshchiki, Ukr.
Zalin, Pol.
Zalozhtsy, Ukr.
Zambrow, Pol.
Zamosc, Pol.
Zaporozhye, Ukr.
Zapyskis, Lith.
Zarasai, Lith.
Zareby Koscielne, Pol.

Zarki, Pol.
Zarnow, Pol.
Zarnowiec, Pol.
Zasavica, Yugo.
Zasiecie, Bel.
Zaslavl, Bel.
Zaslawie, Ukr.
Zasliai, Lith.
Zastavna, Ukr.
Zatrzebin, Pol.
Zavadov, Ukr.
Zavalov, Ukr.
Zavod, Pol.
Zawada (Nowy Sacz area), Pol.
Zawichost, Pol.
Zawiercie, Pol.
Zawitala, Pol.
Zbarazh, Ukr.
Zbaszyn, Pol.
Zbikowice, Pol.
Zborov, Ukr.
Zbrachlin, Pol.
Zdiar, Cz.
Zdolbunov, Ukr.
Zdunska Wola, Pol.
Zdzieci, Pol.
Zeckendorf, Ger.
Zegiestow, Pol.
Zeilitzheim, Ger.
Zeilsheim, Ger.
Zeimiai, Lith.
Zeitlofs, Ger.
Zeitz, Ger.
Zelechow, Pol.
Zelenaya, Ukr.
Zelenitsa, Ukr.
Zelenovka, USSR
Zeliezovce, Cz.
Zelow, Pol.
Zelwa, Bel.
Zemun, Yugo.
Zeran, Pol.
Zgierz, Pol.
Zhdanov, Ukr.
Zheludok, Bel.
Zhidachov, Ukr.

Zhirmuny, Bel.
Zhitomir, Ukr.
Zhlobin, Bel.
Zhmerinka, Ukr.
Zhuravno, Ukr.
Ziarkowice, Pol.
Zidikai, Lith.
Ziegenhain, Ger.
Zielona Gora, Pol.
Zielonka, Pol.
Zielonki, Pol.
Ziezmariai, Lith.
Zilina, Cz.
Zimna Voda, Ukr.
Zirndorf, Ger.
Zittau, Ger.
Zlate Moravce, Cz.
Zmigrod, Pol.
Zmudz, Pol.
Znamenka, Ukr.
Znin, Pol.
Zofyuvka, Ukr.
Zohor, Cz.
Zolkiewka, Pol.
Zolochev, Ukr.
Zolotonosha, Ukr.
Zolotoy Potok, Ukr.
Zolynia, Pol.
Zomba, Hun.
Zossen, Ger.
Zrebice, Pol.
Zrenjanin, Yugo.
Zsambek, Hun.
Zschachwitz, Ger.
Zuromin, Pol.
Zvenigorodka, Ukr.
Zvinyachka, Ukr.
Zweibrucken, Ger.
Zwickau, Ger.
Zwierzyniec, Pol.
Zwiesel, Ger.
Zwolen, Pol.
Zychlin, Pol.
Zylin, Pol.
Zyrardow, Pol.
Zywiec, Pol.

APPENDIX C: TOWNS DESCRIBED IN THE EXTRAORDINARY STATE COMMISSION TO INVESTIGATE GERMAN-FASCIST CRIMES COMMITTED ON SOVIET TERRITORY

Source: U.S. Holocaust Research Institute

Listed below are more than 1,450 towns that provided information to the Extraordinary Commission to Investigate Nazi Crimes Committed on Soviet Territory. Each town was required to document, in detail, the events that transpired. Many reports include not only the events and dates, but also the names of the individuals murdered or deported. Shown below are the town names and, in parentheses, the oblast (province) in which they are located.

Adamovka (Vinnitsa)
Afanasovo (Kalinin)
Aglon (Latvia)
Aisty (Zhitomir)
Akkobez (Krym ASSR)
Aleksandreny (Moldova)
Aleksandria (Kirovograd)
Aleksandrovka (Dnepropetrovsk)
Aleksandrovsk (Chernigov)
Aleksandrovsk (Rostov)
Alekseevka (Voroshilovgrad)
Alekseevskiy (Voronezh)
Amekin? (Rovno)
Amvrosievka (Stalino)
Ananchitsy (Bobruysk)
Andreevka (Zaporozh'e)
Andreevo-Ukr. (Zhitomir)
Andreevsk (Stalino)
Andreevskoe (Chernigov)
Andreyav ? (Lithuania)
Andrievichi (Zhitomir)
Anisovichi (Polesskaya)
Antonovka (Sumy)
Antonovka (Chernigov)
Apostol'skiy (Dnepropetrovsk)
Apzhelino (Zhitomir)

Arbetgeim (Zaporozh'e)
Arkhangel'skoe (Kursk)
Arleyskiy (Polotsk)
Armiansk (Krym ASSR)
Arnautovka (Nikolaev)
Artemovsk (Stalino)
Avangard (Polesskaya)
Avdeevka (Stalino)
Averikhanskiy (Polesskaya)
Azernoye (Bobruysk)
B. Belozerka (Zaporozh'e)
B. Bubnovka (Kamenets-Pod.)
B. Kamyanka (Stanislav)
B. Karakuba (Stalino)
B. Medvezhye (Volynya)
B. Ternovsk (Vinnitsa)
B. Tokmaki (Zaporozh'e)
B. Znamenka (Zaporozh'e)
Babchin (Polesskaya)
Babintsy (Chernovtsy)
Babovnya (Bobruysk)
Babunichi (Polesskaya)
Babushki (Zhitomir)
Bagushev (Vitebsk)
Bakhchisaray (Krym ASSR)
Bakhmach (Chernigov)

Bakilo (Chernovtsy)
Balabanovtsy (Vinnitsa)
Balaklava (Krym ASSR)
Balchan (Vinnitsa)
Baliarka (Zhitomir)
Balki (Zaporozh'e)
Bar (Vinnitsa)
Baran (Vitebsk)
Baranovichi (Baranovichi)
Barovaia Sloboda (Minsk)
Basalychevka (Vinnista)
Bashtany (Nik)
Baturin (Chernigov)
Bayanichi (Bobruysk)
Bel'nichi (Vitebsk)
Bel'skiy (Polotsk)
Beleduya (Stanislav)
Belina Velika (Drogobych)
Belochanski (Moldova)
Belopol'e (Vinnitsa)
Belorechenskaia (Krasnodar)
Belousovka (Nikolaev)
Belousovka (Vinnitsa)
Beltsy (Moldova)
Bendery (Moldova)
Benyakoni (Grodno)
Berdichev (Zhitomir)
Bereshevskiy (Bryansk)
Beresnevka (Bobruysk)
Berestiye (Chernovtsy)
Berestovets (Chernigov)
Berestovitskiy (Grodno)
Berezhynets (Kamenets-Pod.)
Berezinskiy (Minsk)
Bereznoe (Chernigov)
Bero? (Chernovtsy)
Bershad' (Vinnitsa)
Beshenkovichi (Vitebsk)
Betygala (Lithuania)
Beyzimovka (Zhitomir)
Bezliudovka (Kursk)
Bibiki (Polesskaya)
Bil'dugi (Polotsk)
Bit'kov (Stanislav)
Biuk Onlar (Krym ASSR)
Blagoveshchenka (Zaporozh'e)
Blistova (Chernigov)

Blonsk (Minsk)
Bludim? (Polesskaya)
Bobr (Minsk)
Bobrinets (Kirovograd)
Bobrovichi (Polesskaya)
Bobrovitsy (Chernigov)
Bobrovka (Kalinin)
Bobruysk (Bobruysk)
Bogorodets (Nikolaev)
Bogrovka (Stanislav)
Bolekhov (Stanislav)
Bolotintsy (Moldova)
Bolshenitsy (Stanislav)
Borislav (Drogobych)
Borisov (Minsk)
Borisovichi (Mogilev)
Borisovshchina (Polesskaya)
Borivtsy (Chernovtsy)
Borkovicheskiy (Polotsk)
Boroinichi (Mogilev)
Boroskoye (Kursk)
Borovitskiy (Volynya)
Borshchov (Stanislav)
Bortniki (Bobruysk)
Borynya (Drogobych)
Boske (Stanislav)
Botelka-Vyzhne (Drogobych)
Bragin (Polesskaya)
Brailov (Vinnitsa)
Branchitsy (Bobruysk)
Braslov (Polotsk)
Brat___ (Stanislav)
Bratslav (Vinnitsa)
Brenev (Polesskaya)
Brest (Brest)
Brichany (Moldova)
Brigintsy (Chernigov)
Bril'ki (Molodech.)
Britsalovichi (Bobruysk)
Brodnya (Minsk)
Brozhskiy (Bobruysk)
Brushteny (Moldova)
Brusilov (Zhitomir)
Bubialiay (Lithuania)
Bubnovka (Vinnitsa)
Budennovskiy (Stalino)
Budenovka (Chernigov)

Budslav (Molodec)
Bugryn-Maydan (Rovno)
Bukcha (Polesskaya)
Bukhovichi (Polesskaya)
Bukivna (Stanislav)
Bulgatino (Bobruysk)
Bulychi (Polotsk)
Burkovskiy (Polesskaya)
Burshtyn (Stanislav)
Bychkovichi (Mogilev)
Bykhov (Mogilev)
Bykhovskiy (Volynya)
Bystritsa (Molodech.)
Chabruch (Moldova)
Chaplitsy (Bobruysk)
Chashniki (Vitebsk)
Chausy (Mogilev)
Chechelivka (Vinnitsa)
Chechenek (Bobruysk)
Chelnoshchevichskiy (Polesskaya)
Chemer (Chernigov)
Chepeleutsy (Moldova)
Chepeli (Bobruysk)
Chepovichi (Zhitomir)
Cheremkhov (Stanislav)
Cherenkovskiy (Polotsk)
Cherepashentsy Kalinovskiy
   (Chernovtsy)
Cherikov (Mogilev)
Cherkassy (Cherkassy)
Cherniakho (Zhitomir)
Cherniatskiy (Bryansk)
Chernichna (Brest)
Chernigov (Chernigov)
Chernolitso (Stanislav)
Chernovka (Chernovtsy)
Chernovtsy (Chernovtsy)
Cherny Rog (Chernigov)
Chernyashskiy (Brest)
Chernyy Ostrov (Kamenets-Pod.)
Cherven' (Minsk)
Chervonskiy (Sumy)
Cheske (Zhitomir)
Chistiakovo (Stalino)
Chizhevichi (Bobruysk)
Chkalovo (Zaporozh'e)
Chogrov (Stanislav)

Chudey (Chernovtsy)
Chudnov (Zhitomir)
Chutovo (Poltava)
Dadomka/?/ (Chernigov)
Dagda (Latvia)
Dal'skiy (Volynya)
Danovshchina (Mogilev)
Darnitsa (Kiev)
Dashkovtsy (Chernovtsy)
Dashkovtsy (Mogilev)
Datsky (Zhitomir)
David Gorodok (Pinsk)
Davydovichi (Polesskaya)
Debal'tsevo (Stalino)
Dedkovichi (Zhitomir)
Delyatin (Stanislav)
Demidov (Smolensk)
Demidov (Polesskaya)
Derevatskiy (Volynya)
Devochky (Zhitomir)
Diagova (Chernigov)
Diat'kovo (Bryansk)
Dmitrievka (Kursk)
Dmitrovka (Chernigov)
Dneprinskiy (Kherson)
Dnepropetrovsk
Dobolov (Gomel)
Dobroe (Niko)
Dobropol'e (Stalino)
Dobroselts (Brest)
Dobrovelichovka (Kirovograd)
Dobrovol'shchany (Bobruysk)
Dobryy Bor (Baranovichi)
Doibanskiy (Moldova)
Dokol' (Bobruysk)
Dolginovo (Molodech.)
Dolgovichi (Mogilev)
Dolgoye (Bobruysk)
Dolgoye Pole (Chernovtsy)
Dolina (Stanislav)
Dolova (Stanislav)
Domachevo (Brest)
Domanovichi (Bobruysk)
Domanovichskiy (Polesskaya)
Domnikovskiy (Polotsk)
Domnitsa (Chernigov)
Dopty (Moldova)

Doropeevichi (Brest)
Dorozhev (Drogobych)
Dosovichi (Mogilev)
Dotkov (Lithua)
Dovizhuya? (Volynya)
Dovlyakhovskiy (Polesskaya)
Dranka (Vinnitsa)
Drazi (Minsk)
Drissa (Polotsk)
Drogichin (Pinsk)
Drogobych (Drogobych)
Dronukha (Mogilev)
Drozdino (Minsk)
Drutsk (Vitebsk)
Druya (Polotsk)
Druzhkovka (Stalino)
Druzhskiy (Polotsk)
Dubechno? (Volynya)
Dublin (Polesskaya)
Dubossary (Moldova)
Duboviazovka (Sumy)
Dubravno (Vitebsk)
Dubrovitsa (Rovno)
Dubrovna (Stanislav)
Dubrovo (Bobruysk)
Dubrovo (Stalino)
Dubrovskiy (Polesskaya)
Dugiyevo (Bobruysk)
Dukhovshchinskiy? (Smolensk)
Durushtory (Moldova)
Dvyunkovo (Vinnitsa)
Dyakovichi (Polesskaya)
Dyatlovichi (Pinsk)
Dyatlovo (Baranovichi)
Dyblyany (Drogobych)
Dyrdyno (Kiev)
Dyvin (Brest)
Dzelentsy (Kamenets-Pod.)
Dzerzhinskiy (Stalino)
Dzerzhinskiy (Leningrad)
Dzhankoy (Krym ASSR)
Dzvinyach (Stanislav)
Edintsy (Moldova)
Ekaterinovka (Rostov)
Elgava (Latvia)
Emel'chino (Zhitomir)
Enakievka (Stalino)

Eremichi (Brest)
Ezernizany (Vitebsk)
Faleshty (Moldova)
Fastovichi (Polesskaya)
Fatezhskiy (Kursk)
Fedorovka (Zaporozh'e)
Feodosiia (Krym ASSR)
Fes'kovka (Chernigov)
Filipovichi (Brest)
Fraydorf (Zaporozh'e)
Fraydorf (Krym ASSR)
Gadiach (Poltava)
Gadiuchin (Nikolaev)
Galich (Stanislav)
Gantsevichi (Pinsk)
Garmatskiy (Moldova)
Gastyni (Latvia)
Gavinovichi (Baranovichi)
Gavriliak (Stanislav)
Gayshin (Mogilev)
Gaysin (Vinnitsa)
Gerasimov (Stanislav)
Gerasimovo (Stalino)
Germanovichskiy (Polotsk)
Geroi (Tarnopol')
Gervyati (Molodech.)
Girachitsy (Bobruysk)
Glinka (Pinsk)
Glinoya (Moldova)
Glodyany (Moldova)
Gluboka (Stanislav)
Gluboki (Chernovtsy)
Glukhovichskiy (Polesskaya)
Glussk (Bobruysk)
Gnedintsy (Chernigov)
Gniloe (Kursk)
Gnilugin (Chernigov)
Gnoyev (Polesskaya)
Goloskiv (Stanislav)
Golovchin (Mogilev)
Golovino (Zhitomir)
Golynich (Grodno)
Golyshka (Grodno)
Gomel'skiy (Polotsk)
Gopashchev (Zhitomir)
Gorbov (Rovno)
Gorbovo (Zhitomir)

Gorbovo (Chernigov)
Goriglyadi (Stanislav)
Gorki (Mogilev)
Gorkovskiy (Lvov)
Gorlovka (Stalino)
Gornostayev (Bobruysk)
Gorodenka (Stanislav)
Gorodenkovskiy (Stanislav)
Gorodets (Gomel')
Gorodilov (Molodech.)
Gorodishche (Poltava)
Gorodishche (Zhitomir)
Gorodishche (Chernigov)
Gorodishchi (Baranovichi)
Gorodnia (Chernigov)
Gorodnitsa (Zhitomir)
Gorodok (Bobruysk)
Gorodok (Molodech.)
Gorodok (Vitebsk)
Gorodyachi (Bobruysk)
Gorokhovskiy (Volynya)
Gorovicheskiy (Polotsk)
Gorvashy (Zhitomir)
Gorvol'e (Gomel')
Grabovskoe (Chernigov)
Gradzyany (Bobruysk)
Grafovka (Kursk)
Granov (Vinnitsa)
Grechany (Kamenets-Pod.)
Gremiacheskiy (Voronezh)
Grevenev (Mogilev)
Griazevichi (Mogilev)
Grigoriopol' (Moldova)
Grigorovka (Chernigov)
Grinivtsi (Stanislav)
Grit'ki (Minsk)
Griva (Latvia)
Grozentsy (Chernovtsy)
Grozovo (Bobruysk)
Gruz'koe (Vinnitsa)
Gruzevitsy (Kamenets-Pod.)
Gruzyatinskiy (Volynya)
Gubnik (Vinnitsa)
Gudogay (Molodech.)
Guliay Pole (Zaporozh'e)
Guncha (Vinnitsa)
Guriny (Polesskaya)

Gushchenitsy (Vinnitsa)
Gusne-Vyzhne (Lvov)
Guta (Stanislav)
Gvorki/?/ (Chernigov)
Gvozdets (Stanislav)
Iacha (Grodno)
Ianchekra/?/ (Zaporo Kalin)
Ianovichi (Vitebsk)
Ianuspol' (Zhitomir)
Iarun' (Zhitomir)
Iaslonka (Stanislav)
Iasnoe (Zaporozh'e)
Iazviny (Minsk)
Ichki (Krym ASSR)
Ichnia (Chernigov)
Iglitsa (Mogilev)
Iliya (Molodech.)
Ilovaisk (Stalino)
Indra (Latvia)
Iody (Polotsk)
Irklev (Poltava)
Isakov (Stanislav)
Iskra (Poltava)
Islam Terek (Krym ASSR)
Iurchik (Kirovograd)
Iv'ye (Molodech.)
Ivankov (Zhitomir)
Ivankovtsy (Chernovtsy)
Ivanov (Kherson)
Ivanovka (Kursk)
Ivanovo (Pinsk)
Ivantsevichi (Brest)
Ivashkovichi (Polesskaya)
Ivenets (Baranovichi)
Ivotok (Bryansk)
Izvolta (Latvia)
Jekabpils (Latvia)
Jurbarkas (Lithuania)
Kabanzhik (Moldova)
Kabylniki (Molodech.)
Kachkarov (Kherson)
Kaganovicheskiy (Polotsk)
Kaganovskiy (Pskov)
Kakhovka (Kherson)
Kalika (Chernigov)
Kalinindorf (Kherson)
Kalinino (Krym ASSR)

Kalinino (Vinnitsa)
Kalinkovichskiy (Polesskaya)
Kalinovka (Vinnitsa)
Kalitan' (Polesskaya)
Kalmentsy (Chernovtsy)
Kalush (Stanislav)
Kamenka (Moldova)
Kamenka (Stalingrad)
Kamensk (Minsk)
Kamenskiy (Bobruysk)
Kanashov (Vinnitsa)
Kanetsevichi (Bobruysk)
Kaplava (Latvia)
Kapustina (Molodech.)
Kapyaichi (Polesskaya)
Karantil (Moldova)
Karasu Bazar (Krym ASSR)
Karelichi (Baranovichi)
Karil'skoe (Chernigov)
Karisan (Krym ASSR)
Karlov (Stanislav)
Karpilovka (Minsk)
Karpovtsy (Zhitomir)
Karzhilovka/?/ (Chernigov)
Kasherinovka (Zhitomir)
Kashino (Minsk)
Kasynichi (Bobruysk)
Katerinovka (Kamenets-Pod.)
Katuya Ostritsa (Chernovtsy)
Kaunas (Lithuania)
Kazanov (Stanislav)
Kazatin (Vinnitsa)
Kazimirovka (Mogilev)
Kazyry (Minsk)
Kerch (Krym)
Keydanay (Lithuania)
Kharkov (Kharkov)
Khartsyzsk (Stalino)
Kharyumaa (Estonia)
Khatnoe (Kharkov)
Khimov (Bobruysk)
Khislovichi (Smolensk)
Khlibychin (Stanislav)
Khmel'nik (Vinnitsa)
Khmelyska (Tarnopol')
Kholodniki (Polesskaya)
Kholopenichi (Minsk)

Kholoyev (Lvov)
Khomushin (Vinnitsa)
Khotenchitsy (Molodech.)
Khotenskiy (Sumy)
Khotin (Chernovtsy)
Khotsun (Volynya)
Khronovka (Chernigov)
Khuden' (Polesskaya)
Khutor-Budilov (Stanislav)
Khutorov (Vinnitsa)
Kidanov (Stanislav)
Kiev (Kiev)
Kingisep (Leningrad)
Kiselev (Chernovtsy)
Kislovodsk (Stavropol')
Kislyak (Vinnitsa)
Kitsman (Chernovtsy)
Kivertskiy (Volynya)
Kleban' (Vinnitsa)
Klevan' (Rovno)
Klichev (Bobruysk)
Klimov (Bryansk)
Klimovichi (Mogilev)
Klintsy (Bryansk)
Klishkovtsy (Chernovtsy)
Klityshche (Zhitomir)
Klod'kovka (Chernigov)
Klooga (Estonia)
Kluziv (Stanislav)
Kniazhin (Zhitomir)
Kobaki (Stanislav)
Kobeliaki (Poltava)
Kobeliaki (Poltava)
Kochenov (Viteb)
Kociak (Zhitomir)
Kol'chany (Bobruysk)
Kolay (Krym ASSR)
Kolintsi (Stanislav)
Kolki (Volynya)
Kolodievka (Stanislav)
Kolodishansk (Minsk)
Kolomyya (Stanislav)
Kolovchino (Mogilev)
Kolpino (Leningrad)
Kolyshki (Vitebsk)
Komarovtsy (Vinnitsa)
Komarynskiy (Polesskaya)

Komsomol'skoe (Vinnitsa)
Konotop (Sumy)
Kontsevichi (Polesskaya)
Kontsy (Mogilev)
Kopacheny (Moldova)
Koporyn (Polesskaya)
Kopyl (Bobruysk)
Kopys' (Vitebsk)
Korchevka (Zhitomir)
Koren' (Chernigov)
Koriukovka (Chernigov)
Korma (Gomel')
Korneshty (Moldova)
Korochenki (Zhitomir)
Korolevichi (Polotsk)
Korolevka (Zhitomir)
Korolik (Brest)
Korop (Chernigov)
Koropets (Tarnopol')
Koropyatin (Rovno)
Korosten' (Zhitomir)
Korotnoye (Moldova)
Korshev (Stanislav)
Koryshkovo (Vinnitsa)
Koshchichi (Polesskaya)
Koshlakovo (Kursk)
Kosov (Stanislav)
Kostenevichi (Molodech.)
Kostiukovichi (Mogilev)
Kovalevskiy (Bobruysk)
Kovchi (Chernigov)
Kovchitskiy (Bobryusk)
Kovel'skiy (Volynya)
Kovel'skiy (Volyny)
Kozel'tsy (Chernigov)
Kozeltsy (Poltava)
Kozlov (Bobruysk)
Kozminskiy? (Volynya)
Kozyanskiy (Polotsk)
Krakes (Lithuania)
Kramatorsk (Stalino)
Krasilovka (Chernigov)
Krasilovka (Chernigov)
Kraslava (Latvia)
Krasn. Terchek (Krym ASSR)
Krasna (Stanislav)
Krasnaya Sloboda (Bobruysk)

Krasnoarmeysk (Zhitomir)
Krasnodar (Krasnodar)
Krasnodarsk (Polotsk)
Krasnoe (Chernigov)
Krasnoe Znamya (Rostov)
Krasnogvardeyskiy (Leningrad)
Krasnoluki (Minsk)
Krasnopol'e (Zhitomir)
Krasnopol'e (Mogilev)
Krasnopol'e (Mogilev)
Krasnostavtsi (Stanislav)
Krasnoye Selo (Leningrad)
Krasnoye (Molodech.)
Krasnyy Luch (Voroshilovgrad)
Krasnyy Perekop (Krym ASSR)
Kretinga (Lithuania)
Krezhaev/?/ (Chernigov)
Krichev (Mogilev)
Krivaia Ruda (Poltava)
Krivchanskiy (Polesskaya)
Krivets' (Stanislav)
Krivichi (Bobruysk)
Krivichi (Molodech.)
Krivoe (Lvov)
Krivoy Rog (Dnepropetrovsk)
Kromskiy (Orel)
Kronshtadt (Leningrad)
Kruchinets (Zhitomir)
Krugloe (Mogilev)
Krupskiy (Minsk)
Krymno? (Volynya)
Krymskoe (Krasnodar)
Kryzhonov (Vinnitsa)
Kryzhopol'e (Vinnitsa)
Ksaverovka (Stanislav)
Kublich (Vinnitsa)
Kublichy (Polotsk)
Kudinovichi (Bobruysk)
Kulachin? (Stanislav)
Kulaki (Bobruysk)
Kuldiga (Latvia)
Kulikovskij (Zhitomir)
Kuna (Vinnitsa)
Kunka (Vinnitsa)
Kurenets (Molodech.)
Kustovnitsa (Polesskaya)
Kustovtsy (Vinnitsa)

Kutiska (Stanislav)
Kuty (Stanislav)
Kuybyshevskiy (Leningrad)
Kuz'mintsy (Vinnitsa)
Ladozhin (Vinnitsa)
Lakneki? (Polesskaya)
Lanchin (Stanislav)
Larindorf (Krym ASSR)
Lavsk /?/ (Chernigov)
Lazdijai (Lithuania)
Lazhaniye? (Polotsk)
Lazkiv (Poltava)
Lekhva ? (Pinsk)
Lel'chitsy (Polesskaya)
Lenin (Pinsk)
Leningrad (Leningrad)
Lenino (Minsk)
Lenkovets (Chernovtsy)
Leonpol' (Polotsk)
Leovo (Moldova)
Lepetikha B. (Kherson)
Leshinskiy (Molodech.)
Liady (Vitebsk)
Lida (Grodno)
Lidovka? (Moldova)
Likhalki? (Stanislav)
Likhtfeld (Zaporozh'e)
Limbazhi (Latvia)
Liozno (Vitebsk)
Lipkany (Chernovtsy)
Lipkany (Moldova)
Lipovka (Vinnitsa)
Lipovka (Mogilev)
Lipovki (Polotsk)
Lisets (Stanislav)
Lisichansk (Voroshilovgrad)
Liski (Stanislav)
Litin (Vinnitsa)
Litovshchin? (Polotsk)
Liubar (Zhitomir)
Liubecha (Chernigov)
Liubegosh' (Bryansk)
Liubokhna (Bryansk)
Livany (Latvia)
Loev (Gomel')
Logovoe (Kursk)
Logozhskiy (Minsk)

Lokhvitsa (Poltava)
Lokitka (Stanislav)
Lomnitsa (Minsk)
Lopatna (Moldova)
Lozva (Stanislav)
Luchinets (Pinsk)
Ludzy (Latvia)
Luginy (Zhitomir)
Luka (Stanislav)
Luka (Drogobych)
Luzhany (Chernovtsy)
Lvov (Lvov)
Lyadets? (Pinsk)
Lyakhovichi (Polesskaya)
Lyakhovichi (Baranovichi)
Lyakhvovitsy (Volynya)
Lyntupy (Molodech.)
Lysenka (Mogilev)
Lyskovo (Brest)
Lysogorka (NikoLy Teofi)
Lyuban' (Bobruysk)
Lyuboml' (Volynya)
Lyuboml' (Volynya)
Lyudenevichi (Polesskaya)
Lyutsinov (Rovno)
M. Glumcha (Zhitomir)
M. Khotimek (Mogilev)
M. Mliny (Poltava)
M. Solonov (Nikolaev)
M. Ternovsk (Vinnitsa)
M. Zarich'e (Mogilev)
M. Zaslavl' (Minsk)
Maidan (Stanislav)
Makeevka (Stalino)
Makeevskoe (Chernigov)
Makishino (Chernigov)
Makovka (Zaporozh'e)
Malentsy? (Chernovtsy)
Maliatichi (Mogilev)
Malodevitsy (Chernigov)
Malozhinskiy (Polesskaya)
Malyshevichi (Bobruysk)
Man'kov (Kiev)
Maniava (Stanislav)
Mar'ino (Stalino)
Mar'yanovka (Vinnitsa)
Marinka-Gorka (Minsk)

Martynovka (Kamenets-Pod.)
Masevichi (Brest)
Matsiov (Volynya)
Matski ? (Molodech.)
Maxim Gorkiy (Krym ASSR)
Mazheikiai (Lithuania)
Mazurovka (Vin)
Medenichi (Drogobych)
Medni (Latvia)
Medvedovo (Zhitomir)
Medvezhansk (Minsk)
Mel'nikov (Vinnitsa)
Mel'nitsy (Tarnopol')
Melen' (Zhitomir)
Meleshevo (Minsk)
Meleshkovo (Vinnitsa)
Mena (Chernigov)
Mezeevo (Vitebsk)
Mezhdulesie (Brest)
Mikashevichi (Pinsk)
Mikhaylishki (Molodech.)
Mikhaylovka (Vinnitsa)
Mikhnovichi? (Polesskaya)
Mikitintsi (Stanislav)
Mikulichi? (Polesskaya)
Mikulintsi (Stanislav)
Milevichi (Pinsk)
Milhalki (Stanislav)
Miloslavichi (Mogilev)
Milovits? (Baranovichi)
Mineral'nyye Vody (Stavropol')
Minsk (Minsk)
Minus-Yevrejskiy (Krym ASSR)
Miory (Polotsk)
Mir (Baranovichi)
Mishin? (Stanislav)
Mit'kovskiy? (Polotsk)
Mitlinetskaya (Vinnitsa)
Mizoch (Rovno)
Mlinok? (Polesskaya)
Mogel'? (Moldova)
Mogil'noe (Minsk)
Mokashevka (Chernigov)
Mokony/?/ (Chernigov)
Mokrany (Bobruysk)
Mokraya Dubrava (Pinsk)
Mokrenshchina (Zhitomir)

Mokrovo (Pinsk)
Mokryany (Moldova)
Molodechno (Molodech.)
Molodyvil'chitsy (Pinsk)
Molokovo (Bobruysk)
Molovati (Moldova)
Molytkov? (Polesskaya)
Monastirchani (Stanislav)
Moshkany (Vitebsk)
Moszheska? (Volynya)
Motilevo (Chernovtsy)
Mozyr' (Polesskaya)
Mrochki (Minsk)
Mstislav (Mogilev)
Mukany (Lvov)
Murom (Kursk)
Murovany Kurilovtsy (Mur.Kurilovt. Vinnitsa)
Myadel' (Molodech.)
Myastkovka (Vinnitsa)
Mykolayev (Drogobych)
Myslevichi? (Molodech.)
Mytkov (Vinnitsa)
N. Chirskiy (Stalingrad)
N. Verbizh (Stanislav)
N. Bubnovka (Kamenets-Pod.)
N. Petrovka (Nikolaev)
N. Pikov (Vinnitsa)
N. Vasilevka (Zaporozh'e)
N. Zlatopol' (Zaporozh'e)
Nadinovka (Chernigov)
Nadorozhniv (Stanislav)
Nadvornaya (Stanislav)
Nakhovsk? (Polesskaya)
Naliboki (Baranovichi)
Narayevka (Vinnitsa)
Narovlya (Polesskaya)
Naseka Dvorchani (Grodno)
Navgoliye (Bobruysk)
Naydeny (Latvia)
Nayn Lebn (Kirovograd)
Nedaichkov (Chernigov)
Negin (Mogilev)
Nekliudovo (Kursk)
Nekrashy (Zhitomir)
Nemki (Bobruysk)
Neretas (Latvia)

Nesterovka (Vinnitsa)
Neveselki (Rovno)
Neyz (Krym ASSR)
Nezavertaylovka (Moldova)
Nezhetgol' (Kursk)
Nezhin (Chernigov)
Nezviska (Stanislav)
Nikolaev (Nikolaev)
Nikolaev (Kamenets-Pod.)
Nikolayevskiy (Leningrad)
Nikoryany (Moldova)
Nizhnyaya Zhora (Moldova)
Novaya Zhuchka (Chernovtsy)
Novgorod Sev. (Chernigov)
Novo-Akhtyrsk (Voroshilovgrad)
Novo-Astrakhanskiy
   (Voroshilovgrad)
Novo-Borisov (Minsk)
Novo-Chudnov (Zhitomir)
Novo-Donbassovsk (Stalino)
Novo-Pskov (Voroshilovgrad)
Novo-Tavolzhanka (Kursk)
Novocherkassk (Rostov)
Novogrudok (Baranovichi)
Novomoskovskiy (Dnepropetrovsk)
Novopol' (Zhitomir)
Novorezhskiy (Pskov)
Novoselitsa (Chernovtsy)
Novoselitsa (Stanislav)
Novoselki (Polesskaya)
Novoselki (Mogilev)
Novoselkovskiy (Polotsk)
Novoselok (Volynya)
Novosepki (Polesskaya)
Novosvetlovskiy (Voroshilovgra)
Novye Mamoyavtsy? (Chernovtsy)
Novyy Bug (Nikolaev)
Obertin (Stanislav)
Obol'tsy (Vitebsk)
Obolon'e (Chernigov)
Ochakov (Nikolaev)
Ocheretovka (Dnepropetrovsk)
Odai (Stanislav)
Odessa (Odessa)
Odessa (by city distr)
Oktiabr' (Zaporozh'e)
Oktyabrsk (Bobruysk)
Oktyabrskiy (Leningrad)

Ol'khovatka (Kharkov)
Ol'shevo (Brest)
Oldin (Stalino)
Olesha (Stanislav)
Oleshchino (Stanislav)
Olev (Zhitomir)
Oleyniky (Kamenets-Pod.)
Oloneshty (Moldova)
Onushkis (Lithuania)
Oposhki (Poltava)
Oratov (Vinnitsa)
Ordzhonikidze (Rostov)
Orekhovo (Stalino)
Orel (Orel)
Orelets (Stanislav)
Orsha (Vitebsk)
Oshmyana (Molodech.)
Osintorf (Vitebsk)
Osniki (Zhitomir)
Osoka (Minsk)
Osovaya? (Pinsk)
Osovets (Bobruysk)
Osovets (Novobasanskiy (Chernigov)
Ostashkovichi (Polesskaya)
Oster (Chernigov)
Ostrauten (Chernigov)
Ostrinya (Stanislav)
Ostritsa (Chernovtsy)
Ostroglyady (Polesskaya)
Ostroshitsko (Minsk)
Ostrovki (Bobruysk)
Ostrovskiy (Polotsk)
Ostrozhanka (Polesskaya)
Osveya (Polotsk)
Otinya (Stanislav)
Otuzy (Krym ASSR)
Pakhutentsy (Kamenets-Pod)
Palagichi (Stanislav)
Palanga (Lithuania)
Panashishki (Lithuania)
Panevezhys (Lithuania)
Panka (Chernovtsy)
Parafianovo (Polotsk)
Parichi (Bobruysk)
Parkova (Moldova)
Pasechnaya (Stanislav)
Pasichna (Stanislav)
Pastava? (Rovno)

Patsikov? (Stanislav)
Pavelche (Stanislav)
Pavlograd (Dnepropetrovsk)
Pavlov (Leningrad)
Pavropol' (Brest)
Pechenezhin (Stanislav)
Pecheryani (Moldova)
Pekhinitskiy (Leningrad)
Pepeny (Moldova)
Peratin (Lvov)
Pereshchepino (Dnepropetrovsk)
Perskopskiy (Sumy)
Pervomaysk (Krym ASSR)
Pervomaysk (Voroshilovgrad)
Peschanokopskiy (Rostov)
Peskovskiy (Brest)
Pesochnoye (Bobruysk)
Petrikov (Polesskaya)
Petrivtsy (Chernovtsy)
Petrokrepost' (Leningrad)
Petropavlovka (Dnepropetrovsk)
Petrovka (Vinnitsa)
Petrovka (Voroshilovgrad)
Piatka (Zhitomir)
Pidluzhe (Stanislav)
Pinsk (Pinsk)
Pisliatino? (Mogilev)
Plavsk (Tula)
Pliski (Minsk)
Pliski (Chernigov)
Plissa (Polotsk)
Ploskoye (Chernovtsy)
Plyavinyas (Latvia)
Pniv (Stanislav)
Pobolov (Gomel)
Pochapintsy (Tarnopol')
Pochinok (Smolensk)
Pochunbeny (Moldova)
Podberez'ye (Molodech.)
PodlesniyIaltushkov (Vinnitsa)
Podol (Chernigov)
Podpechary (Stanislav)
Podverbtsy (Stanislav)
Pogost (Bobruysk)
Pokrashevo (Bobruysk)
Polchino (Zhitomir)
Polesse? (Polesskaya)
Polikarov (Bobruysk)

Politotdelovo (Stalino)
Polivanovka (Dnepropetrovsk)
Polotsk (Polotsk)
Polvisoka? (Stanislav)
Ponornitsa (Chernigov)
Popasna (Voroshilovgrad)
Popeliv (Stanislav)
Popovets (Chernovtsy)
Popovka (Sumy)
Popovtsy (Vinnitsa)
Porechye (Grodno)
Porogi (Stanislav)
Porozovo (Grodno)
Postavy (Molodech.)
Poteyki (Bobruysk)
Potichok (Stanislav)
Potoki (Molodech.)
Povita/?/ (Kiev)
Preili (Latvia)
Preslav (Zaporozh'e)
Pridruja (Latvia)
Priluki (Chernigov)
Prislup (Stanislav)
Pristen' (Kursk)
Priutin (Zaporozh'e)
Prodzinskiy (Bobruysk)
Prokhody (Pinsk)
Proletarsk (Voroshilovgrad)
Proskurov (Kamenets-Pod.)
Prozhektor (Bobruysk)
Prozoroki (Polotsk)
Prybyliv (Stanislav)
Pskov (Pskov)
Pukov (Bobruysk)
Pupkovskij (Bryansk)
Purkari (Moldova)
Pustokhi (Zhitomir)
Pustynki (Mogilev)
Putila (Chernovtsy)
Putivlia (Sumy)
Putniki (Stanislav)
Puzhniki (Stanislav)
Pyarnu (Estonia)
Pyatnitsy (Bobruysk)
Pyldeno? (Latvia)
Rad'kovka (Chernigov)
Radekhov (Lvov)
Radlinsk (Vinnitsa)

Radomysl' (Zhitomir)
Radoshkovichi (Molodech.)
Radukhovka (Rovno)
Radulo (Chernigov)
Radun (Grodno)
Rakhnovka (Vinnitsa)
Rakivchik (Stanislav)
Rakov (Molodech.)
Rakovchin (Stanislav)
Rakovets (Stanislav)
Raudondvaris (Lithuania)
Raygorod (Zhitomir)
Rech'ye (Minsk)
Rechitsa (Gomel')
Rechki (Molodech.)
Rechki (Zhitomir)
Redkovichi (Bobruysk)
Removo (Stalino)
Repki (Chernigov)
Rezeny (Moldova)
Riasna (Mogilev)
Ribla (Stanislav)
Ribne (Stanislav)
Richev (Polesskaya)
Rietavas (Lithuania)
Riga (Latvia)
Rim?' (Stanislav)
Rimovichi (Bobruysk)
Rizhiv (Zhitomir)
Rogachev (Gomel')
Rogachev (Rovno)
Rogachi (Kherson)
Rogoska? (Chernovtsy)
Rogozno (Brest)
Romanovskiy (Rostov)
Romeny (Sumy)
Roshkova (Stanislav)
Rosil'na (Stanislav)
Rositsa (Polotsk)
Roslavl' (Smolensk)
Rossko (Vitebsk)
Rostov na Donu (Rostov)
Rovno (Vinnitsa)
Royter Shtern (Kherson)
Rozhes? (Tarnopol')
Rubas (Latvia)
Rubezhnoe (Voroshilovgrad)
Rubilki (Minsk)

Ruditsy (Mogilev)
Rudka (Kamenets-Pod.)
Rudniki (Bobr)
Rudnya (Polesskaya)
Rukhotin (Chernovtsy)
Rul' Krasna (Rovno)
Rungury (Stanislav)
Rusov (Stanislav)
Rybnitsa (Grodno)
Rychsha? (Polesskaya)
Ryshkany (Moldova)
Rysv'anka (Rovno)
Ryzhyv (Drogobych)
Sadgura (Chernovtsy)
Sadzavka (Stanislav)
Saki (Krym ASSR)
Sal'nitsty (Vinnitsa)
Salantai (Lithuania)
Samgorodka (Vinnitsa)
Samoshki (Leningrad)
Samotevichi (Mogilev)
Sed'moye (Bobruysk)
Sedyanski? (Stanislav)
Selidove
Semenovka (Stanislav)
Senets (Mogilev)
Seniukov (Chernigov)
Senno (Vitebsk)
Serbinovka (Zhitomir)
Serby (Zhitomir)
Sevastopol' (Krym)
Seytler (Krym ASSR)
Shabinskaia (Krasnodar)
Shabokruki? (Stanislav)
Shakiai (Lithuania)
Shamovo (Mogilev)
Sharkovshchina (Polotsk)
Shatava (Kamenets-Pod.)
Shatilov (Bobruysk)
Shatilovskiy (Polotsk)
Shatsk (Minsk)
Shauliay (Lithuania)
Shchedrin (Bobruysk)
Shebekino (Kursk)
Shembulovo (Vitebsk)
Shenarivtsi (Stanislav)
Shershevo (Brest)
Shibensk (Kamenets-Pod.)

Shilovtsy (Chernovtsy)
Shipinki (Vinnitsa)
Shirovtsy (Cherno)
Shklov (Mogilev)
Shkuptinskiy (Polotsk)
Shkuraty (Polesskaya)
Shmal'ki (Zaporozh'e)
Shorskiy (Dnepropetrovsk)
Shostka (Sumy)
Shtatlag N 352 (Minsk)
Shukotin? (Stanislav)
Shumianskiy? (Smolensk)
Shvedchikivskiy? (Bryansk)
Shvenchionis (Lithuania)
Sil'tsy (Polesskaya)
Silianshchina (Zhitomir)
Silorad ? (Stanislav)
Simakivka (Zhitomir)
Simferopol' (Krym ASSR)
Simonovichi (Bobruysk)
Sinevichi (Pinsk)
Sinne (Sumy)
Skalat (Tarnopol')
Skel'sk (Zaporozh'e)
Skeyev? (Tarnopol)
Skopino (Moscow)
Skopivka (Stanislav)
Skrichalovo (Polesskaya)
Skrundas (Latvia)
Skuodas (Lithuania)
Skuratov (Zhitomir)
Sladkovodnia (Zaporozh'e)
Slavov (Zhitomir)
Slavyanoserbsk (Voroshilovgrad)
Slavyansk (Stalino)
Slipchintsy (Zhitomir)
Slobinka (Stanislav)
Sloboda (Polesskaya)
Sloboda (Smolensk)
Sloboda (Polesskaya)
Sloboda (Minsk)
Slobodka Lisna (Stanislav)
Slobodka (Stanislav)
Slobodka (Polesskaya)
Slobodskiy (Polotsk)
Slobodzeya (Moldova)
Slutsk (Minsk)
Smabara (Polesskaya)

Smela (Kiev)
Smile (Sumy)
Smilovichi (Minsk)
Smol'iany (Vitebsk)
Smolensk (Smolensk)
Smolevichi (Minsk)
Smolichi (Bobruysk)
Smorgon' (Molodech.)
Smorzhov (Rovno)
Snezhniany (Stalino)
Snyatin (Stanislav)
Sobakintsy (Grodno)
Sokirchik (Stanislav)
Sokol (Lvov)
Sokuryany (Chernovtsy)
Sol'tsy (Novgorod)
Solonianskiy (Dnepropetrovsk)
Solonovtsy (Chernigov)
Solotvina (Stanislav)
Solotvinskiy (Stanislav)
Soloviev (Kamenets-Pod.)
Soly (Molodech.)
Sopiv (Stanislav)
Sopotskin (Grodno)
Sopronovichi (Mogilev)
Sosenka (Molodech.)
Soshitskiy (Brest)
Sosnitsa (Chernigov)
St. Liubar (Zhitomir)
St. Beshevo (Stalino)
St. Bratushany (Moldova)
St. Chartoryisk (Zhitomir)
St. Dubova (Grodno)
Staklishkes (Lithuania)
Stal'novtsy (Chernovtsy)
Stalingrad (Stalingrad)
Stalino (Stalino)
Stanislav (Stanislav)
Stanislav (Stanislav)
Stanislavskiy (Stanislav)
Stanitsy Dol'shni (Chernovtsy)
Starask (Bobruysk)
Staraya Russa (Novgorod)
Staraya Zhuchka (Chernovtsy)
Staraya Doroga (Bobruysk)
Staritsy (Bobruysk)
Starobel'sk (Voroshilovgrad)
Starobesheve (Stalino)

Starobin (Bobruysk)
Starodverskiy (Polotsk)
Staroil'e (Mogilev)
Starozhukov (Rovno)
Starskoy (Bryansk)
Stary Kuty (Stanislav)
Staryy Krym (Krym ASSR)
Staryye Broskovtsy (Chernovtsy)
Stavki (Brest)
Staykovtsy (Zhitomir)
Stazhkovki (Vitebsk)
Steblikovskaya (Krasnodar)
Stetseva (Stanislav)
Stinceni (Moldova)
Storolichi (Polesskaya)
Storozhinets (Chernovtsy)
Strigovo (Brest)
Strimba (Stanislav)
Studenok (Sumy)
Styrty (Zhitomir)
Subotniki (Molodech.)
Sudak (Krym ASSR)
Sukhinichi (Smolensk)
Sukhoverkhova (Chernovtsy)
Sukhovichi (Polesskaya)
Sukhovolia (Zhitomir)
Supovne (Vinnitsa)
Susleny (Moldova)
Sutov (Vitebsk)
S. Stanislav (Stanislav)
Svatoshizy (Vitebsk)
Svatovo (Voroshilovgrad)
Sverdlovsk (Voroshilovgrad)
Svidichi (Bobruysk)
Svil'skiy (Polotsk)
Svisloch (Grodno)
Synzheriskiy (Moldova)
Taganrogskiy
Tal'china (Chernigov)
Tallinn (Estonia)
Talyy (Bobruysk)
Tampal (Latvia)
Tarasovka (Nikolaev)
Taravukha (Polotsk)
Tarkany (Polesskaya)
Tarnovitsa (Stanislav)
Tarnovitsa (Stanislav)
Taslitskiy (Leningrad)

Tekhovka (Bobruysk)
Tel'man (Krym ASSR)
Tel'man (Krym ASSR)
Tel'shiai (Lithuania)
Telekhany (Pinsk)
Temirgoevskaia (Krasnodar)
Temriuk (Krasnodar)
Teofipol' (Kamenets-Pod.)
Terblicha (Chernovtsy)
Ternov (Vinnitsa)
Tikhinichi (Gomel)
Tikhonov (Chernigov)
Tikhonovka (Zaporozh'e)
Tishanov (Vitebsk)
Tishovka (Mogilev)
Tlumach (Stanislav)
Tluste (Stanislav)
Tolkachevka (Chernigov)
Tolmachev (Leningrad)
Tomakovskiy (Dnepropetrovsk)
Tomashovka (Brest)
Tomashpol' (Vinnitsa)
Toporivka (Chernovtsy)
Torgovitsa (Stanislav)
Trakay (Lithuania)
Trebeski (Kalinin)
Tretel'nyki (Kamenets-Pod.)
Trishinskiy (Brest)
Troianov (Zhitomir)
Trostianets (Vinnitsa)
Trostianets (Sumy)
Trostyanitsk (Minsk)
Troychany (Bobruysk)
Truba (Polotsk)
Trudov (Kherson)
Tselevichi (Minsk)
Tsessava (Latvia)
Tsigira (Moldova)
Tsintsovichi (Molodech.)
Tsyr (Volynya)
Tul'govichi (Polesskaya)
Tulichovo (Baranovichi)
Tupichev (Chernigov)
Tur (Volynya)
Turchinovka (Zhitomir)
Turginov (Kalinin)
Turov (Polesskaya)
Tyastovskiy (Polotsk)

Tyfmar (Vinnitsa)
Tyrlovka (Vinnitsa)
Uborki (Chernigov)
Udnazh? (Polesskaya)
Ugorniki (Stanislav)
Ugorniki (Stanislav)
Ukmerge (Lithuania)
Ukrainskoe (Vinnitsa)
Ungeny (Moldova)
Unizh (Stanislav)
Urapka? (Volynya)
Usaya (Polotsk)
Ushachi (Polotsk)
Ushna (Chernigov)
Uspensk (Zaporozh'e)
Ustilug (Volynya)
Ustinka (Kursk)
Ustinovka (Kharkov)
Utena (Lithuania)
Uzda (Minsk)
V. Burimsk (Poltava)
V. Verbizh (Stanislav)
V. Volytsa (Zhitomir)
Valentirovka (Moldova)
Valmiera (Latvia)
Valynets (Polotsk)
Varatik (Moldova)
Varenikovskaya (Krasnodar)
Varkava (Latvia)
Varva (Chernigov)
Varvarovka (Krasnodar)
Varvarovka (Zhitomir)
Varvarovka (Nik)
Vas'kovichi (Mogilev)
Vashkovtsy (Chernovtsy)
Vasil'evka (Zaporozh'e)
Vasil'kov (Dnepropetrovsk)
Vasilevskiy (Leningrad)
Vasilishki (Grodno)
Vasilishki (Polesskaya)
Vatutino (Zhitomir)
Vcherayshe (Zhitomir)
Vel'dzizh (Stanislav)
Velesnitsa (Stanislav)
Velichkovichi (Bobruysk)
Veliko-Mikhailovskiy Bobruysk)
Verebushskiy (Molodech.)
Veresnitsa (Polesskaya)

Verkhnedneprovsk (Dnepropetrovsk)
Verkhnyaya Zhory (Moldova)
Verkholesiye (Brest)
Verkhovtsy (Vinnitsa)
Vesna (Bobruysk)
Vetanka (Bobruysk)
Vetrino (Polotsk)
Vidinov (Stanislav)
Vikno (Stanislav)
Vileyka (Molodech.)
Vilnius (Lithuania)
Vinnitsa (Vinnitsa)
Visoko (Zhitomir)
Vitebsk (Vitebsk)
Vizhnitsa (Chernovtsy)
Vizhviv (Stanislav)
Vladimir-Volynsk (Volynya)
Vladimirets (Rovno)
Voduluy Vody (Moldova)
Vodychky (Kamenets-Pod.)
Volchek (Chernigov)
Volina (Stanislav)
Volkovo (Kursk)
Volkovysk (Grodno)
Volma (Grodno)
Volnovakha (Stalino)
Volodarskiy (Leningrad)
Volodarskiy (Stalino)
Volodievtsy (Vinnitsa)
Volostkiv (Drogobych)
Volozhin (Molodech.)
Volsk (Zhitomir)
Vornyani (Molodech.)
Vorob'evo (Chernigov)
Vorob'yevskiy (Molodech.)
Vorokhta (Stanislav)
Vorona (Stanislav)
Voronezh (Voronezh)
Voronezhskiy (Polotsk)
Voronokskiy (Bryansk)
Voronov (Stanislav)
Voronovo (Grodno)
Voroshilovgrad (Voroshilovgrad)
Voroshilovskiy (Stalingrad)
Vorotyn (Bobruysk)
Vorov (Zhitomir)
Voru (Estonia)
Vovchinets (Stanislav)

Vozden'ky (Kamenets-Pod.)
Vyborgskiy (Leningrad)
Vychkov (Stanislav)
Vygoda (Bobruysk)
Vyrovka (Sumy)
Vyshki (Latvia)
Vyshpol' (Zhitomir)
Yablonitsy (Chernovtsy)
Yablonov (Stanislav)
Yagorlyk (Moldova)
Yakoveni (Moldova)
Yakuty (Minsk)
Yalta (Krym ASSR)
Yaltushkova (Vinnitsa)
Yamno (Brest)
Yampol'sk (Vinnitsa)
Yampole (Vinnitsa)
Yarmolintsy (Vinnitsa)
Yatsivka (Stanislav)
Yatskovichi (Molodech.)
Yaznenskiy (Polotsk)
Yefingar' (Nikolaev)
Yelno (Pinsk)
Yerkhi (Molodech.)
Yevlichi (Minsk)
Yevpatoriya (Krym ASSR)
Yevpatoriya (Krym ASSR)
Yugin (Rovno)
Yurevichi (Polesskaya)
Yurkevichskiy (Polesskaya)
Yurkovtsy (Chernovtsy)
Yuzefov (Polotsk)
Zabava (Lvov)
Zablysheno (Mogilev)
Zabolot'e (Gomel)
Zabolotov (Stanislav)
Zabolotye (Volynya)
Zaboslot? (Grodno)
Zabrechen (Moldova)
Zabrezhye (Molodech.)
Zabuzh'e (Vinnitsa)
Zagol'ye (Bobruysk)
Zagor'e (Minsk)
Zagorye (Stanislav)
Zagrebel'e (Chernigov)
Zakapchany (Moldova)

Zakrinich'e (Zhitomir)
Zalesye (Tarnopol)
Zaluchye-Dolishne (Stanislav)
Zamogil'ye (Bobruysk)
Zamostki (Vitebsk)
Zapol'ye (Polesskaya)
Zaporozh'e (Mogilev)
Zaprutie (Stanislav)
Zarasai (Lithuania)
Zarechye (Stanislav)
Zarubichi (Mogilev)
Zarubinka (Kharkov)
Zaskevichi (Molodech.)
Zasteb'ye (Bobruysk)
Zavale (Stanislav)
Zaytsevo (Dnepropetrovsk)
Zborov (Tarnopol')
Zelenoe (Chernovtsy)
Zelenyy Gay (Polesskaya)
Zembin (Minsk)
Zgurov (Poltava)
Zhabevo (Bobruysk)
Zhabinka (Brest)
Zhabokrich (Vinnitsa)
Zhavolki (Bobruysk)
Zhilinay (Lithuania)
Zhiriatino (Bryansk)
Zhirichi (Volynya)
Zhitkovichi (Polesskaya)
Zhivachev (Stanislav)
Zhmerinka (Vinnitsa)
Zhovninskiy (Polotsk)
Zhovten (Stanislav)
Zhukovskiy (Bryansk)
Zhuravka (Chernigov)
Zhuravlevka (Vinnitsa)
Zhurzhovichi (Zhitomir)
Zhutovo (Stalingrad)
Ziborovka (Kursk)
Zolotonosha (Poltava)
Zubochi (Brest)
Zugres (Stalino)
Zuysk (Krym ASSR)
Zverevskiy (Rostov)
Zyatkovtsy (Vin)

APPENDIX D
LIBRARIES WITH LARGE COLLECTIONS OF YIZKOR BOOKS

Harvard University
Widener Library
Judaica Department, Room M
Cambridge, MA 02138
(Their yizkor book collection is not
open to the general public)

Hebrew College
Jacob & Rose Grossman Library
43 Hawes Street
Brookline, MA 02146
Total books: 129

Brandeis University
Goldfarb Library
Waltham, MA 02254
Total books: 387

Jewish Theological Seminary
3080 Broadway
New York, NY 10027
Total books: 250

New York Public Library
Jewish Division
42nd Street & Fifth Avenue
New York, NY 10018
Total books: 607

Yeshiva University
Mendel Gottesman Library
500 West 185th Street
New York, NY 10033
Total books: 500+

YIVO Library
555 West 57th Street
New York, NY 10019
Total books: 800+

Center for Judaic Studies
University of Pennsylvania
420 Walnut Street
Phildelphia, PA 19106
Total books: 250

Tuttleman Library of Gratz College
Old York Road & Melrose Avenue
Melrose Park, PA 19126
Total books: 76

Library of Congress
African and Middle Eastern
    Division—Hebraic Section
Adams Building, 110 Second St. SE
Washington, DC 20540
Total books: 800+

U.S. Holocaust Memorial Museum
100 Raoul Wallenberg Place, SW
Washington, DC 20024-2150
Total books: 360

Baltimore Hebrew University
Joseph Meyerhoff Library
5800 Park Heights Avenue
Baltimore, MD 21215
Total books: 118

Price Library of Judaica
406 Smathers
University of Florida
Gainesville, FL 32611
Total books: 475

Jewish Federation of Nashville
801 Perry Warner Blvd
Nashville, TN 37205
Total books: 59

Hebrew Union College
Jewish Institute of Religion
Klau Library
3101 Clifton Avenue
Cincinnati, OH 45220
Total books: 600+

Hatcher Graduate Library
Near East Division
University of Michigan
Ann Arbor, MI 48109-1205
Total books: 119

Holocaust Memorial Center
6602 W. Maple Road
West Bloomfield, MI 48322
Total books: 900+

Hebrew Theological College
Saul Silver Memorial Library
7135 Carpenter Road
Skokie, IL 60076
Total books: 200+

Spertus College
Asher Library
618 South Michigan Avenue
Chicago, IL 60605
Total books: 250

University of Texas
Perry Castaneda Library
P.O. Box P, University Station
Austin, TX 78713
Total books: 300+

Hebrew Union College
Frances Henry Library
3077 University Avenue
Los Angeles, CA 90007
Total books: 225

UCLA
University Research Library
405 Hilgard Avenue
Los Angeles, CA 90024
Total books: 500

University of Judaism
Jack M. & Bell Ostrow Library
15600 Mulholland Drive
Los Angeles, CA 90077
Total books: 300

Simon Wiesenthal Center
Yeshiva University Library
9760 W. Pico Boulevard
Los Angeles, CA 90035
Total books: 120

Canada

Jewish Public Library
5151 chemin de la Cote
    Ste-Catherine
Montreal, H3W 1M6 Quebec
Total books: 1,000

Jewish Public Library
4600 Bathurst Street
Willowdale, M2R 3V3 Ontario

John T. Robarts Research Library
University of Toronto
130 St. George Street
Toronto, M5S 1A5 Ontario
Total books: 130

France
Bibliotheque Nationale
58, rue Richelieu
75002 Paris, France

Bibliotheque Medem
52 rue Rene Boulanger
75010 Paris, France

Centre de Documentation Juive
    Contemporaine
17 rue Geoffroy L'Asnier
75004 Paris, France
fax 48-87-12-50

Israel
Library
Yad Vashem
P.O. Box 3477
91034 Jerusalem, Israel
Total books: 1,000+

APPENDIX E
HOLOCAUST RESOURCE CENTERS
THROUGHOUT THE WORLD
Source: Association of Holocaust Organizations

Holocaust resource centers have been established in many cities throughout the world, especially in the United States and Canada. Facilities available at these locations include a library of books, microfilm and microfiche, and an oral history collection of the remembrances of Holocaust survivors. Many centers provide educational services, such as lectures, speakers' bureaus, videos, exhibits and teacher workshops. They also publish newsletters and magazines.

Most belong to an umbrella organization, the Association of Holocaust Organizations (AHO). Through AHO, they keep in constant contact, informing each other of their latest acquisitions. Plans are being developed to include their holdings in a common computer database. When this is implemented, it will be possible to know in which resource center information of interest to you is available.

Listed below are those organizations that indicate they have resource centers where research can be performed. The list is in sequence of postal (or zip) code within each country. New resource centers are being created every year. If there is not one near you, write to AHO to determine if a new one has been established. The address is Association of Holocaust Organizations; Holocaust Resource Center and Archives; Queensborough Community College; The City University of New York; 56th Avenue and Springfield Blvd.; Bayside, NY 11364.

Argentina
Simon Wiesenthal Center
Maipu 853
1006 Buenos Aires, Argentina
fax: (541) 312-6777

Australia
Jewish Holocaust Center
13 Selwyn Street
Elsternwick, Melbourne
3185 Victoria, Australia
528-1985
fax: 528-3758

Canada

Holocaust Education and
   Memorial Centre of Toronto
4600 Bathurst Street
Willowdale, Ontario
Canada M2R 3V2
(416) 635-2883 ext. 144
fax: (416) 635-1408

Simon Wiesenthal Center
8 King Street
Toronto, Ontario M5C 1B5
(416) 864-9735

Vancouver Holocaust Centre for
   Education and Remembrance
950 West 41st Avenue
Vancouver, B.C. V5Z 2N7
(604) 264-0499
fax: (604) 264-0497

France

Simon Wiesenthal Center
64, Avenue Marceau
75008 Paris, France

Israel

Beit Lohamei Haghetaot
Kibbutz Lochamei-Haghetaot
D.N. Oshrat
25220 Israel
972+4-820412, 825542
fax: 972+4-820455

Holocaust Education Center
State Teachers College
Seminar Hakibbutzim
Namir Road 149
62057 Tel Aviv, Israel
972+3-6902369
fax: 972+3-6990269

Yad Vashem
The Holocaust Martyrs' and
   Heroes' Remembrance Authority
P.O. Box 3477
91034 Jerusalem, Israel
972+2-751611
fax: 972+2-433511

Simon Wiesenthal Center
1 Mendele Street #1
92147 Jerusalem, Israel

Russia

Holocaust Research and
   Educational Center of Moscow
Bulatnikovsky pr 14-4-77
Moscow 113403 Russia
(095) 383-6262
fax: (095) 229-0457

United States

Holocaust Center of the North
   Shore Jewish Federation
McCarthy School
70 Lake Street, Room 108
Peabody, MA 01960
(508) 535-0003

Facing History and Ourselves
   National Foundation
16 Hurd Road
Brookline, MA 02146
(617) 232-1595
fax: (617) 232-0281

Rhode Island Holocaust Memorial
   Museum
JCC of Rhode Island
401 Elmgrove Avenue
Providence, RI 02906
(401) 861-8800
fax: (401) 331-7961

Holocaust Resource Center
Keene State College
Box 3201, 229 Main Street
Keene, NH 03431
(603) 358-2490
fax: (603) 358-2257

Holocaust Human Rights
  Center of Maine
Box 825
Palermo, ME 04354
(207) 993-2620
fax: (207) 993-2620

Holocaust Resource Center of
  the Jewish Federation of
  Greater Clifton-Passaic
199 Scoles Avenue
Clifton, NJ 07012
(201) 777-7031
fax: (201) 777-6701

Holocaust Resource Center of
  Kean College
Thompson Library, Second Floor
Kean College
Union, NJ 07083
(908) 527-3049

Center for Holocaust and Genocide
  Studies
Ramapo College Library
505 Ramapo Valley Road
Mahwah, NJ 07430
(201)529-7409
fax: (201)529-6717, -7508

Center for Holocaust Studies
Brookdale Community College
765 Newman Springs Road
Lincroft, NJ 07738
(908) 224-2769

Metrowest Holocaust Education &
  Remembrance Council
901 Route 10
Whippany, NJ 07981
(201) 884-4800 ext. 178
fax: (201) 884-7361

Holocaust Resource Center of the
  JCRC of South Jersey
2393 W. Marlton Pike
Cherry Hill, NJ 08002
(609) 665-6100
fax: (609) 665-0074

Holocaust Resource Center
The Richard Stockton College of
  New Jersey
Pomona, NJ 08240
(609) 652-4699
fax: (609) 652-4958

The Julius and Dorothy
  Koppelman Holocaust/Genocide
  Resource Center
Rider University
2083 Lawrenceville Road
Lawrenceville, NJ 08648
(609) 896-5345
fax: (609) 895-5684

Joseph H. and Belle R. Braun
  Center of Holocaust Studies
Anti-Defamation League of
  B'nai B'rith
823 United Nations Plaza
New York, NY 10017
(212) 490-2525
fax: (212) 867-0779

Leo Baeck Institute
129 East 73rd Street
New York, NY 10021
(212) 744-6400
fax: (212) 988-1305

The Rosenthal Institute for
Holocaust Studies/CUNY
Graduate School and
University Center
City University of New York
33 W. 42nd Street, Room 1516GB
New York, NY 10036
(212) 642-2183

A Living Memorial to the
Holocaust
Museum of Jewish Heritage
342 Madison Avenue, Suite 706
New York, NY 10173
(212) 687-9141
fax: (212) 573-9847

Simon Wiesenthal Center
342 Madison Avenue, Suite 633
New York, NY 10173
(212) 370-0320

Holocaust Studies Center
Bronx High School of Science
75 West 205th Street
Bronx, NY 10468
(212) 367-5252

Rockland Center for Holocaust
Studies
17 South Madison Avenue
Spring Valley, NY 10977
(914) 356-2700

Holocaust Resource Center and
Archives
Queensborough Community
College
56th Avenue & Springfield Blvd
Bayside, NY 11364
(718) 225-1617
fax: (718) 631-6306

Holocaust/Genocide Studies Center
John F. Kennedy High School
50 Kennedy Drive
Plainview, NY 11803
(516) 937-6382
fax: (516) 937-6382

Holocaust Survivors and Friends
in Pursuit of Justice
800 New Loudon Road, Suite #400
Latham, NY 12110
(518) 785-0035

Holocaust Resource Center of
Buffalo
2640 North Forest Road
Getzville, NY 14068
(716) 688-7020
fax: (716) 634-0592

Holocaust Resource Center
Bureau of Jewish Education
441 East Avenue
Rochester, NY 14607
(716) 461-0290
fax: (716) 461-0912

Holocaust Center of the United
Jewish Federation of Greater
Pittsburgh
242 McKee Place
Pittsburgh, PA 15213
(412) 682-7111
fax: (412) 681-3980

Allentown Jewish Archives/
Holocaust Resource Center
702 N. 22nd Street
Allentown, PA 18104
(215) 821-5500
fax: (215) 821-8946

Halina Wind Preston Holocaust
  Education Center
101 Garden of Eden Road
Wilmington, DE 19803
(302) 478 6200
fax: (302) 478-5374

United States Holocaust Memorial
  Museum
100 Raoul Wallenberg Place, SW
(15th Street and Independence
  Avenue)
Washington, D.C 20024-2150
(202) 488-0400
fax: (202) 488-2690

Joseph Meyerhoff Library
Baltimore Hebrew University
5800 Park Heights Avenue
Baltimore, MD 21215
(301) 578-6936
fax: (301) 578-6940

Zachor Holocaust Center
1753 Peachtree Road NE
Atlanta, GA 30309
(404) 873-1661
fax: (404) 874-7043

Fred R. Crawford Witness to the
  Holocaust Project
Emory University
Atlanta, GA 30322
(404) 329-6428

Holocaust Memorial Resource &
  Education Center of Central
  Florida
851 N. Maitland Avenue
Maitland, FL 32751
(407) 628-0555
fax: (407) 628-0555

Holocaust Documentation and
  Education Center
Florida International University
North Miami Campus
3000 N.E. 145 Street
North Miami, FL 33181
(305) 940-5690
fax: (305) 940-5691

Simon Wiesenthal Center
13499 Biscayne Blvd.
North Miami, FL 33181
(305) 944-4500

Holocaust Learning Center
David Posnack Jewish Center
5850 South Pine Island Road
Davie, FL 33328
(305) 434-0499 ext. 314
fax: (305) 434-1741

Tampa Bay Holocaust Memorial
  Museum and Educational Center
5001-113th Street (Duhme Road)
St. Petersburg, FL 33708
(813) 392-4678
fax: (813) 393-0236

Holocaust Resource Center
  of Greater Toledo
6465 Sylvania Avenue
Sylvania, OH 43560
(419) 885-4485, 841-6585
fax: (419) 885-3207

Dayton Holocaust Resource Center
100 East Woodbury Drive
Dayton, OH 45415
(513) 278-7444
fax: (513) 832-2121

Holocaust Memorial Center
6602 W. Maple Road
West Bloomfield, MI 48322
(810) 661-0840
fax: (810) 661-4204

Holocaust Resource Center of
Minneapolis
8200 West 33rd Street
Minneapolis, MN 55426
(612) 935-0316
fax: (612) 935-0319

Holocaust Memorial Foundation of
Illinois
4255 West Main Street
Skokie, IL 60076
(708) 677-4640
fax: (708) 677-4684

St. Louis Holocaust Museum and
Learning Center
12 Millstone Campus Drive
St. Louis, MO 63146
(314) 432-0020
fax: (314) 432-1277

The Dallas Memorial Center for
Holocaust Studies
7900 Northaven Road
Dallas, TX 75230
(214)750-4672
fax: (214) 368-4709

Holocaust Education Center and
Memorial Museum of Houston
2425 Fountainview Drive, Suite 105
Houston, TX 77057
(713) 789-9898
fax: (713) 789-8502

El Paso Holocaust Museum and
Study Center
405 Wallenberg Drive
El Paso, TX 79912
(915) 833-5656
fax: (915) 584-0243

Holocaust Awareness Institute
University of Denver
2199 S. University Boulevard
Denver CO 80208
(303) 871-3013
fax: (303) 871-3037

Simon Wiesenthal Center
9760 West Pico Boulevard
Los Angeles, CA 90035
(310) 553-9036
fax: (310) 533-8007

Friends of Le Chambon
8033 Sunset Boulevard, #784
Los Angeles, CA 90046
(213) 650-1774

Martyrs Memorial and Museum of
the Holocaust of the Jewish
Federation Council
6505 Wilshire Blvd.
Los Angeles, CA 90048
(213) 852-3242
fax: (213) 951-0349

The Rosen Holocaust Center of
Southern California
1385 Warner Avenue, Suite A
Tustin, CA 92680
(714) 259-0655
fax: (714) 259-1635

The Holocaust Center of Northern
California
639 14th Avenue
San Francisco, CA 94118
(415) 751-6040, 751-6041
fax: (415) 751-6735

Noma State University Holocaust
Studies Center/Alliance for the
Study of the Holocaust
Rohnert Park, CA 94928
(707) 664-4076/664-2160

Oregon Holocaust Resource Center
2900 SW Peaceful Lane
Portland, OR 97201
(503) 244-6284
fax: (503) 246-7553

Washington State Holocaust
  Education Resource Center
2031 Third Avenue
Seattle, WA 98121
(206) 441-5747
fax: (206) 443-0303

APPENDIX F
JEWISH GENEALOGICAL SOCIETIES AND SPECIAL INTEREST GROUPS

Source: Association of Jewish Genealogical Societies

Jewish genealogical societies are organizations of persons who are tracing their family histories. These societies typically meet once a month from September to June. At these meetings, members help each other solve problems in documenting their ancestors. Because the Holocaust has had such a profound affect on contemporary Jewish families, many members of these societies have expertise in Holocaust research. Genealogical special interest groups (SIGs) are organized by geographic area of ancestry. Members are located throughout the world; consequently, regular meetings are not held, and the principal method of communication is their publications. Members of these SIGs have expertise in Holocaust research for the particular region.

The address of most smaller societies in the list below is the address of the current president of the organization (as of March 1995). For a current list of societies, including any newly formed societies, send a self-addressed stamped envelope to Association of Jewish Genealogical Societies, P.O. Box 900, Teaneck, NJ 07666.

NORTH AMERICA

Arizona, Phoenix/Mesa: Arizona Jewish Historical Society, Committee on Genealogy; Carlton Brooks; 720 West Edgewood Avenue, Mesa, AZ 85210; (602) 969-1201.

Arizona, Tucson: Jewish Historical Society of Southern Arizona, Committee on Genealogy; Alfred E. Lipsey; 4181 E. Pontatoc Canyon Drive, Tucson, AZ 85718; (520) 299-4486.

British Columbia, Vancouver: Jewish Genealogical Institute of British Columbia; Cissie Eppel; 950 West 41st Avenue, Vancouver, B.C. V5Z 2N7. (604) 266-3529.

California, Los Angeles: Jewish Genealogical Society of Los Angeles; P.O. Box 55443, Sherman Oaks, CA 91413; (818) 784-7277.

California, Orange County: Jewish Genealogical Society of Orange County; Dorothy Kohanski; 2370-1D Via Mariposa West, Laguna Hills, CA 92653; (714) 855-4692.

California, Sacramento: Jewish Genealogical Society of Sacramento; Iris Bachman; 5631 Kiva Drive, Sacramento, CA 95841; (916) 484-0572.

California, San Diego: Jewish Genealogical Society of San Diego; Carol Davidson Baird; 255 South Rios Avenue, Solana Beach, CA 92075; (619) 481-8511.

California, San Francisco: San Francisco Bay Area Jewish Genealogical Society; Robert Weiss; 3916 Louis Road, Palo Alto, CA 94303; (415) 424-1622.

Connecticut: Jewish Genealogical Society of Connecticut; Jonathan Smith, 394 Sport Hill Road, Easton, CA; (203) 874-4572.

D.C., Washington: Jewish Genealogy Society of Greater Washington; P.O. Box 412, Vienna, VA 22183-0412; (301) 654-5524.

Florida, Fort Lauderdale: Jewish Genealogical Society of Broward County; P.O. Box 17251, Ft. Lauderdale, FL 33318; (305) 791-8209.

Florida, Miami: Jewish Genealogical Society of Greater Miami; Arthur Chassman; 8340 SW 151 Street, Miami, FL 33158; (305) 253-1207.

Florida, Orlando: Jewish Genealogical Society of Greater Orlando; P.O. Box 941332, Maitland, FL 32794; (407) 671-7485.

Florida, South Palm Beach: Jewish Genealogical Society of Palm Beach County, Inc.; Albert Silberfeld; 6037 Pointe Regal Circle #205, Delray Beach, FL 33484.

Georgia, Atlanta: Jewish Genealogical Society of Georgia; Peggy Freedman; 245 Dalrymple Road, Atlanta, GA 30328; (404) 396-1645.

Illinois, Chicago Area: Jewish Genealogical Society of Illinois; P.O. Box 515, Northbrook, IL 60065-0515; (708) 679-1995.

Illinois/Indiana: Illiana Jewish Genealogical Society; Henry Landauer, 404 Douglas, Park Forest, IL 60466; (708) 748-5962.

Kansas, Kansas City: Jewish Genealogical Society of Kansas City; Steven B. Chernoff; 14905 West 82nd Terrace; Lenexa, KN 66215; (913) 894-4228.

Louisiana, New Orleans: Jewish Genealogical Society of New Orleans; Jacob and Vicki Karno; 25 Waverly Place; Metarie, LA 70003.

Manitoba, Winnipeg: Genealogical Institute of the Jewish Historical Society of Western Canada; Suite 404, 365 Hargrave Street, Winnipeg, Manitoba R3B 2K3; (204) 942-4822.

Maryland, Baltimore: Genealogy Council of the Jewish Historical Society of Maryland; Carol Rider; 2707 Moores Valley Drive, Baltimore, MD 21209.

Massachusetts, Boston: Jewish Genealogical Society of Greater Boston; P.O. Box 366, Newton Highlands, MA 02161; (617) 784-0387.

Michigan, Detroit area: Jewish Genealogical Society of Michigan; David Sloan; 8050 Lincoln Drive, Huntington Woods, MI 48070; (810) 544-9356.

Nevada, Las Vegas: Jewish Genealogical Society of Las Vegas, Nevada; P.O. Box 29342, Las Vegas, NV 89126; (702) 871-9773.

New Jersey, New Brunswick: Jewish Historical Society of Central Jersey; 228 Livingston Avenue, New Brunswick, NJ 08901; (908) 249-4894.

New Jersey, Wayne: Jewish Genealogical Society of North Jersey; Evan Stolbach; 1 Bedford Road, Pompton Lakes, NJ 07442; (201) 839-4045.

New York, Albany: Capital District Jewish Genealogical Society; Rabbi Don Cashman; 420 Whitehall Road, Albany, NY 12208; (518) 482-5295.

New York, Buffalo: Jewish Genealogical Society of Greater Buffalo; Muriel Selling; 174 Peppertree Drive #7, Amherst, NY 14228; (716) 691-4828.

New York, Long Island: Jewish Genealogy Society of Long Island; Renée Steinig; 37 Westcliff Drive, Dix Hills, NY 11746; (516) 549-9532.

New York, New York: Jewish Genealogical Society, Inc.; P.O. Box 6398, New York, NY 10128; (212) 330-8257.

New York, Rochester: Jewish Genealogical Society of Rochester; Bruce Kahn; 265 Viennawood Drive, Rochester, NY 14618; (716) 461-2000.

Ohio, Cincinnati: Jewish Genealogical Society of Greater Cincinnati; Nancy Felson Brant; Bureau of Jewish Education, 1580 Summit Road, Cincinnati, OH 45237.

Ohio, Cleveland: Jewish Genealogical Society of Cleveland; Arlene Blank Rich; 996 Eastlawn Drive, Highland Heights, OH 44143; (216) 449-2326.

Ontario, Toronto: Jewish Genealogical Society of Canada; P.O. Box 446, Station "A", Willowdale, Ontario M2N 5T1; (416) 638-3280.

Oregon, Portland: Jewish Genealogical Society of Oregon; Lorraine Greyson; 5437 S.W. Wichita Street, Tualatin, OR 97062; (503) 692-6515.

Pennsylvania, Philadelphia: Jewish Genealogical Society of Philadelphia; Jon E. Stein; 332 Harrison Avenue, Elkins Park, PA 19027-2662; (215) 635-3263.

Pennsylvania, Pittsburgh: Jewish Genealogical Society of Pittsburgh; Julian Falk; 2131 Fifth Avenue, Pittsburgh, PA 15219; (412) 471-0772.

Quebec, Montreal: Jewish Genealogical Society of Montreal; Stanley M. Diamond; 5599 Edgemere Avenue, Montreal, Quebec H4W 1V4; (514) 484-0100; fax (514) 484-7306.

Texas, Dallas: Dallas Jewish Historical Society; Jewish Genealogy Division; David Chapin, 7900 Northaven Road, Dallas, TX 75230; (214) 739-2737, Ext. 261.

Texas, Houston: Jewish Genealogical Society of Houston; Myra T. Ephross; 11727 Riverview Drive; Houston, TX 77077; (713) 496-3466.

Utah, Salt Lake City: Jewish Genealogical Society of Salt Lake City; Thomas W. Noy; 3510 Fleetwood Drive, Salt Lake City, UT 84109.

Virginia: Jewish Genealogical Society of Tidewater; Jewish Community Center; 7300 Newport Avenue, Norfolk, VA 23505; (804) 622-3202.

Washington, Seattle: Jewish Genealogical Society of Washington; Jerome Becker; 14222 NE 1st Lane, Bellevue, WA 98007; (206) 562-0533.

Wisconsin, Milwaukee: Wisconsin Jewish Genealogical Society; Penny Deshur; 9280 N Fairway Drive, Milwaukee, WI 53217; (414) 351-2190.

EUROPE

France: Cercle de Genealogie Juive; Micheline Gutmann; B.P. 707, 75162 Paris Cedex 04, France.

Netherlands: Nederlandse Kring voor Joodse Genealogie; Rudi Cortissos; da Costalaan 21, 3743 HT Baarn, Holland.

Russia: Jewish Genealogical Society in Moscow; VAAD, 71 Varshavskoye Str., 113556 Moscow, Russia. Fax: 095 161-2106.

Switzerland: Schweizerische Vereinigung für Jüdische Genealogie; P.O. Box 876 CH-8021 Zurich, Switzerland. Telephone: 01/462.78.83; fax: 01/463. 52.88.

United Kingdom: Jewish Genealogical Society of England; Graham Jaffe; 36 Woodstock Road, Golders Green, London NW 11 8ER, England. Telephone: 081-455-3323.

SOUTH AMERICA

Brazil, São Paolo: Jewish Genealogical Society of Brazil; Dr. Guilherme Faiguenboim; Rua Jardim Ivone 17 #23; 04105-020 Sao Paolo, Brazil. Telephone: 574-8554.

AUSTRALIA

Australia, Sydney: Australian Jewish Genealogical Society; P.O. Box 154, Northbridge 2063, NSW, Australia. Fax: 612) 967-2834.

ISRAEL

Jerusalem: Israel Genealogical Society; Esther Ramon; 50 Harav Uziel Street, 96424 Jerusalem, Israel. Telephone: 02-424147.

Galilee: The Galil Genealogical Society; P.O. Box 135, 19312 Mizra, Israel. Telephone: 06-599883; fax: 06-429719.

SPECIAL INTEREST GROUPS

Gesher Galicia: Organization name: Gesher Galicia; Suzan Wynne; 3128 Brooklawn Terrace, Chevy Chase, Maryland 20815; (301) 657-3389; fax: (301) 657-3658.

Germany: Harry Katzman; 1601 Cougar Court, Winter Springs, Florida 32708-3855; (407) 365-4672.

Hungary: Louis Schonfeld; P.O. Box 34152, Cleveland, Ohio 44134; (216) 661-3970; fax (216) 291-0824.

Romania: Gene Starn; P.O. Box 520583, Longwood, Florida; (407) 788-3898; fax (407) 831-0507.

Suwalk-Lomza: Focuses on the 19th-century Suwalki and Lomza guberniyas which today constitute an area of southwestern Lithuania and northeastern Poland. Marlene Silverman; 3701 Connecticut Avenue NW #228, Washington, DC 20008.

APPENDIX G
THE STATISTICS OF THE HOLOCAUST
Source: Yad Vashem

Country	Total Jewish Population	Total Killed	Total Survivors	Percent Killed
Austria	185,000	50,000	135,000	27.0
Belgium	65,700	28,900	36,800	44.0
Bohemia/Moravia	118,310	78,150	40,160	66.1
Bulgaria	50,000	0	50,000	0.0
Denmark	7,800	60	≈7,740	>1.0
Estonia	4,500	2,000	2,500	44.4
Finland	2,000	7	≈1,993	>1.0
France	350,000	77,320	272,680	22.1
Germany*	566,000	141,500	424,500	25.0
Greece	77,380	67,000	10,380	86.7
Hungary	825,000	569,000	256,000	69.0
Italy	44,500	7,680	36,820	17.3
Latvia	91,500	71,500	20,000	78.1
Lithuania	168,000	143,000	25,000	85.1
Luxembourg	3,500	1,950	1,550	55.7
Netherlands	140,000	100,000	40,000	71.4
Norway	1,700	762	≈938	44.8
Poland	3,300,000	3,000,000	300,000	91.0
Romania	609,000	287,000	322,000	47.1
Slovakia	88,950	71,000	18,000	80.0
Soviet Union	3,020,000	1,000,000	2,020,000	33.1
Yugoslavia	78,000	63,300	14,700	81.2
Total	**9,797,000**	**5,860,000**	**3,937,000**	**59.8**

* The total number murdered for Germany is undoubtedly low given the fact that the *Gedenkbuch* identifies by name just over 128,000 persons. This book omits most German Jews who lived in the towns and cities of the former East Germany and also omits a number of West Germans known to Holocaust survivors for which the authors were unable to find any documentation.

Isaac and Bronka Mokotow. *Warsaw ghetto victims.*

APPENDIX H
MEMORIAL TO THE MEMBERS
OF THE MOKOTOW FAMILY
MURDERED IN THE HOLOCAUST

If you were Jewish and living in Europe in 1939, it is unlikely that you would have been alive in 1945. The Mokotow family was no exception. Listed below are the names of more than 250 men, women and children, all descendants of Tuwia (Tobiasz) Dawid Mokotow (c1774–1842), who were murdered during that period. Following the necrology is a list of sources used to acquire information about these individuals.

From Warsaw, Poland:
The descendants of Tobiasz Mokotow, including:
    Mendel Mokotow, his eldest son, and his wife Rosa
        Heniek Mokotow, son of Mendel Mokotow
    Moshe Mokotow, son of Tobiasz, and his wife Chava
        Lola Mokotow, daughter of Moshe
        Reginka Mokotow, daughter of Moshe
        Rozka Mokotow, daughter of Moshe
        Heniek Mokotow, son of Moshe
        David Mokotow, son of Moshe and his wife Mania
            Son of David, name unknown
            Son of David, name unknown
    Isaac Mokotow, son of Tobiasz Mokotow
        Bluma Mokotow Cukierman, daughter of Isaac, and her husband Heniek
            Galilah Cukierman, daughter of Bluma
        Bronka Mokotow, daughter of Isaac
    Josef Mokotow, son of Tobiasz, and his wife Pesa
        Son of Josef, name unknown
        Son of Josef, name unknown
        Daughter of Josef, name unknown
    Ite Mokotow Wąhochier, daughter of Tobiasz, and her husband Baruch
        Beniek Wąhochier, son of Ite
        Leon Wąhochier, son of Ite

Moshe Wąhochier, son of Ite, and his wife Adele
  Abraham Wąhochier, son of Moshe
  Zenon Wąhochier, son of Moshe
Abraham Wąhochier, son of Ite
Simcha Wąhochier, son of Ite
Faygele Mokotow Maysner, daughter of Tobiasz Mokotow, and her husband, name unknown
Chava Maysner, son of Faygele
Galilah Maysner, daughter of Faygele

The descendants of David Mokotow and his wife Dyna
Joshua Mokotow. His wife died in 1936
  Zysza Mokotow, eldest son of Joshua and his wife, name unknown
    David Mokotow, their son
    Daughter of Zysza, name unknown
  Miriam Mokotow Rękaw, daughter of Joshua, and her husband Yankel
    Fayge Rękaw, Miriam's daughter
    Gedale Rękaw, Miriam's son
  Zosia Mokotow Stoma, daughter of Joshua, and her husband Yankel
    Heniek Stoma, Zosia's son
    David Stoma, another son
    Rivka Mokotow, daughter of Zosia
  Kielman Mokotow, son of Joshua and his wife, name unknown
    Heniek Mokotow, son of Kielman
    David Mokotow, another son of Kielman
  Dora Mokotow Fuks, daughter of Joshua, and her husband Mendel
    David Fuks, a son of Dora
    Heniek Fuks, another son
    Chaia Sura Mokotow Rom, daughter of Joshua, and her husband, name unknown
    Fayge Rom, daughter of Chaia
    David Rom, son of Chaia
  Cesia Mokotow, daughter of Joshua Mokotow
  Gita Mokotow, youngest daughter of Joshua Mokotow
Kalman Mokotow (died before Holocaust)
  David Mokotow, son of Kalman
Shlomo Mokotow (may have died before Holocaust)
  Leibel Mokotow, son of Shlomo
  Sara Mokotow, daughter of Shlomo
  Moniek Mokotow, daughter of Shlomo
  Feivel Mokotow, son of Shlomo
  Chana Mokotow, daughter of Shlomo
  Heniek Mokotow, son of Shlomo
  Tzluva Mokotow, daughter of Shlomo

Descendants of Hirsik Mokotow, including:

Judel Mokotow, son of Hirsik and his wife Ruchla
    Menasze Mokotow, son of Judel

Moshe Mendel Mokotow and his wife Miriam
    Joseph Mokotow, son of Mendel
    Helr Mokotow, daughter of Mendel
    Esther Mokotow, daughter of Mendel
    Sara Mokotow, daughter of Mendel
    Leah Mokotow, daughter of Mendel
Sarah Mokotow Augenszajn, sister of Moshe Mendel Mokotow
    Joseph Augenszajn, son of Sarah
    Myndl Augenszajn, daughter of Sarah
Gitla Mokotow, a second sister of Moshe Mendel Mokotow

Meir Mokotow and his wife Rachel Zuckerman
    Irka Mokotow, Meir's daughter
    Salek Mokotow, Meir's son

From Otwock, Poland:
The descendants of Yehosie Efraim Monkitow, including:
Shmuel Mokotowski and his wife Ester Raizel
        Unknown number of children of Shmuel Mokotowski, names unknown
Aron Shmuel Mokotowski
Szeja Mokotowski
Idel Mokotowski and his wife, name unknown
    Itshe Mokotowski, daughter of Idel and her husband
        Unknown number of children of Itshe, names unknown
    Hanna Mokotowski
    Jehoshua Mokotowski
Tobiasz Mokotowski and his wife Masha
    Jehoshua Mokotowski
    Reizel Mokotowski and her husband, name unknown
        Child of Reizel, name unknown
        Child of Reizel, name unknown
        Child of Reizel, name unknown
        Child of Reizel, name unknown
Chaia Sara Mokotowski Cieszynski, and her husband, name unknown
    Gittel, daughter of Chaia Sara and her husband, name unknown
        Feigele, daughter of Gittel
    Rivka, daughter of Chaia Sara and her husband, name unknown
        Unknown number of children of Rivka, names unknown
    Jehoshua Cieszynski and his wife, name unknown
        Unknown number of children of Jehoshua, names unknown

Descendants of Eleazar Mokotowski, son of Yehosie Efraim
Tshurna Edel Mokotowski, daughter of Eleazar

Ester Mokotowski, daughter of Edel, and her husband David Hirsh Zaler
    Reizel Zaler, daughter of Ester
    Haja Zaler, daughter of Ester
    Minda Zaler, daughter of Ester
Minda Mokotowksi, daughter of Edel and her husband Mendel Malniak
    Frieda Malniak, daughter of Minda
    Hershel Malniak, son of Minda
    Mottel Malniak, son of Minda
    Rachel Malniak, daughter of Minda
    Dorah Malniak, daughter of Minda
Leah Mokotowski, daughter of Edel and her husband Menashe Mirel
    Irka Mirel, daughter of Leah
    Lolek, son of Leah
Yitzhak Yrachmiel Mokotowski and his wife Hava
    Leibel Mokotowski, their son
    Joshua Mokotowski, their son and his wife Zlata
        Daughter of Joshua, name unknown
        Daughter of Joshua, name unknown
        Daughter of Joshua, name unknown
        Daughter of Joshua, name unknown
    Pincas Mokotowski, son of Yitzhak Yrachmiel and his wife, name unknown
        Daughter of Pincas, name unknown
    Yente Mokotowski, daughter of Yitzhak Yrachmiel
Leibel Mokotowski and his wife Rachel
    Mendel Mokotowski, son of Leibel
    Zvi Mokotowski, son of Leibel
    Fayge Mokotowski, daughter of Leibel
    Yenta Mokotowski, daughter of Leibel

From Garwolin, Poland:
The descendants of Yechiel Tuvia Mokotow, including:
His wife, Rachel
    Zlata, the wife of Moshe Mokotow, son of Yechiel Tuvia (Moshe died in the
    late 1930s)
    Shmuel Hirsh Mokotow, son of Moshe and his wife Ester
        Yrachmiel Mokotow, son of Shmuel Hirsch
    Chaim Dan Mokotow, son of Moshe and his wife Mania
        Guza Mokotow, daughter of Chaim Dan
        Moshe Mokotow, son of Chaim Dan
    Shalom Mokotow, son of Moshe and his wife Bayla
    Asher Mokotow, son of Moshe
    Dovtza Mokotow, daughter of Moshe
Leibe Mokotow, son of Ychiel Tuvia
Dan Mokotow, son of Ychiel Tuvia

From Kalisz, Poland:
Berish Mokotow and his wife Dova
Esther Mokotow Jacobowsky and her husband, name unknown
   Daughter of Esther, name unknown
   Daughter of Esther, name unknown
Rayzele Mokotow Brand and her husband David

The Szare family whose origins are Kalisz, Poland:
The descendants of a daughter of Berek Mokotow (name unknown) who married
   Menachem Szare, including:
Samuel Szare and his wife, Ite
   Hennis Szare, daughter of Samuel
   Paula Szare
Rachel Zemelowicz Szare (husband died before Holocaust)
   Samuel Szare, son of Isaac, and his wife Jetka
   Paula Szare Briefman, daughter of Isaac, and her husband, name unknown
     Marguerite Briefman, daughter of Paula
   Josef Szare, son of Isaac, and his wife, name unknown
     Zelda Szare, daughter of Josef
     Another child of Josef
   Juda Szare, son of Josef
   Hela Szare, daughter of Josef
   Riwka Szare, daughter of Josef
   Berta Szare, daughter of Josef and her husband, Jurek Rokman
     Their child, name unknown
   Bella Szare, daughter of Josef and her husband, Herman Simon
     Max I. Simon, son of Bella
     Salli Simon, son of Bella

From Warka, Poland (the ancestral town of the Mokotow family):
Godol Mokotow, son of Tobiasz Berek Mokotow
Rysza Royza Zeitman, great-granddaughter of Rysza Royza Mokotow, youngest
   child of Tuwia Dawid Mokotow (c1774–1842)
Undoubtedly other persons from Warka named Zeitman who were victims are
   part of the Mokotow family

From Lublin, Poland:
Rafael Mokotowski, brother of Eliyahu Kitov
Four sisters of Elyahu Kitov and their families, details not known

From Paris, France:
Raymonde (Rivka/Rebecca) Mokotowicz

The descendants of Natan Monkotowicz, including:
Esther Monkotowicz Grajcar and her husband, name unknown
   Maurice Grajcar, son of Esther

Claudine Grajcar, daughter of Esther
Therese Grajcar, daughter of Esther
Jacqueline Grajcar, daughter of Esther
Mindl Monkotowicz, daughter of Natan, and her husband
Child of Mindl, name unknown
Moshe Monkotowicz, son of Natan, and his wife, name unknown
Child of Moshe, name unknown
Child of Moshe, name unknown
Child of Moshe, name unknown
Child of Moshe, name unknown
Leizer Monkotowicz, son of Natan and his wife, name unknown
Child of Leizer, name unknown
Child of Leizer, name unknown

From Strassbourg, France:
Sarah Mokotow, daughter of Tobiasz Berek Mokotow and her husband, Dawid
Winter
Child of Sarah, name unknown
Child of Sarah, name unknown
Child of Sarah, name unknown

From Frankfurt-am-Main, Germany:
Israel Mokotow, relationship to family unknown
Morris Mokotow, brother of Tobiasz Berek Mokotow
Bernard Mokotow, son of Morris and his wife Gitel

From London, England:
Leonard Mokotow. Properly not a Holocaust victim. Because of the increased
anti-Semitism in Germany, he was sent by his parents from his native Berlin
to live with cousins in England. He was killed in a 1941 London bombing raid.
His parents survived the Holocaust by escaping Germany and hiding out in
France. They did not discover the fate of their son until after the war. Both
died shortly afterwards.

SOURCES OF INFORMATION
ABOUT MOKOTOW VICTIMS AND SURVIVORS

Holocaust Records

1. Interviews and correspondence with living members of the Mokotow family.
2. Pages of Testimony at Yad Vashem.
3. Yizkor book for Garwolin, Poland.
4. Yizkor book for Otwock, Poland.
5. Yizkor book for Przedecz, Poland.
6. *Gedenkbuch.*
7. *Memorial to the Jews Deported from France.*

8. Jewish Agency survivor lists.
9. Records of the International Tracing Service, Arolsen, Germany.
10. List of Persons who died after the liberation of Bergen-Belsen.
11. Records and efforts of the Search Bureau for Missing Relatives.

Genealogical Sources.

1. Birth, marriage and death records of the Jewish population of Warka, Poland, located at the regional archives in Radom. Birth records of Przedecz, Poland, located in the local records office. The records of the Jewish population of Garwolin and Otwock appear to have been destroyed during World War II.
2. Census of non-Aryans taken in 1In 1936, at the age of 16, 938 in Germany.
3. Passenger arrival records for the Port of New York.

SELECTED BIBLIOGRAPHY

REFERENCES

Rosaline Schwartz and Susan Milamed. *A Guide to YIVO's Landsmanshaftn Archive*. New York: YIVO Institute for Jewish Research, 1986.

Cohen, Chester G. *The Shtetl Finder*. Los Angeles: Periday Company, 1980; Bowie, Md.: Heritage Books, 1989.

Sack, Sallyann Amdur and the Israel Genealogical Society. *A Guide to Jewish Genealogical Research in Israel, Revised Edition*. Teaneck, NJ: Avotaynu, 1995.

Guide to Unpublished Materials of the Holocaust Period. Jerusalem: Hebrew University of Jerusalem and Yad Vashem, 1975–81.

BIBLIOGRAPHIES OF THE HOLOCAUST

The Holocaust has been called the most documented event in history. The documentation is so extensive, books have been published consisting exclusively of works in print about the subject.

Edelheit, Abraham J. and Hershel Edelheit. *Bibliography on Holocaust Literature*. Boulder, CO: Westview Press, 1986. This two-volume work identifies more than 14,500 works on the Holocaust.

Gar, Joseph. *Bibliography of Articles on the Catastrophe and Heroism in Yiddish Periodicals*. 3 vols. New York: Yad Vashem/YIVO, 1969.

Robinson, Jacob and Philip Friedman. *Guide to Jewish History Under Nazi Impact*. New York: Martin Press, 1960. Lists sources of information about the Holocaust.

Szonyi, David. *The Holocaust: An Annotated Bibliography and Resource Guide*. New York: Ktav, 1985.

BOOKS ON THE HOLOCAUST

Listed below are books about the Holocaust not mentioned elsewhere in this book. The are primarily beneficial to the researcher for background purposes. None contains information about individuals but may provide useful background material about the circumstances involving individuals.

——————. *Pinkassim HaKehillot* (Encyclopedia of Towns). Jerusalem: Yad Vashem. Multi-volume—15 as of 1995—of history of Jewish communities of Central and Eastern Europe. Not all areas are covered although additional volumes are planned.

Czech, Danuta. *Auschwitz Chronicle 1939–1945*. New York: Henry Holt & Co., 1990. Documents day by day events at Auschwitz, identifying incoming and outgoing transports, individual deaths and escapes.

Friedlander, Henry and Sybil Miton. *Archives of the Holocaust*. New York: Garland. Lists archives holding Holocaust-related material.

Gutman, Israel. *Encyclopedia of the Holocaust*. New York: MacMillan, 1990. Four-volume work giving information about events, noted individuals and towns.

Hilberg, Raoul. *Destruction of European Jewry*. New York: Holmes & Meier Publishers, 1985. Considered one of the best books on the history of the Holocaust.

Mogilanski, Roman. *Ghetto Anthology*. Los Angeles: American Congress of Jews from Poland and Survivors of Concentration Camps, 1985. Describes events at more than 600 ghettos and concentration camps.

Mokotoff, Gary and Sallyann Amdur Sack. *Where Once We Walked: A Guide to the Jewish Communities Destroyed in the Holocaust*. Teaneck, NJ: Avotaynu, Inc. 1991. Gazetteer of 21,000 towns in Central and Eastern Europe where Jews lived before the Holocaust.

BOOKS ON HOW TO LOCATE PEOPLE

Ferraro, Eugene. *You Can Find Anyone!* Santa Ana, CA: Marathon Press, 1986.

Hoyer, Frederick Charles, Jr. and John D. McCann. *Find Them Fast, Find Them Now! The Handbook for Finding Missing Persons*. Secaucus, NJ: Citadel Press, 1988.

Ullman, John and Jan Colbert. *The Reporter's Handbook: An Investigator's Guide to Documents and Techniques*. New York: St. Martin's Press.

INDEX

Below is an index to pages that have references to specific localities and organizations. Excluded from the index are appendixes A–C which are themselves liistsof towns.